With very best wishes

Philip Upton

Reviews of *Gates of Bronze*

'I intended to hold off reading this book until I had completed some other work but could not resist and, once started, could not put it down. It is a compulsive and inspirational account of how a tragedy became a powerful force for good, turning around not just one life, the one most immediately affected, but hundreds of others in a different continent.

'Anyone who has suffered a bereavement, particularly a suicide, or seen depression at close hand and wants to make sense of the unimaginable should read this extraordinary and poignant book to find inspiration and hope. It's about loyalty, redemption, extreme suffering and abuse as well as carrying a torch for a departed loved one. It also contains much advice about ordinary life including helpful information regarding setting up a charity, mixed religion marriages and moving not just home but continents.

'But do not read it as a self-help volume this is far more inspiring and moving.

'Philip Holmes is a natural storyteller but also a fighter with endless enthusiasm which shines through these pages. It's impossible not to read this book without believing that some people have the power to move mountains. He may be one of them.'

- Anne Sebba, journalist and historian biographer most recently of *That Woman, A life of Wallis Simpson* and *Les Parisiennes, How the Women of Paris lived loved and died in the 1940s* – www.annesebba.com

'A heroic, heartfelt journey through personal loss to the salvation of a thousand children on the other side of the world: caring, compassionate and inspirational.'

- Rory MacLean, bestselling author of *Stalin's Nose, Falling for Icarus* and *Gift of Time* – www.rorymaclean.com

'Over the years, *Nepali Times* reporters have accompanied Esther Benjamins Trust and ChoraChori on many stories to do with children's welfare. Some of those collaborations are mentioned in the manuscript. It was not until I read the manuscript of *Gates of Bronze* that I learnt about the background to Philip's total commitment to the cause of children. I never knew that side of the story: of his wife's tragic passing, her love of children, her despair at not being able to have them herself,

Philip's affection for Nepal through his neighbours at Church Crookham, and how the activities evolved as time went on and as the need of children changed.

'This is a very important book, and in a lot of ways a piece of investigative journalism. It chronicles in meticulous detail, in an intimate and personal way, the vulnerabilities faced by Nepali children. It exposes the predators, their political protectors and the cross-border nature of trafficking. This book is important because it will alert governments, charities, international child welfare groups, as well as potential do-gooders and donors about the need to be careful with where they put their money.

'*Gates of Bronze* will also be a high-profile expose of the security agencies and powers that be that profit from the abuse and exploitation of our children. It also needs to be translated into Nepali and local Indian languages for fuller impact.'

- Kunda Dixit, Editor of English language weekly *The Nepali Times* – www.nepalitimes.com

'Philip's account is a raw insight into an underworld in Nepal. An honest narrative of his own journey towards establishing ChoraChori, it is an eye opener to the power of human resilience. Proud to be an Ambassador of Philip's charity, *Gates of Bronze* was my introduction to the years of work he has put into empowering the lost children of Nepal and equipping them for a future. Having visited his centre in Kathmandu myself, I have seen first-hand how much has already been done by the strong team Philip has built. I know Philip's account will pique interest and more awareness towards the unspeakable horrors children are going through and what it takes to help them.'

- Amrita Acharia, Ukrainian-Nepalese actress, of ITV's *Good Karma Hospital* and HBO's *Game of Thrones*

Philip Holmes was born and brought up in Northern Ireland. Immediately after qualifying as a dentist from Queen's University, Belfast in 1982 he joined the British Army, seeing service in UK, Germany and Belize. He was promoted to Lieutenant Colonel in 1995. In response to the suicide of his first wife, Esther Benjamins, in January 1999 Philip resigned his commission to set up a charity for Nepalese children in her memory. He married Beverley in September 2002 and in 2004 the couple moved to live in Nepal so that Philip could lead his charity's anti-child trafficking operations on the ground. Philip and Bev returned to UK in 2012 with their adopted Nepalese children, Alisha and Joe. Their life's work in Nepal continues through the UK registered charity ChoraChori which they founded in January 2015. ChoraChori is currently at the forefront of the fight against child rape in Nepal.

The Holmes family now live near Kingsbridge in Devon, UK.

GATES OF BRONZE

One man's journey from heart-breaking loss to finding
redemption and purpose in Nepal

Philip Holmes

Bhagwati Temple, Tansen, Nepal

GATES OF BRONZE

Published in the United Kingdom by Philip Holmes through Juntara Ltd
Visit our websites at www.juntara.co.uk and www.gatesofbronze.com

First Edition: May 2019

The events and conversations in this book have been set down to the best of the author's ability, although some names and details have been changed to protect the privacy of individuals. Every effort has been made to trace or contact all copyright holders. The publisher will be pleased to make good any omissions or rectify any mistakes brought to their attention at the earliest opportunity. The views expressed are entirely personal and not necessarily shared by ChoraChori in UK or Nepal.

Cover photographs © Dermot Tatlow and Graham Uden
Cover design by Simon Avery at www.idobookcovers.com
Line illustrations by Philip Holmes
Printed and bound in UK by Biddles, King's Lynn, Norfolk.

Photo credits:

Graham Uden (Hong Kong) Images 5 – 10
Herbert Grammatikopoulos (Germany) Images 14 - 15
Min Bajracharya (Nepal) Images 13, 27-37
Tom Bell (Nepal) Images 21 - 22
Philip Horgan (UK) Image 23
Mark Robson (*Inept Gravity*) Image 50

ISBN: 9781071157565

AUTHOR FOREWORD

Through Gates of Bronze I have tried to distil and unite highlights from over three decades of my life into some 260 pages. Inevitably, I have had to sacrifice detail in the interests of brevity and flow of the narrative. The content is derived from contemporaneous notes but also from memory. Of course, memories fade and my perceptions may on occasions have been distorted by the episodes of extreme emotion that I experienced. These ranged from the depths of despair and heartache to moments of sublime triumph and absolute jubilation. Therefore, I offer apologies for any errors and omissions that may have crept into this memoir; I am happy to amend and include any facts in subsequent editions if I agree their authenticity and import.

I must point out that, through the need to respect privacy and anonymity, some names and identities have been changed, events might have been compressed and dialogue has been recreated. Most importantly, in the interests of child protection I have changed children's names. Some of the children's stories that are interspersed between chapters should be read as being illustrative of actual children's sufferings that I have witnessed after family life disintegrates in Nepal or when criminals descend to prey on vulnerable people. These vignettes represent a fusion of experiences and do not relate to specific, identifiable children and their families but are nonetheless totally real-world.

Within these constraints this is entirely a true record of one-off activities and human endeavours which I have been privileged to join and lead. I feel honoured to document and indeed salute achievements by remarkable people who would otherwise go unrecognised - and before memories fade further. Most importantly, I assert the authenticity of the synchronicities that I record. These might seem far-fetched or fanciful, and, frankly, I would not have believed these accounts had I not experienced them personally. They spanned the gulf with the divine and ensured that mine would be a very spiritual journey.

To Bev, Alisha and Joe, with all my love

The prayer wheel, Three Ways
Dulce Domum

Contents

Acknowledgements

In spite of the dreadful personal trauma and loss that I experienced in January 1999 and subsequent challenges, I consider myself to have had a blessed life. Unlike so many of the children in Nepal whom I would come to meet, I enjoyed a happy and stable childhood and every opportunity in my upbringing, education and career. I have been happily married twice and am the proud father of two wonderful children. My life and work has purpose and above all I have found myself spiritually. Therefore, I could write paragraphs in gratitude to the family members, friends, charity supporters who have helped me along life's path. However, I hope they can forgive me if, in the interests of brevity, I confine my appreciation to those who have helped me write and produce this memoir.

Encouragement has been for the most part gentle, but one individual in particular, Els Horst, has been more robust than the rest and I am deeply grateful to her for a directness that jolted me out of a certain degree of literary inertia. My main reader has been my wife, Bev, who has not only supported and sustained me, as ever, but has superb editing skills. I recognise how well she has performed this role, one that will have been particularly challenging for her in the early chapters of the book.

My other main readers have been my wonderful, ever-loyal, big brothers, Tom and Willie, church ministers Willie McNaughton and Graham Dear, and friends Angela Sherman, Abha Karki, Grace Mulchrone, Neal Gillespie, Simon Boyd and Susie Wren. I am particularly indebted to literary consultant Victoria Roddam and author Rory Maclean for their transformative inputs.

I would like to thank those whose photographs have been reproduced, namely Dermot Tatlow, Graham Uden, Herbert Grammatikopoulos, Tom Bell, Philip Horgan, Mark Robson and Min Bajracharya.

Prologue

'Do you not see how necessary a world of pains and troubles is to school an intelligence and make it a soul?'

- John Keats, letter to George and Georgiana Keats

Dear Esther,

I t's been 20 years since you passed over and here is my belated response to the one-liner you left me on the day of your death. How those stark words of yours have haunted me ever since in their pathos, their excruciating brevity.

At the end you had convinced yourself that you'd become worse than worthless, a liability who stood to ruin my future. I couldn't persuade you otherwise or help you to shake off this false perception. Ultimately it dragged you under. Through this memoir you will realise that, on the contrary, you were my inspiration not just in life, but also in death. Although I can't imagine taking a greater, more traumatic, body blow, your loss didn't become my nemesis. On the contrary, I became stronger, more focussed and resolute. Your death proved to be my redemption. It's tough for me to make such an observation, but it is undeniably true. For I found a professional and personal fulfilment that undoubtedly wouldn't have happened if our marriage had continued beyond those first, sublime, ten years. While you were at rest, I lived life in abundance, on a bizarre and remote path that neither of us could have anticipated.

Do you remember how I used to joke with you that you'd never find a job with the KGB as you were too secretive? I laughed at the methods you adopted to protect your privacy, flushing shredded paperwork down the loo or encoding your diary notes into Hebrew. I hope you will understand and forgive the candour of this memoir, some of which relates to our private life. Actually, intimate details have already been in the public domain, cruelly so, and there's no privacy to lose. But this is a memoir that I believe is worth sharing in tribute to you and to document what has been essentially your legacy.

I have no idea how much of all this you know already. It felt as if you remained with me for a while following your death but after a year or so I sensed you'd moved on. Did you stay around in those first few months to make sure I was okay? If so, thank you, it helped, for I seemed to absorb some of your strength and wisdom and that sustained me through eight years of living in Nepal. Yes, Nepal – somewhere that you once told me you'd love to visit. It's not the Shangri La you'd visualised, and not all the locals are as decent and endearing as the Nepali neighbours we knew in England. But Nepal is never boring, ever challenging, and the country I was always destined to adopt. It continues to draw me back, a lodestone and second home that has taken possession of my soul. When I'm there I meet up with special people that I can't wait to tell you about.

Is that persistent blue tit tapping at my bedroom window anything to do with you?

Part 1

the A-Kerk, Groningen

'Oh gentle child, beautiful as thou wert
Why didst thou leave the trodden paths of men
Too soon, and with weak hands though mighty heart
Dare the unpastured dragon in his den?'

- Percy Bysshe Shelley, *Adonais*

Zurich. August 1931.

The psychiatrist stole a glance at the clock on the mantelpiece in his consulting room. Only twenty minutes of his session had elapsed; it felt like double that.

He just wasn't getting through to the woman who sat so upright and uptight before him, maintaining a flow of rhetoric that prevented him from getting more than a few words in edgeways. She clearly considered herself his intellectual superior, drawing upon a high education grounded in rationalism to inform her stream of consciousness. Yet he knew that underneath it all she was as buttoned-up as the bodice of her plain grey dress. Faced with this intense and unnatural monologue, there was no prospect of his delivering therapy short of her receiving a jolt of the irrational. Something unexpected.

He took off his little round spectacles and polished them meticulously as he considered his options. The clock's dreary tick seemed positively joyous compared to this assault on his senses that continued unabated. Replacing his spectacles, he sat back and considered the randomness of the specks of dust in the shafts of sunlight that probed the darkness of his consulting room. He was awaiting inspiration or, if truth be told, the stroke of three that would mark the end of this tedious consultation.

Just then the woman appeared to digress.

'Last night I had the strangest dream.'

'Oh yes? Do tell me about it,' he replied, relieved at the change in tack.

'I dreamt that a man in a grey suit handed me an expensive piece of jewellery. It was a golden scarab of all things.'

To his surprise she paused, and in the brief silence he noticed a gentle tapping on the window behind him. This offered a welcome diversion for him to investigate the sound. Through the lowest pane he could see a winged beetle that seemed to be as determined to enter the room as he was keen to escape it. Glad of the company, he opened the sash and it flew in languidly. It was an easy catch. He opened his hand to reveal a golden-green scarab, highly

unusual in central Zurich. He had only ever seen one before near rose bushes and his practice was in a non-residential area.

'Here's your scarab,' he said, as he handed the now-compliant insect to her.

His client's mouth fell open as she accepted it and placed it on her lower left sleeve. Then she undid the top two buttons of her high collar and appeared to ease in her chair. With both the woman and her iridescent companion in harmonious relaxation the therapeutic session could at last begin.

After she'd gone, Carl Jung wrote up her case notes and then paused to reflect on what he had witnessed. This hadn't been the first time he'd experienced a *meaningful* coincidence that had transformed his interaction with a client. He recalled how he had once been walking through a wood with a patient as he was describing a dream featuring a spectral fox. No sooner had the words been uttered than a fox crossed their path. He allowed himself a chuckle as he remembered the occasion he had been sitting alongside another woman on a park bench, her shyness preventing her from describing the sexual nature of her dreams. The ice had been broken when two sparrows had landed close to their feet and started to copulate before them.

He was all too aware of how his colleagues had experienced similar coincidences but were shy of sharing them for fear of obloquy. An exception had been his friend Wolfgang Pauli, who had first consulted him the previous year in the wake of his mother's suicide. After getting to know one another over the course of many sessions, Pauli joked openly about how experimental equipment routinely broke down when he was in its vicinity. This was a major limitation in life for such a prominent physicist.

Jung opened his notebook and wrote down and underlined the word 'synchronicity', followed by an account of what he had just seen alongside reference to the earlier examples. Then he added, 'When coincidences pile up in this way, one cannot help being impressed by them – for the greater the number of terms in such a series, or the more unusual its character, the more improbable it becomes.'

1.   Return to Groningen

I watched from the departures lounge at Heathrow airport as baggage handlers loaded Esther's plain hessian-covered coffin on to the plane. They joked as they manhandled the box, unaware that I was looking on. The profound sense of the surreal that had started three days previously, when I found her body, continued unabated. I felt lifted out of time.

Friends had offered to join me as I returned Esther's remains to her native Holland but I declined. I preferred to make this intimate homecoming with her alone. This would be her last international trip, the sad culmination of a weekly international commute that had started ten years before. She'd always hated flying and would start reading her beloved, battered little prayer book the moment she was seated. However, in her final months those same prayers had come to feel futile, and the prayer book remained in her bag, redundant. Nevertheless, I'd taken it with me to help guide me through the Jewish rites that lay ahead.

As I leafed through the pages, the passenger beside me turned in her seat and smiled at me. She was a pleasant young Dutch nurse and determined to chat. I had no interest in a conversation – but I was polite, if taciturn. I couldn't tell her the real reason I was going to Holland, travelling with my deceased wife's body in the hold.

Arriving in Groningen my thoughts turned inevitably to the visits I'd made in happier times. The last of these had been in late 1988 when we'd hosted a small drinks reception for Esther's Dutch friends to celebrate our marriage. She'd been so full of vitality and hopes for the future as she presented me to her parent Jewish community. What it lacked for in numbers and youth it made up for in character. The Chairman, Manuel, was full of good humour, Esther's friend Rosie more reserved but clearly solid. And then there was Frouk. On the face of it a little old lady with wispy hair, she introduced herself with a firm handshake, a confident voice and impeccable English. In her eyes I sensed an inner strength, some vestige of youth. Esther told me afterwards that she was a survivor of Westerbork Concentration Camp.

Everyone had received me warmly, Esther's choice respected, regardless of the religious mismatch. Now it felt like I had betrayed their acceptance. I was bringing this vivacious young woman back to them in a

10

coffin. An undeniable element of this dark tapestry of tragedy was a feeling of embarrassment and failure. Here was I, a central actor in the downfall of a girl who'd had so much to give and to live for. Over the coming 24 hours I would have to be at my most robust. She'd have expected nothing less of me.

On the Friday morning at the funeral parlour in Groningen the undertaker showed me into a low-lit room that contained the sealed casket. In keeping with Jewish custom, it was a plain one, although it had the temporary drape of a velvet cloth bearing the Star of David. She who had adored antique oak and elm furniture was now confined in a plywood box. This was my final opportunity to spend a few private moments with her.

Standing next to the casket, I felt the echo of our former Sabbath pre-dinner Kiddush. On Friday evenings Esther would prepare the table with wine and bread and light the ceremonial candles. Then, the lights similarly dimmed, she would recite the blessing in Hebrew in a low voice, graceful hands moving with reverence over the flame and finally to her closed eyes. It was a time of domestic privacy and stillness when we'd exclude the world and draw a line under a busy week. Now it was just the two of us again at the end of the most draining of weeks. This time it fell to me to lead the ceremony in that darkened room. I donned the ornate embroidered skullcap she'd given me for Jewish ceremonies and, resting my hand on her coffin, opened the prayer book. The Mourner's Kaddish was on the back page. She had once pointed it out to me:

'Listen to these incredible words,' Esther had said. 'They're so moving.' And she read: 'Blessed, praised and glorified, exalted, extolled and honoured, magnified and lauded be the name of the Holy One, blessed be he; though he be high above all the blessings and hymns, praises and consolations which are uttered in the world.'

She put the book down.

'There's no hint of sadness in the Kaddish, or any mention of the deceased. Instead, even when we're confronted by the pain of death and bereavement, we have to focus on praising God.'

Death didn't come much more painful than this. Just like the Sabbath blessing, I closed by bidding her *shalom*. I would strive to allow Esther to find final peace.

An indifferent flurry of snow greeted my arrival at the cemetery gate. The walk along the path was wearisome as I approached the graveside where I was to meet the few friends who knew of our tragedy. There, among some other members of the Jewish community, stood Rosie and Frouk. The day before, the two of them had conducted one of the last rites for Esther, the ceremonial washing of her body, performed under a sheet to preserve the dignity of the deceased. Rosie told me how, as Frouk had tenderly sponged Esther's body, she'd kept repeating, 'Why, Esther, why?'

The scene blends now into shades of grey, but the piece of colour that remains vivid in my memory was the rabbi's red beard. He looked uneasy - I didn't know it at the time, but he'd tried to prevent Esther being buried in the cemetery - because her death had been a suicide. Rosie and Frouk had over-ruled him, insisting that Esther had been a central member of the congregation, and should remain so in death.

The Holocaust had so decimated the Groningen community that Esther couldn't have a full religious ceremony, as there weren't enough male adults available to form a *minyan*[1]. Instead we had to settle for an inauspicious brief burial conducted by a young rabbi who'd come from Amsterdam for the occasion. He recited a few sentences in Hebrew that I didn't understand, leaving me feeling even more like an uncomfortable extra as I stared into the open grave. Then we took turns to shovel sand over the coffin, heaping misery upon misery.

As the rabbi left, he offered me a loose handshake. There was no hint of compassion in his eyes. As far as he was concerned, he wasn't bidding farewell to a newly bereaved widower since, according to his religion, our marriage wasn't valid anyway, with my not being Jewish. I asked him if I could say something at the gathering afterwards; with a shrug he replied I was free to say what I liked. He wouldn't be there as, his duty done, he had to hurry back to Amsterdam before sunset. It was forbidden for him to drive a car on the Sabbath.

We reassembled half an hour later at a nearby café. One of Esther's oldest friends, Hannah, came over straight away.

'But she was so strong,' she whispered. 'How is this possible?'

The funeral, dismal in every respect, left me feeling wretched, indignant and marginalised. Granted, there had been unavoidable

---

[1] A quorum of ten men over the age of 13 required for traditional Jewish public worship.

limitations over the lack of a *minyan*, but Esther deserved better after her remarkable life and all that she had done for people. I couldn't send her off with such a whimper. Besides, I owed Frouk, Hannah and the other mourners an explanation as to why she, at the peak of her profession and in the most loving of relationships, had ceased to be. I felt the need to say something on her behalf. Once everyone was seated, I arose to deliver a spontaneous, unscripted eulogy, suddenly finding words from I knew not where:

'No one knew Esther better than me, and I think I know what she would wish me to say to you all today.

'Esther was grieving for a very long time over her childlessness and no amount of support, be it medical, from friends and family or indeed the intense love we felt for one another could provide her with a child. For her, this seemed to be the only escape for her troubled soul. Esther did not believe in the concepts of either self-pity or blame and would certainly not wish anyone now to be blaming themselves or thinking "if only".

'So, how are we to respond to this tragedy? Although Esther and I had different religious faiths, we shared a common belief in God and in what was right and wrong, kosher or not kosher. For all of her working life and for long before we met, she worked and struggled for what was good and just. She was the most selfless person I have ever met, with a God-given talent for reaching into other people's troubled souls, showing compassion and easing burdens. This was reflected in her work with the Jewish community in Holland, in her work as a lawyer and indeed in the many people's lives, including my own, which she touched. We must thank and praise God for the gift of Esther; what happened last Monday was nothing to do with God and we must continue to praise Him in the face of this evil.

'If I could have taken away Esther's pain when she was alive, I would gladly have done so. But now I will shoulder the burden of her suicide and accept her unselfish wish to be free from anguish. Her bright light has been extinguished but I can assure you now – I will rekindle it. I will not allow both of us to be broken by this terrible tragedy.

'I wish you all strength and peace as she herself is now at peace, her soul-pain over. I leave you with Esther's favourite passage from her prayer book:

'Lord of the Universe, He reigned
Before creation's teeming birth;
Erst when His fiat all ordained,

13

Acknowledged King supreme on earth.
And, when these worlds shall pass away,
He still shall govern, sole, sublime,
Who was, who is, and will be aye,
All-glorious to the end of time.
One only God, with none beside
To equal Him, or share His throne;
Beyond the reach of time and tide,
Pow' r and dominion His alone.
Without compare or parallel,
Ne'er knowing variance or change,
No power can lessen, increase swell
His mighty empire's boundless range.
My God and my Redeemer lives,
A sheltering Rock when woes befall;
My banner, He a refuge gives,
A cup of solace, when I call.
To Him my spirit I consign,
Or when I sleep, or vigils keep,
Yield with my soul this frame of mine,
My God is near, I shall not fear.'

'My God is near, I shall not fear,' would become my simple mantra for the rest of that year. I was clinging to a core faith; I had nowhere else to turn.

As the mourners were filing out, two of them came over to speak with me. The first was a young woman who said:

'After hearing your speech, I will treasure my children all the more. May God bless you.'

The second was an elderly man who had been hovering in the background for a couple of minutes, awaiting his turn.

'I just wanted to say to you that when I moved to live in Groningen in 1980, I sought out the Jewish community and attended synagogue on my first Saturday morning. I found the members to be a very sad group, living in the past. Nonetheless I still joined the congregation and that was only because I'd met Esther there.'

His smiling eyes began to well up.

'She was full of warmth and enthusiasm taking me around to introduce me to everyone. I will never forget her lovely personality and the kindness she showed to me as a stranger.'

I was deeply moved by this simple tribute in which I completely recognised the Esther I had known and loved.

After I returned to the UK a couple of days later, I took a room at the Officers' Mess in Aldershot. Reflecting on the past week I knew that I had completed all that Esther would have expected of me in spite of the time constraints and geographical challenges. Not to mention the emotional ones. Furthermore, I'd ensured that she had received a fitting send-off.

That first night, at around two in the morning, I experienced the definite sensation of the bedclothes being tucked about me. It felt like how Esther used to fuss over me if I was ill in bed. This was not frightening; instead it came with a feeling of tenderness, a reward, after this most arduous of weeks. For sure this wasn't a dream, and I had the clear sense of a message:

'Well done.'

R amesh's home was on the *Terai*, Nepal's southern plains that stretch the length of the country from west to east. The fertile soil makes it a breadbasket for the rest of the country. At certain times of the year the fields dazzle with the lime-green of rice plants and the yellow surge of mustard blossom.

But appearances can be deceptive and it is an inhospitable place for people like Ramesh, whose family home was a mud hut. In May, temperatures soar into the mid-forties, with a humidity to match. June sees the onset of three months' worth of monsoon rains, a downpour that, while bringing life to the fields, can also deliver death to those who live on the edge of them. A surprising number of villagers die through lightning strikes, reflecting how exposed the poor are to the elements. Many succumb to snake bites. The Terai is also home to the venomous krait and to cobra that try to escape rising water levels by heading for the higher ground of the villagers' settlement. During floods the snakes are often washed into their homes.

Most insidious is the arrival of the diseases carried by mosquitos or in contaminated water. These include malaria, Japanese encephalitis, dengue fever, dysentery and typhoid. After the monsoon there's a brief pleasant respite in October before the temperature plummets. In December and January the Terai is shrouded in thick fog as the mercury drops to just above freezing. Mud huts offer little protection to old people and infants, who perish in the ruthless cold.

The tribulations of the cruel Terai were only part of Ramesh's tough legacy of birth. He'd been born into the *Badi* community, an ethnic group that lives in the far west of Nepal. The Badis are 'untouchables' who had once earned their living singing, dancing, telling stories and playing music at festivals, weddings and parties. It is quite normal for Badi girls to become prostitutes in the community after they reach puberty and within the higher ranks of Hindu culture this practice is accepted as just another service delivered by a lower caste. Their role in the sex trade condemns the Badis as lowest of the low within untouchability. The paradox is that an upper caste Hindu won't even accept a glass of water from an untouchable yet think nothing of having sex with a Badi girl. Reprobates can arrive in groups at a Badi family home to take turns with a daughter since she charges by the hour, not by the client.

In the late twentieth century demand waned for the live entertainment offered by the men when recorded music and video became both cheaper and more fashionable. Parentally endorsed prostitution became the staple source of income. This grim prospect is viewed or presented as being the girls' fate, and therefore immutable. It would be heretical to presume to intervene in destiny by offering more positive alternatives like education or skills training. Besides, options such as these rarely lead to work. As for the menfolk, many of them have left to join the desperate thousands who leave Nepal to enter grueling manual labour in India or the Gulf States. Nearly every day one of these pays the price of poverty and returns to Kathmandu airport in a coffin. Those young men who choose to stay at home end up with idle hands that can readily turn to crime. And that was how Ramesh found himself in Tulsipur prison.

Ramesh thought that his parents had done something really bad the day the police arrested them. His mother couldn't be separated from his infant brother, Sameer, and the four of them had gone to the police station. There he'd overheard the word 'murder', and from the station they'd all been taken straight to the jail. Ramesh didn't understand that it's easy to be imprisoned in Nepal on the strength of a denunciation and a bribe paid in the right direction. Poor people can't afford to fight their corner or pay their way out of trouble. It can take up to three or four years for a case to come to trial and in the meantime family life disintegrates.

This was already happening – Ramesh's older sister, Anju, hadn't joined them in jail where the regulations state that children of ten or above couldn't stay with their parents. Anju had turned ten the previous month so she'd gone to his uncle's home, an unwelcome addition to his brood of five children. Still, before long she'd have some earning potential.

Ramesh would never forget that first day in prison when he'd walked around the inside of the grey perimeter wall, looking up at the intimidating watchtowers and armed guards. It only took him a few minutes to complete the circuit that defined the limits of a world where there could be no breeze on his face. He faced up to six years' imprisonment although he knew that he'd done nothing wrong. During that time, he wouldn't see his friends outside and there'd be no school. His prospects were bleak, with the highlight of the day a meagre daily ration of a handful of rice eaten in the company of criminals. Sameer, who was still being breast-fed, had gone with his mother into the women's section of the prison while Ramesh had joined his father. Even so, he didn't feel safe and was frightened by how some of the prisoners looked at him. He dreaded nightfall.

2.   A downfall observed

Dinner over, Esther reached for the cigarette packet that lay between us. Finding it empty, she rose with a sigh and went off to find a replacement from her trove of duty-free. Esther used to hide them from me. Although she had the enviable self-discipline that allowed her to smoke no more than two or three a day, she knew that unsmoked cigarettes were very poor companions for me. A Dutch friend told me that just after she'd got to know Esther, she'd asked her if I smoked too. She'd replied, 'My dear, he'd smoke the packaging, if he got the chance.'

She returned to the table and began to pick the seal off the new packet. In that last month of her life she was smoking twenty cigarettes a day, maybe more. An uneasy silence sat over the table, Esther preoccupied with thoughts that she was loath to share. At last I tried to lighten the atmosphere with a gentle, almost teasing, question:

'What am I to do with you?'

Her outburst took me aback.

'Get rid of me, find another woman and have children.' She continued, 'I'm so sorry, love, but you've married a depressive. You need to find someone else and start again.'

She lit up from the candle on the table but, distracted, didn't offer me one. I reached for the packet and our smoke mingled over the table, as if adding physicality to the communication barrier between us. I took a few minutes to work out a reply that wouldn't inflame the exchange.

'You don't have to apologise,' I said. 'This isn't your fault. And if this is depression you can find a place for it and still have a very full life. Look at Churchill. He was shadowed all his life by the black dog. This doesn't need to be a show-stopper, by any means.'

A perfunctory shrug from across the table.

'And whatever solutions you might have, divorce isn't one of them. It's you I love, and I don't want to be married to anyone else.'

She drew again on the cigarette and looked away. I was losing once again. I took a deep breath.

'Don't you think it's time to seek some proper professional help, a psychiatrist rather than a counsellor?'

There was a rare flicker of anger as she stubbed out the half-smoked cigarette, grinding it in her brass mortar and pestle ashtray. She was as disgusted with the cigarette as she had become with herself.

'No,' she muttered, 'Not unless he can offer me a baby. He'll only give me more medication and write a long report.' She looked up. 'I don't want to end up sectioned.'

In spite of my attempt at optimism I could see I wasn't connecting with her anymore. She'd withdrawn into a shadowy world that I could do nothing to illuminate, where reassurance fell on deaf ears. Then the conversation took a dark twist. With a furtive glance she said:

'What would you do, if I wasn't here?'

I sprang from the table and began to clear away the dishes, a displacement activity. I feigned irritation to conceal my terror. She'd told me already that she was having the darkest of thoughts.

Esther's cataclysmic downfall had really started in January 1998, one year before her death. She'd seen her GP in Holland complaining of fatigue, or what she believed to be a kind of burn-out. This was hardly surprising after the excesses of the previous year, with an already taut lifestyle further stretched by the exhaustive selection process necessary to become a Judge. Moreover, she'd taken on the burden of running our home while I had been on my residential Masters' degree course in London. The GP had diagnosed depression and she had been devastated. He prescribed a course of the anti-depressant Seroxat. She'd soon feel better with this latest wonder drug, the successor to Prozac, safe and non-addictive.

Esther knew that tablets weren't the solution. She'd have been content with a break, a sabbatical, but that wasn't possible as the Dutch Ministry of Justice was bearing down on her. She was under instruction to take up her Judge appointment in April in Middelburg, which meant completing a house move to the other end of Holland. Concurrently she'd have to apply a weary mind towards reading her way into what was for her a different legal discipline, criminal law. Esther knew only too well that taking tablets meant dodging issues that wouldn't go away, something that was anathema for her; but she was in a trap and, with no other options on the table, surrendered to the medical advice.

The doctor's prescription didn't help. Worse, she began to disintegrate, swept up in a steep, inexorable descent that alarmed me. A loss of mental equilibrium by day compounded by chronic sleeplessness made her exhaustion intractable. The doctor sent her for a CAT scan to investigate splitting headaches and stabbing eye pains that added to the misery. What was going on? Medical investigations revealed nothing. In the midst of this turmoil she had a deadline to respond to the Ministry of Justice's directive. There was no alternative but to turn it down. From here on she'd have to deal with the bitter pill of having fallen after crossing the finish line.

I persuaded Esther that she had to stop commuting. After nine years it was time for us to live together and enjoy life as a more conventional couple. We didn't need this strain and we'd manage very well on my income alone. She agreed and transferred her effects from her *pied à terre* in Leeuwarden, north Holland, to our house in Church Crookham. She retained the flat though; this was her last vestige of independence and she wasn't quite ready to relinquish that.

By the middle of that year Esther was adrift, her despondency deepening by the day. I did everything possible to support her, thinking through problems and trying to reason with her. Most of the time, though, I was a frustrated bystander, witness to an unrelenting grief for all she had lost, or been denied. Personally, and now also professionally.

In July, plagued with a sense of desperation and morbid thoughts, she had consulted a clinical psychologist, Emma Rigby. After she died, I asked Emma if I could read her clinical notes in my quest for clues. The content shocked me. Esther had told Emma that she thought her situation might be God's punishment for having married a Gentile. She had taken personal responsibility for our circumstances. In those sessions Esther had clearly talked much more with Emma about her despair at being childless than she did with me. And for the first time she had admitted considering suicide but said that she wouldn't go through with it because of its potential impact upon me.

Eventually Esther decided that Emma, much as she respected her, had nothing to offer. I suggested we take a break in the sun and found an art holiday in Greece. The venue was a lovely old villa at Candili on the island of Evia. It's the home of the expatriate Noel-

Baker family and full of history and atmosphere. Previous visitors had included Maria Callas and Virginia Woolf. Our tutor would be a New English Art Club artist called Patrick Cullen.

My idea seemed to work. Esther had thrown herself into working in oils and pastel with her girl-like enthusiasm for colours and textures. Indeed, she had reverted to her former outgoing self, curious to engage with the other guests. She'd talk with them and even ended up counselling a couple of them on the quiet. No one on that holiday could have guessed at the inner torment she appeared to have left at home.

No sooner were we back than she regressed to an even worse state. Insomnia had started to take a toll on her appearance. Now she couldn't conceal her inner turmoil and she turned ever more insular. The cosy home that had been a sanctuary became her prison. Esther would run to hide from the doorbell. There was no need to avoid the telephone as, to her deep disappointment, no one was calling her. Friends had been important to her but, sadly, by the end of her life she'd come to believe that the majority of them had let her down. She felt abandoned.

In November we tried a further break, revisiting a National Trust cottage we knew near Beatrix Potter's former home in the English Lake District. On previous visits Esther had been like a puppy in her excitement at the prospect of Lakeland walks. This time around I couldn't coax her out of the door. On our first morning she sat on the kitchen floor, lifeless and absent in spirit, a coffee growing cold by her side. Warming her back against a radiator panel she gazed into space, rasping her lower lip with her front teeth. In a bid to jolt her out of this inertia I urged her outdoors and up a hillside trail. I was determined to encourage her upwards, desperate to make her prove to herself that she could still climb mountains both physical and metaphorical. She had to rediscover her true self and regain the fighting spirit that everyone knew her by. She protested all along the path, at one point even calling me cruel, but she reached the top. Ultimately, though, my strategy failed. I may have won that particular battle, but I lost the war. That Lakeland summit would be her last.

By December Esther was sharing with me, shamefaced, that she had contemplated suicide.

'May you never, ever feel as I do now,' she'd whispered one morning.

I was in a quandary. She wasn't going to seek specialist support herself and if I forced her to it risked tipping her over the edge. Any suggestions I made fell on deaf ears. All she would do was continue to see her GP in England who was as disturbed as me at her deterioration. She phoned me up to discuss her concerns but Esther wouldn't budge. They doubled the dose of Seroxat and it was then that I awoke one morning to find her already awake. She was gazing at me across the pillows with faded eyes after yet another sleepless night. When I asked what she was staring at she gave no answer. That look has stayed with me ever since, and I know now what it meant: I love him so much but I've got to leave him.

Christmas 1998 arrived with both of us short on festive spirit. In previous years she'd tuned out from being a practising Jew and thrown herself into the preparations with trademark good cheer. However that year, for the first time, we had neither decorations nor turkey. We were sitting in the kitchen on Christmas morning, lounging in our dressing gowns, sullen over our coffees, harbouring persistent colds. At last I took the initiative.

'We *will* have Christmas lunch!' I announced.

I dressed and drove to a garage to see what was left on the shelves. All I could find was a packet of stir-fry turkey strips, but that was enough. Back home, with culinary ingenuity, I assembled these into a stuffed turkey roll. Afterwards we agreed that it had been one of our best and most memorable Christmas lunches. We laughed at how we'd pulled ourselves out of the inertia. Somehow, I sensed we were becoming a couple once again.

Esther's demeanour improved over the next few days and I had felt we'd turned a corner. We even began to research adoptions from China on the internet. Furthermore, we discussed my suggestion to apply for another Army posting on the Continent to reduce her travelling. She'd registered for classes in Tai Chi and interior design that were due to start in January.

We'd never been much into New Year revelry but on the eve of 1999, Esther insisted on sitting up to watch the celebrations on television. She even dressed up for the occasion and put on some makeup. Just before midnight, she went out of the room to return on the hour bearing a tray with two glasses of sherry. She proposed a toast to the future with words that are embossed in my memory:

'I want you to have a great 1999.'

S even year-old Dinesh had never known pain like this before. An older street kid called Ashok had caught him and tried to find out where he'd hidden his money. He hit him again and again, but Dinesh had refused to tell. Then, as two other boys held Dinesh down, Ashok wrapped plastic paper around his legs and set it alight. His attackers laughed and clapped at his excruciating dance as he tried to put out the flames, eventually succeeding only by rolling in the dust. The boys had run away after that, leaving him to pick at his burns and peel off shreds of plastic. Later he was able to use some hidden rupees to buy bandages. These had stuck to his wounds and he could only get them off by pouring water onto them. The supply of bandages lasted for a few days and after that he resorted to using mud as a dressing on the raw areas.

After six months on the street, Dinesh had thought that he'd already hit rock bottom. Life hadn't always been so bad. He had vague, but happy, memories of living in a village in the hills with his parents. To his child's mind everything there had seemed tranquil, green and clean in contrast with his current existence on the bustling, dangerous streets of Butwal. By village standards his father, Indra, had been quite well off as a former Gurkha soldier in the Indian army.

Then, one day, Maoist rebels had called at his house to extort money. His father had paid up but decided it was time for the family to move out as the hills had become unsafe. On their next visit they might be looking for him as a conscript into their People's Army. He left his home in the hands of his elderly parents and moved with Dinesh's mother, older brother and sister to find somewhere to live in Butwal. There was sure to be work to be found in this busy, sprawling southern town that lies at the intersection of Nepal's main east-west highway with a trade route that ran north-south into India. And with its major military presence the Maoists would stay well away.

When Indra arrived in Butwal he found that many other families from west Nepal had had the same idea. A shanty town had sprung up on stony barren land on the outskirts of the town. He had no choice but to use some of his savings to build a makeshift hut in this urban slum before beginning to look for a job. That search proved fruitless. There only seemed to be poorly paid seasonal labour available for those who were willing to harvest boulders from the bed of the nearby large river that almost dried up in the dry season. This activity was not worthy of his

25

status as an ex-serviceman, so he stayed unemployed and the family got by on his tiny pension. Squatting in this wasteland was not a lifestyle that Indra's mother was prepared to endure. One day she was gone, eloping with someone who she hoped might offer her a better life.

The family tried to struggle on. Dinesh's fourteen-year-old brother left for India to find an income for himself and the family. They'd never hear of him again. His twelve-year-old sister Ashmita dropped out of school to make some money washing dishes in a small hotel. She didn't earn much, but it was enough to help keep Dinesh at school. That was the way it worked in other families, too; girls labouring to educate brothers.

The family's hopes seemed to rest on Dinesh getting a good education but from what he could see there wasn't much prospect of finding that in the local government school. There were fifty other children in his class and – as is common in Nepali schools - the teacher often just didn't turn up. When she did, she was quick with the cane even for minor offences. Soon Dinesh followed her example and started playing truant himself, in his case exploring Butwal's back streets.

The next downturn for Dinesh came when his father suddenly remarried. All was fine for a few weeks but then alcohol-fuelled arguments began between his father and stepmother. It became clear that this woman didn't want Dinesh or his sister around the place. Dinesh was beaten at home and at school.

A relative came to the house one day to offer a solution. He said that he could take Ashmita and Dinesh to an orphanage in Kathmandu where they'd be well looked after and access one of the best educations in Nepal. It would be totally free and the children would be able to come home for the main religious festivals. The fact that they weren't really orphans didn't seem to matter much as the relative said they would be linked to overseas sponsors who would be none the wiser. Dinesh's father and stepmother agreed that the children could begin the seven-hour journey to Kathmandu the next day. But Dinesh was having none of that. He'd enjoyed the little taste of freedom that accompanied his school truancy, and early the next morning he ran away from home.

At first, street life seemed pretty good. He met some children of around the same age who shared their food and introduced him to their survival methods. But before long, it was clear that he'd have to pull his weight and earn some money too. The children were 'rag-pickers', working (often at night) to rummage through filthy garbage in search of recyclables, mainly plastic bottles. Sacks of these would be taken to an

26

agent who would pay them according to weight. On a good day they'd earn 80 rupees (50 pence). That was enough to live on when your existence consisted of sleeping rough in doorways, begging for food and buying cigarettes, *ganja* (marijuana), glue and alcohol. It was a case of money in, money out, as they had nowhere safe to keep it. Sometimes they'd treat themselves to a trip to the cinema where they'd be mesmerised by the India presented by Bollywood. But the reality of life in Butwal was tough and the nights were bitter in winter. Dinesh and his mates would get by through lighting bonfires and huddling around these, the drugs staving off the pangs of hunger.

Very rarely a rag-picker might stumble upon something decent while trawling through the rubbish. Dinesh couldn't believe his eyes when one day he found a gold ring by the roadside. He only told a couple of his friends about his treasure and later that day tried his chances in offering to sell it to a passer-by. The man accused him of theft and slapped him, but Dinesh ran away. He didn't get very far before the police caught up with him and they, too, beat him and took the ring. Later he saw the passer-by and police chatting and laughing together. The news of his find and alleged relative wealth had got out, though, and it was this that had led to Ashok pouncing on him.

As Dinesh dressed his burns it dawned on him that he hadn't found freedom at all. Instead he was trapped in the culture of the streets, unable to return home and with no way out of his predicament. Being rejected by your family was bad enough but when everyone else in the community was your enemy matters became ten times worse. He hated the nickname that people attached to him and his fellow street children: *Khate* – 'scum'.

4th January 1999.

3.   'Unbearable'

So many times I have turned over in my mind how Esther's final moments unfolded on the 4th January 1999. I remember the greyness of our bedroom as I left her that Monday morning, how I told her to rest while I got myself up and out to work. A brief parting kiss destined to be our last. That morning I wasn't at all concerned about leaving her, as her mood had improved over the previous few days. I didn't know then this is a common observation before a suicide. Nor did I know that early January is a peak time for people to kill themselves, confronted by the return of sad realities after all the hype of Christmas and New Year.

How long did she stay in bed after I'd gone? Did she lie there debating what to do or was the sound of the front door closing the signal to launch her plan? My guess is that she arose straight away, determined this time that there'd be no mistakes. That's why she chose the extension cable. Afterwards, I found the unwashed dishes by the sink that evidenced a last breakfast. It was strange that she bothered; or had tea and toast been her companions as she wrote a valedictory note to me?

Sometimes I wonder if there was a final trigger at the end. Perhaps she'd looked out the kitchen window and seen a neighbour go past with a pram at school-run time? In the months after her death, off work and in our quiet house, I came to realise how exuberant children at this time each morning must have been a cruel intrusion. This was for sure a painful daily reminder of the void in her life, mocking her failure to realise her main wish of bearing a child. She who had been so expert at finding solutions for others couldn't solve her own.

Did Esther's spirit linger in the hallway to witness my return that terrible lunchtime? If so, it must have been dreadful anticipating my shock and horror at the grotesque sight of her body hanging in the stairwell. She'd have been surprised by my calm, and involuntary response, 'Och, love…', as I opened the door. More than anything I felt a desperate, aching pity for her. This was a grisly, ignominious end for someone who deserved nothing but the richest rewards from life. She'd have been a tremendous Judge, and a mother to dream of, yet was denied both opportunities.

I didn't freeze, or collapse in a heap. Instead I became focussed, mechanical, after that initial outburst of emotion. I checked her hand but

28

it was already cold, so there was no point in cutting the body down or attempting resuscitation.

Then my mind began to work quickly as I concentrated on the need to protect myself. I knew from my military training that I was in the middle of the classic scenario for developing Post-Traumatic Stress Disorder. I had expected nothing other than lunch that day but, in an instant, I'd been wrenched from the mundane into circumstances of surreal horror. It is this sudden jolt from one extreme to the other that leaves lasting damage, and I knew it was imperative for me to minimise the impact by reducing further visual exposure to that horrifying scene. I picked up the portable phone, went into the kitchen and closed the door while I called the police. I only glimpsed Esther's body - for the final time ever - when I passed it again to let them in.

Before he interviewed me, the policeman took a quick look around upstairs. When he returned to the kitchen, he told me he'd found a note by our bedside. I asked him not to show it to me until I had given my statement. Although we'd been a private couple, the time had come for openness and I wanted the note to reflect what I had to say to him, as confirmation of my own analysis of events as much as anything else.

For the purposes of the statement I began the story in 1988, when we were newly-married and living in Catterick Garrison on the edge of the Yorkshire Dales. I told the policeman how happy we were, so in love with one another – yet Esther was becoming frustrated professionally. The recently acquired Masters in Dutch Law, achieved at such personal sacrifice, seemed to have been a waste of time. There were no jobs for Dutch lawyers in rural north England and the small-world existence of the Army officer's wife was stifling.

Six months into the marriage, a friend phoned to tell her a vacancy for a Civil Service senior lawyer had arisen at the Province House in Leeuwarden, north Holland. The job would be for four days a week. We believed this to be workable, particularly if the flexibility was there to work from Tuesday of one week through to Thursday of the next. This routine would involve our being apart a great deal and sacrificing alternate weekends, but I'd be away a lot on military exercises in any case. To mitigate the demands of Esther's travelling I could timetable my leave to stay with her in Holland. On balance the opportunity appeared to be a godsend and she'd jumped at the offer.

We planned on this arrangement lasting only for a couple of years. By the end of that time she'd be pregnant, and our normal family life could resume then. Little did we guess that this would become the start of a decade of international commuting. Week after week she'd emerge from airport Arrivals, an elegant whirlwind, bustling and busy, yet with not a hair out of place in the storm. Burberry coat, bespoke gold jewellery, Hermès scarf, Chanel and duty-free bags. Some people assumed she must be earning vast sums of money but her salary almost vanished into travel costs. Others believed she was wed to her career. I remember once how crestfallen Esther had been at an Army cocktail party when a woman commented on her jet set lifestyle: 'You're lucky you don't have children,' she had said, laughing.

Esther's main wish, by far, was to be a mother. Had she become pregnant she'd have been overjoyed to stop work. The sad reality was that her job was also an attempt to fill the vacuum of childlessness. In practice, with all our separation and associated stress, it ended up contributing to it. For, as I told the policeman, finding ourselves in different countries at the right time of the month didn't help with conceiving. None the less, we convinced ourselves we'd get away with it. We had faith.

Eventually, we put that faith in medical expertise and the specialists at Groningen University's teaching hospital advised us to go straight for IVF. Twenty-five years ago, the technique was in its infancy. We paid a high price financially, emotionally and, for Esther, physically. I couldn't believe how members of a caring profession could harvest eggs from her without any sedation at all. It was brutal. Still, the procedure appeared to work first time with the outcome of three 'good' fertilised eggs. The medics showed us our nascent offspring on a screen before implantation. We were overjoyed at the prospect of triplets. In my premature excitement I'd suggested names, joked at how I would teach them to take turns singing 'London's Burning' as a trio.

But the cycle failed and Esther had been devastated.

Our second attempt, at which we managed only one fertilisation, didn't implant either. We took a break from the process. The whole business was causing us to live under a strain and disrupting our domestic harmony. Moreover, we didn't like how Esther was experiencing artificial emotions through the hormones I needed to inject into her. And we were both worried about the unknown possible long-term risks of the drug therapy. Besides, we'd heard so many encouraging stories of couples who'd conceived after dropping out of the stress of IVF and maybe we'd have similar good fortune. We reverted to where we'd been before, enjoying one another's company and a quality lifestyle. The rationed time we had together was precious and we packed a great deal into it, treating ourselves to a good few luxuries to offset the privations.

By 1992, when the Army moved us back to UK from a posting in Dortmund, Germany, Esther had turned 37. We were almost out of time. In fact, she was approaching the upper age limit for most IVF clinics. She'd never expected not to have a baby. Indeed, she'd been clear in our early meetings that she didn't just want a child or two – she hoped for a large family. Her maternal instinct was profound and of longstanding. She told me once how even as a little girl she'd bring the neighbours' kids around for her mother to admire. 'Aren't they sweet?' she'd say, and her mother would give them cookies.

Continuing the statement, I explained to the policeman how, once settled in the UK again we'd surrendered to the temptation of 'one last go' with IVF. We hoped that the British specialists might be using different techniques from the Dutch, but London's Harley Street failed us too, without a single fertilisation to show for the effort. We'd finally reached the end of the line for conception. We resolved to move on, and be satisfied with enjoying one another. Adoption or fostering didn't feel right for us.

In 1994 the Army sent us to Aldershot, 'The Home of the British Army', in reality a bland nineteenth-century military town. We chose to live five miles away in the more rural Church Crookham, the UK headquarters of the Brigade of Gurkhas. We had Nepali neighbours.

Esther's weekly flights resumed although she reduced her commitment to three days a week to allow us to spend weekends together. Even so, this travelling which might have appeared glamorous was nothing of the sort. Church Crookham was an hour's drive from Heathrow from where she had a one-hour flight to Holland, followed by a three-hour train journey to get to Leeuwarden. Factor in the inevitable flight delays, missed trains and time changes and a Monday lunchtime departure from home involved arriving around midnight at her flat in Leeuwarden. On the way she'd have to buy her groceries for the next three days. Then she'd do it all in reverse on the Thursday, returning home in time to finish her domestic chores before the start of the Sabbath on Friday evening. Amazingly, she always managed to pause en route to shop for little presents for friends; she had such attention for detail in the midst of that punishing schedule.

I rounded off my tragic statement by outlining Esther's rapid deterioration in 1998, her physical and emotional burn-out.

31

It took me a couple of hours to tell the story, and the policeman recorded everything, pausing only occasionally to confirm a detail. At the end he complimented me on my composure, and then took the note from his pocket and passed it across the table for me to read Esther's final words:

'Darling, life without children is unbearable for me.'

A riti's family was falling apart. The disintegration had started when her mother died soon after the birth of her brother, Santosh. The rate of maternal and infant mortality is high in rural Nepal and especially within her ethnic community, the Tamangs. Girls who marry young die young, victim also to unhygienic home deliveries. In Ariti's village, it was normal to smear the freshly severed umbilical cord with dung. The cow was sacred in her faith and there could be no better seal to the wound.

The death of a young mother is a disaster in any family but so much worse in a developing world country such as Nepal. In the absence of state social security, it falls to the extended family to share the burden of the tragedy. An aunt cared for baby Santosh allowing Ariti's father, Raju, to continue to work as a tractor driver. During the day Ariti and her sister Rita, seven, could be cared for by their eleven-year-old sister Muna while they worked around the home. None of them wanted to attend school and in backwoods Bara District no one cared much about truancy.

This domestic arrangement might have worked if Ariti's father hadn't started drinking. Alcohol abuse is common in impoverished rural areas, and endemic within the downtrodden Tamangs. As far back as 1854, Nepal's Civil Code classified this ethnic group as being 'enslavable alcohol drinkers'. The alcohol dependency is affordable through the local hooch – *raksi* - that's made from fermented rice or barley within even the poorest households. Ariti knew families where the parents drank raksi from sunrise to sunset and beyond. To her horror her father began doing the same, unable to cope with his grief and the pressure of being a single parent in full-time employment.

Before long, his employer realised and he lost his job; he was unfit to be entrusted with a tractor. Moreover, his drinking stretched the goodwill and sympathy of the extended family to the limit. Caring for Santosh and keeping an eye on the girls after bereavement was one thing; supporting a drunkard quite another.

Then one day as the three sisters foraged in the jungle for firewood, a man called Dani Gurung approached them. They recognised him as he passed through the village every few months, so they weren't shy about chatting with him. He made these regular visits to recruit children as performers for Indian circuses. They knew a few girls whom he'd already taken south of the border, and a couple of women who'd come back home after completing their time at the circus. This

33

procurement had been going on for a long time. Dani groomed the girls with stories about the glamorous lifestyle of the big top and what it offered in terms of an income, good food, travel to exotic places and the bright lights. They might become stars just like the dazzling Bollywood actresses they had seen on a friend's television. The circus would teach them exciting new skills and tricks, even educate them if they so wished. The girls weren't interested in studying, but he left them to think over the other attractions.

By the time Dani Gurung caught up with them the next day, Muna had decided this was what she wanted to do. She found village work backbreaking, daily life dreary, and she resented the added burden of acting as a surrogate mother to Rita and Ariti. Her sisters were too little to make up their minds about going south, but Dani said he'd discuss the matter with their father. As per the convention in Nepali families, the final decision rested with him. He asked Muna to speak with him in the meantime and that's what she did, again and again, determined to get her way.

It didn't take long for him to become bored with her pleas and he was quite compliant on the evening that Gurung called by. Dani knew to time his visit to be sure of Raju Lama being drunk, and more likely to accept his offer. If Raju allowed Muna to go to the circus, said Dani, he'd give him 3,000 rupees (£20) up front, that being the going rate for a girl. If he gave him another sister, he'd pay the same again with a 1,500-rupee bonus. Gurung suggested that he took Muna and the youngest sister, Ariti, leaving Rita to look after the housework. Raju agreed: 7,500 rupees bought a lot of whisky and he'd be free of a nagging daughter and the burden of caring for a small girl. And Dani promised that there'd be more regular money in the pipeline to compensate for his lost income.

Gurung produced a contract he'd already prepared. It looked impressive with a circus logo and Indian postage stamps affixed to it. The document was written in English which Raju Lama didn't understand so Gurung explained the content to him. Raju thumb-printed his agreement; he couldn't read or write, even when sober. The following morning Raju struggled to remember the exact terms of the contract but by then Muna and Ariti had already gone. He felt fairly certain, though, that they'd be away for ten years. He reached for the bottle of raksi that lay by his bed.

An hour beforehand, an excited Ariti had crossed into India, feeling safe in the company of her *didi*[1] who had always looked out for her. There's an open border between the two countries allowing the free passage of Indian and Nepali nationals in both directions. Dani had

34

warned them beforehand of the small possibility of the police questioning them at the checkpoint, but that they shouldn't worry. They only had to speak up and tell the truth, saying that their uncle was taking them for circus work. In the end no one stopped them, and they were on their way to The Great Indian Circus which was playing in a place called Kerala. It was a long journey but Ariti didn't mind. She'd never been on a train before, and Dani Uncle looked after them well.

From the outside the circus appeared tantalising. The tent itself was enormous, held up by eight poles and surprisingly drab. It was the perimeter fence that was so fascinating. It was about twenty feet high, the bottom half consisting mainly of railings. Ariti assumed the bars must be there to prevent the animals from escaping. The top half was a series of panels advertising the range of tricks that took place inside. One showed a girl playing with dogs that were performing tricks balancing on their hind legs. Another, a girl held aloft by an elephant, its trunk entwined around her thighs. Beside that a panel showed a performer blowing fire from her mouth. All of the girls on the signs wore exotic clothing, more revealing than she had expected. The image that most surprised her was of a girl driving a tractor over a broad plank that was on top of another performer. She didn't like the idea of being the human fulcrum to such a seesaw, but she was thrilled at the possibility of driving a tractor like her father. Nevertheless, with that thought came also her first pang of homesickness.

35

Once inside the compound, Dani took Muna and Ariti to meet the circus manager who was known as *Malik* ('the boss'). His twisted face frightened Ariti and she was scared when met them holding a stick. He told them that he was now their god and to be obeyed without question. Their training would start the next morning, and they were to get up with the other girls before sunrise. When Ariti looked around for reassurance from Dani she saw he had slipped away. She burst into tears, whereupon Malik set about her with his stick. When Muna tried to stop him, he beat her, too. Ariti had never had a thrashing like this in her life and it only stopped after Malik's stick broke. Later on, she met a Nepali boy her age called Santosh. He told her she'd got off lightly. When he'd cried on the day he joined the Great Indian Circus, Malik had kicked him across the ground like a football.

That night, as Ariti lay on the floor of her tent, she glimpsed the clear night sky through its leaking canvas roof. She looked at the brilliant stars, longing for what she had so recently lost. Her dreams had been dashed too for, although only five years old, she could see that she would find neither glamour nor happiness in this circus and her thoughts returned to that high perimeter fence. She was imprisoned, confined by the physicality of the fence and the apparent legality of her father's thumb-print. She had no adult protector, and was far away in a foreign country where she didn't speak the language. Most frightening of all, she was at Malik's mercy.

4.   Dreams

As I stole through the rooms, I felt part-detective, part-intruder within a sanctuary. I needed to explore the stillness of the house that had lain untouched, just as Esther had left it exactly one week before. All my senses were alert to any clue that she might have left relating to how her final moments had unfolded. I knew the policeman must have missed something; I couldn't quite believe that she hadn't had more to say to me than the contents of that short note. We'd talked over everything in her final months, of course, but she had been a prolific and diligent letter writer and I guessed there was a second one hidden somewhere. My instinct told me that the suicide note was for public consumption and there had to be a longer, private message that was for my eyes only. Nothing or no one would distract me in my search. I placed a sign on the door requesting no callers and disconnected the phone.

Esther's presence, her style, pervaded the whole house, expressed through her remarkable gift for interior design Most officers could tolerate military furnishings supplemented with a few things of their own. Not us. Esther's philosophy had been that life was too short to live like Spartans. We always moved into unfurnished quarters, so that Esther could start with a blank canvas. She'd rip out utility fittings and put them into storage for reinstatement when we left; she'd have the walls repainted. Once we even re-carpeted a house to freshen it up. After the basics were sorted the removals men would transplant our furniture into the rooms under Esther's fastidious guidance. These items had to be handled with extreme care as they were quality antiques, some bought by Esther not long after she'd first started work, supplemented by our purchases in married life. Together, we'd bought around 30 original art works until eventually we ran out of wall space.

The beauty had now gone out of the room, the silence disturbed only by the tick of our ornate gilt French mantel clock. The house held its breath. As I looked around, my eye paused on various items. The oval Flemish oak dining table with three carved fox heads on the pedestal, above which hung a brass lamp on chains. It was suspended over a hand-painted Chinese bowl. Once, Esther would have been down on her knees dusting the foxes' ears with a large paintbrush, then polishing their heads until they gleamed. That interest had waned in the previous year and now they had accumulated a layer of dust. In the corner stood her

beloved *secretaire*, also Flemish, its little drawers home to her expensive stationery and cards. She would sit there writing letters of appreciation for the smallest gesture of hospitality or kindness, sometimes cards of condolence that she could script with such finesse and intimacy. A brass menorah stood on the *secretaire*, next to the Kiddush cup we used on the Sabbath evening. On the wall alongside there was a dramatic watercolour, loose strokes depicting the Torah rolls on display in a synagogue at Safed in Israel. Underneath it the artist's scribble, '*Les Rouleaux Sacrés sont exposés*'.

Three framed photographs side-by-side on the window sill were stepping-stones through the halcyon early years of our relationship. The first showed Esther, lithe on skis, a picture taken in Fieberbrunn in March 1985. We'd first met one another by a ski lift and agreed to share a chair ride. I had started chatting with her in my pidgin German – that seemed to be the right overture in the Austrian Tirol. We were both relieved to establish one another's nationality, and able to switch the conversation to English.

Initially she'd been cool and circumspect behind her sunglasses, perhaps showing even then some tendency towards that ingrained secrecy. But by mid-morning she had invited me to join her and her brother Peter for coffee in a favourite little mountain restaurant. Once at the table she took off the sunglasses and for the first time I gazed into those dazzling blue eyes. After a few minutes she excused herself for a moment. After she returned, I was pleased to note a hint of interest; she'd applied lipstick.

After that, we kept company over the few days that remained of their holiday. There were many laughs, usually linked in some way to my skiing technique, or lack of it. I was a novice skier, and well behind both Esther and her brother in ability. She could glide down the slopes with the strong legs that are the lot of a Dutch cyclist, confident and fearless. For my part, it was a case of a great deal of heroic effort and spills as I was determined to keep up with this intriguing woman. On our final evening in Fieberbrunn we had dinner together. By this stage Esther was

in full flow and chatted easily with me. She talked excitedly of where she lived, the northern Dutch university town of Groningen, which she described as being like a mini Amsterdam.

The second picture on my window-sill was of Esther sitting by the canal in her street, the Hoge der A, a turn-of-the-century sailing ship moored in the background, eighteenth -century warehouses reflected timeless in the water. On that last night in Fieberbrunn, as we chatted over dinner, Esther said I'd have to come and visit her, to see her flat, which was in one such converted warehouse. She told me of how she was working as a social worker with a welfare organisation for the survivors of the Holocaust and their families. In her spare time, she was studying law.

She was exciting company, but I couldn't understand what she saw in me. At the time I was a 25-year-old British Army dental officer, stationed in Minden, Germany. I was five years her junior, but the age gap may as well have been a decade, given her maturity and composure. As a new Captain in the British Army I had more money than was healthy for me and was a bit too pleased with myself. By contrast, she was getting by on a very modest income yet had a much richer life, and a more fulfilling profession.

The next morning, I had got up early to say goodbye to Esther and Peter as they started the long drive back to Holland. Esther gave me her contact details; she wanted my assurance that I would come to see her, that I really meant it. I promised I would call by within the coming few weeks. We cheek-kissed, and she was gone.

By the time I returned to the Officers' Mess in Minden four days later there was already a postcard of Groningen waiting for me. I've still got it. There could be no doubt how keen she was to see me again. I was excited, but nervous. For sure I was intrigued – but I was also young, and cautious about getting into a serious relationship. Nevertheless, I kept my word and I went to see her.

Esther's lovely flat in the 'Hoge der A' spoke volumes about her good taste and values. From the rear balcony there was a lovely view of the distinctive yellow-striped tower of the 'A-Kerk'[2]; but it was the inside of the flat that startled me as it displayed Esther's sophisticated, precocious design sense. That juxtaposition of antique and modern, oil paintings on the wall, polished wood and brass. As for Groningen itself, it was full of vitality and a bit of anarchy, with its helter-skelter cyclists and

---

[2] A-Church

40

graffiti. The weekend was nothing short of magical and my visit would be the first of several over the ensuing six months.

Soon afterwards, Esther reciprocated with a trip to the Officers' Mess in Minden and had been quite appalled. This was her first exposure to British Army social life and she witnessed dissolute behaviour that was far removed from the restrained style of Dutch socialising that she enjoyed. She commented on how some of my fellow officers at that first party were getting inebriated (if she hadn't been there, I'd have been as bad as the rest of them). She made quite an impression in the Mess; she was a head-turner at parties, with her natural dress sense and charisma.

On a subsequent visit to Minden she'd fixed me with those blue eyes and tried to draw out of me the feelings I had for her. Was this merely a friendship, and a weekend travel opportunity? I was alarmed when she pressed me for a commitment; I wasn't prepared to give anything of the sort.

If truth be told, I was quite relieved when the Army posted me back to the UK in November 1985. Even better, the transfer was to Fort George, near Inverness in north Scotland, a long way from Holland. Or so I thought. Not long after I got there, I received a letter from Esther inviting herself to drop in; she would be accompanying a group of disabled kids on a visit to London and could take some time out. She couldn't really have studied the map that closely. To my surprise, the visit worked out well for and was something of a turning point. She returned several times, giving us the chance to explore the Highlands, Skye and the Orkney.

Wherever I went, Esther clung to me with a terrier's determination. Those first couple of years were more like a pursuit than a courtship. It continued even after the Army sent me further afield with a six-month posting to Belize in Central America. I wasn't getting away from her that easily, and there she was in San Jose, Costa Rica, waiting to meet me on my two-week 'R&R' break. It was on that holiday that we became an item. I shouldn't have been so surprised when *she* proposed to *me* before we parted. I agreed, for by this stage a series of subtle but mistakable signs went some way to allaying my reservations about settling down and making a commitment. They were trivial, it is true, but they were undeniably there. We felt destined to be together.

In the stillness of our sitting room, sighing heavily, I picked up the third framed photograph. It was a wedding picture showing us standing, full of optimism, on the steps of the Registry Office in Richmond, North Yorkshire. Given our different religions we couldn't marry in either a church or a synagogue, so opted for a civil ceremony. It was very private with just two witnesses. We married on the fourth of August 1988, and ever after that the fourth of the month was a special day for us. Childlike, we'd vie to see who would be the first to remember and whisper 'Mazel Tov' to the other – just as I had declared it to her on the day of our wedding. As I gazed at that third picture, I realised that we'd forgotten the date on her final morning. By the 4th January 1999 our luck had long since run out.

The drift into nostalgia over, I turned all three pictures face down. It was just too painful to loiter in those memories. I resumed checking the cupboards in the downstairs rooms for a letter, for something unusual. I even looked under the cushions of our Chesterfield suite. But there was nothing to be found.

I headed upstairs, a shiver running down my spine as I passed the stairwell. Upstairs, everything in our bedroom was in its place. She'd spread her exquisite gold jewellery on the dressing table ready for polishing. Inside the cupboards her pullovers and cardigans were folded and arranged on top of one another. Running my fingers over those garments, I recalled how she pined for me when I was away from home. Her friend Christine had told me that Esther had confessed how, when I was away from home, she'd bury her nose in my clothes just to feel closer to me. Now these items retained her scent. She felt so near.

A copy of *Captain Corelli's Mandolin* was lying beside the bed, the book that had given some rare pleasure in her final days. When I picked it up a bookmark I hadn't seen before dropped out. It showed an icon depicting 'The hospitality of Abraham' with the benediction from Numbers 6: 24-26:

'The Lord bless you and watch over you;
the Lord make his face shine upon you
and be gracious to you;
the Lord look kindly on you and give you peace.'

Was this a hint of farewell, a valediction of enduring love and benevolence?

In a drawer I found Esther's microcassette recorder. She'd used it for work but once she'd recorded her own version of Marilyn Monroe's breathless 'Happy Birthday, Mr President' for JFK and played it to wake me up on my birthday. I wondered if maybe she'd recorded a final message there. But there was nothing apart from the recording of a work meeting. The quality wasn't good, and the conversation was in Dutch so I couldn't make out all that was being said, but over the subsequent months I would listen to it again and again just to hear her velvet timbre, her easy charm. It was all I had apart from photographs and I longed to feel close to her, a little oasis of sound that I could return to in the barren desert of loss.

It was time to suspend the search – I had other pressing tasks to be getting on with. Foremost amongst these was the need to write to our wider circle of friends and let them know what had happened.

I also wanted to write to those who knew of Esther's death but whose offer of attendance at the funeral I had declined. These included my brother Willie in Northern Ireland. He'd only met Esther a couple of times but the two of them experienced an immediate rapport, maybe because they shared a certain delightful eccentricity. They'd been fascinated by one another. But when I phoned him on the 4th of January he'd exclaimed, 'You didn't deserve that'. In a way he was right – but I wanted calmness and considered reactions, with no suggestion of Esther having done anything wrong to me. A suicide sends out a huge shockwave and I wished to still the waters - she wanted to leave us with the minimum commotion and upset. Writing to Willie, and the others was part of that calming process. My duty.

It took a great deal of time and emotion both to compose the letter and to work out the addressees. I worked my way through Esther's little black diary, trying to decipher the scrawl of her handwriting. The task wasn't made any easier by my not knowing many of these people or even if they still mattered to her; I hadn't a hope with the bits that were in Hebrew. In my letter I explained why I'd kept the funeral private out of respect for Esther's wishes. Then, from memory, I wrote a short account of what I had said that day, offering the same frank explanation as to why I believed she had taken her own life. To protect myself I asked the recipient to help me by not responding for at least a month, to prevent me from becoming swamped in an exchange of correspondence that I didn't have the time or emotional energy to answer.

At the end of the afternoon I met up for a drink with Neal Gillespie, my best friend from university. He, too, had joined the Army after graduation – in his case as a doctor. Despite our firm friendship, Army life had conspired to keep us apart and at that time he was stationed in Scotland.

It would have been hard to imagine two more sober guys to be sitting in the rural pub at a place called Well. Our carefree student days seemed far distant He listened carefully as I told him the bleak back story, one that came as a revelation to him. Usually buoyant, with an irrepressible good humour, I was moved to see tears in his eyes. This was the first time I'd seen that emotion in this very tough man.

'The Army's over for me, Neal. It's all become meaningless. I have to change my life,' I began. 'I knew that within a day or two of Esther's death.'

'What'll you do?' he asked. 'Carry on in dentistry?'

'No, that's pointless. I need to find real purpose in life. And I must respond to that suicide note. It's so haunting.'

For all Neal's joker facade, I knew that underneath it all he was level-headed and blessed with a high degree of common sense. He'd always been a great sounding-board and wouldn't hesitate to tell me to my face if he thought an idea was mad.

'I've decided I'm going to set up a children's charity in Esther's name, for Nepali children.'

He raised his eyebrows.

'But you've never been to Nepal!'

'No, but I'm drawn to it. It's such a poor country *and* there's the Army connection. Esther was fascinated by our Nepali neighbours, she told me a couple of times that she'd love to visit it. So, why not?'

Neal knew much more about Nepal than I did, having served as a Regimental Medical Officer with the Gurkhas. He could probably think of lots of reasons not to become involved there as a total novice, but if he did, he didn't share them. At least he hadn't shot the idea down. Many years later, a mutual friend told me that Neal had said to him then that he hadn't the slightest doubt I would make a go of it. I was surprised and flattered. I continued:

'I think I can do this. I'll have a small pension from the Army and I won't need much to get by. I can use the lump sum I get on retirement as start-up funding – it's worth around £35,000. There's nothing or no one holding me back.'

Neal took a long gulp to finish off his pint; it was time for him to go.

'Philip, my advice to you – and don't take this the wrong way – is to go and see a psychiatrist. You've been through a terrible trauma and before you make any hasty decisions you need to talk to someone, to talk about your feelings, your plans.'

'Do you know anyone?' I asked.

'There's a guy called Ian Palmer – I think he's the best military psychiatrist we've got. He's outstanding. If you like, I can have a word with him and organise a private visit.'

I agreed, we parted and I returned to the Officer's Mess in nearby Aldershot that had become my temporary home. I was using our house, at least for the time being, as an office that offered the privacy I needed to apply myself without distraction to sorting out Esther's affairs as well as my own. Instinctively, it seemed sensible to sleep at the Mess and keep a healthy distance from memories and tasks. Above all, I was determined to keep a tight grip on the situation. I suppose I realised my vulnerability and I couldn't allow the tiniest chink to develop in my armour lest I disintegrate. I followed a strict domestic and personal discipline, keeping myself fit and preparing proper meals even though I was now cooking for one.

My emotional strategy was to avoid burning up energy with the negative sentiments of guilt, anger or blame. There was no need for these in any case as I felt everyone, myself included, had done all that we could - or that Esther would allow us to do - to save her. Most of all I refused to surrender to self-pity, the one sentiment that Esther detested the most.

It was during this surreal period that I experienced three significant dreams. In the first I dreamt in full colour that I saw Esther sitting writing at that secretaire. As I approached, she looked up and grinned. I knew then that she was okay. The second arose from that penultimate holiday at Candili. During the holiday I had attempted to paint the garden scene, clambering out of bed very early each morning to catch the light at its best. In my dream I was standing at my easel, the lawn shimmering with dew as I had remembered it. Someone was beside me and I turned to this person to say 'Isn't it beautiful?' I awoke with the realisation that things *were* still beautiful; it was just my perceptions that had become distorted. I'd have to give myself a boost. When I returned to the house the next morning, I righted those pictures again and played the classical music we had always adored. The caress of Barber's Violin Concerto banished the chill from the rooms.

The third dream was deeply unsettling. In it, I heard a knock on my bedroom door in the Officers' Mess. I opened it expecting to see a friend whose visit I had anticipated the previous evening. Instead a black dog brushed past me into the room. This woke me with a start and, shaken, I got dressed and went outside to recover. I wandered around the neighbourhood in the darkness of the early hours, an urban fox's eerie child-like cry somewhere nearby. Was this dream a message, too? If I let depression enter my life I'd be finished. I had to keep the black dog from stalking me. That was fine in theory, but the experience left me rattled. I knew I could maintain control by day but was I going to be a martyr to nightmares? I needed that appointment with the psychiatrist.

I quickly came to realise that my daily routine and off-site sleeping arrangements just meant swapping one type of sadness for another. I'd become a woebegone widower slipping in and out of the Mess to occupy a soulless room in a characterless building, avoiding company and eating unhealthy takeaway meals. I couldn't allow myself to become a recluse, living a posthumous life. The only way ahead was to emerge from the shadows, reclaim my home and sleep there once again. The prospect of staying in the house where Esther had hanged herself was daunting, but I had to overcome this psychological hurdle. I wasn't prepared to run from anything – 'My God is near, I shall not fear.' Still, I didn't sleep much on my first night back in my own bed.

Something else I had to do as part of the moving forward process was to transform *our* house into *mine*. This would be no reliquary; I'd cherish Esther's memory in a much more meaningful way. I packed up all her expensive clothes and sent them to a charity shop. During this clear-out came two discoveries. The first was a large store of antidepressants and sleeping pills she'd concealed behind the tidy piles of clothes. Had she been stockpiling tablets, exploiting her parallel contacts with doctors in UK and Holland? Had she played a game of asking for a resupply from one practice by claiming she'd left her medication in the other country? For the first time I wondered about the effect all those drugs had had on her body and mind.

The other discovery was the final letter that I had known all along had to be hidden somewhere. As I pulled a box out of a wardrobe two handwritten sides of A4 dropped out. The opening sentences:

'I'm so tired I just want to go. I can't live with this empty womb.'

In the letter she described how she had fought against childlessness, leading a hectic lifestyle as a way of addressing the emptiness within. However, now that work was over, she wrote that she'd felt the full impact of the failed IVF attempts. She added:

'There is darling you who loves me, needs me, wants me even now. Here I am, loving you, needing you, but empty, completely empty to do or give more. An inner voice is telling me that my time is over and enough is enough.'

Och love, indeed.

Sangita felt that it was somehow her fault when her mother walked out on her father. The youngest of five children, she had been 'Daddy's girl' and, as such, a soft target for some of her mother's jibes, spat out during repeated rows between her parents. Then, one day, just like Dinesh's mother, she was gone, believed to have left for the Gulf to take up work as a domestic assistant. Sangita's father had a decent job as a carpenter but it would still be a struggle for him to provide for the family. Although she was only eight, she wanted to help him. But what could she do?

Then one evening Sangita's uncle had suggested that she might like to join an Indian circus. He knew a woman across the border who acted as an agent, and he could take Sangita to meet her. Her father wasn't at all sure, but he could see that Sangita was enthusiastic and he trusted his brother's judgement.

Within days they were crossing the border to meet an elderly woman called Phul Maya, who was also Nepali. She in turn took them to the Great Western Circus where they met the owner, Sujit. He seemed friendly enough and certainly unthreatening – he was wheelchair-bound. Sujit explained that he had once been a performer who had fallen from the trapeze, a silly mistake that would never have happened if he had obeyed his instructor. He told Sangita and her uncle that obedience was important if a girl was to enjoy a safe, fulfilling and enriching life at his Circus. A contract was produced and Sangita's uncle immediately thumb-printed it in agreement. The agent gave him 2000 rupees to give to his brother. Sangita was very pleased.

Sangita's training started the following day with an early morning call at 4 a.m. There was a foretaste of the training method that lay ahead as the trainer went around each sleeping girl, tapping them with a thick bamboo cane called a *latti*. Half-an-hour later she and another new girl, Bikki, were learning how to ride bikes inside the main ring. It should have been fun, but their trainer kept them focussed by clipping them on the calves every time he caught a foot touching the ground. They had to learn quickly, and move quickly to get away from him. After an hour of this they switched to juggling skills with a different trainer, who took equal pleasure in using the latti. Then it was time to muck out and feed the elephants and horses. Sangita would soon discover that their welfare took priority over that of the children.

By the time she and Bikki sat down for their mid-morning meal they had been going for six hours and Sangita was ravenous. The food was disgusting. Each girl was given a tiny portion of rice and the thinnest lentil soup that she had ever tasted, with a pot of dried oats - the same gritty oats that she had fed to the horses. A trainer supervised their meal to make sure there was no waste. He noticed Sangita's hesitation.

'What's up?' he demanded.

'There's a creepy-crawly in my oats,' Sangita replied, 'a grub.'

'That's extra protein, good for building up your muscles. Get used to it, get on with it!' He rolled the latti in his hands.

The rest of that first training day was given over to tightrope training. The rope was positioned at about the height of an elephant and stretched for twenty feet between two raised platforms. Even wearing a harness those twenty feet looked to Sangita like 200. She fell off at her first attempt and dangled there in her harness. The trainer didn't even wait for her to return to the ground. He set about her with the latti as she dangled there, helpless to resist.

'How much worse can this get?' wondered Sangita.

Training finished at 11 that night and they went straight to bed, physically and emotionally wrung out. They were allowed five hours' sleep.

Sangita's gruelling captivity would last for another two years. She'd perform in two, sometimes three shows a day, with training and rehearsals between shows. This unrelenting routine continued through the public holidays and festivals that only meant extra performances to cope with the added demand. The beatings were severe but the punishment she hated the most was being told that the circus owner needed a massage. A trainer would take her to his tent where Sujit would already be laid out naked on his bed, ready for his fat body and hairy back to be oiled. Because of his disability it never went beyond a massage but Sangita would have preferred ten beatings over the grotesque intimacy, indignity and embarrassment of that ordeal.

5.   Tsedekah

Consultant psychiatrist Ian Palmer must have encountered few new patients as self-controlled as me in his consulting room at the military hospital in Portsmouth. Based on the background Neal Gillespie had given him, he might reasonably have expected to meet a broken man, unsure as to where to turn, wracked with guilt and remorse, full of anger against God and everyone around him. I was nothing of the sort. In fact, I was calm about the past while confident that I could deal with the future. I had a clear sense of direction and resolve. Most importantly for my sense of equilibrium, I was also in a spiritual place, relying on the simple faith I had expressed in Esther's eulogy.

Straight away I could see he was a caring man. He listened to my story, to my concerns about developing PTSD after the trauma, taking notes as we went along. A couple of times he commented, 'So sad, so sad.' Finally, he closed his notebook and looked at me directly.

'I'm sorry, Philip,' he said. 'There are no easy answers or quick fixes. I'm afraid you're in the shit, and you just have to wade through it. From what I know about PTSD, I can tell you it's really important that you acknowledge your feelings. Make sure you act on them. That what you say and do and how you feel inside are one and the same.'

His advice confirmed what I already knew and had shared with Neal. There was no way I could return to my former lifestyle or continue in the Army. My heart had gone out of it and if I carried on as before I'd be living a lie.

Our session at an end, I got up to leave, but he motioned me to remain seated. After a short pause, he asked:

'What do you think Esther would most want for you now?'

With a surprising lack of hesitation, I exclaimed:

'Freedom. Freedom from the Army, freedom from being dragged down by others, freedom to find my own way in life, freedom to be fulfilled on every level.'

Army life had been good for me, but it could be tiresome. Often, I'd become annoyed by an unfair or inappropriate decision from a superior against which there was little real redress. You simply accepted the injustices, the occasional ineptitudes, and got on with it. Orders were orders. Before, at those moments when I might feel deflated, Esther would say to me, 'Don't forget, you're a free man'. Now, out of this awful tragedy I saw the chance to grasp liberty. If it didn't work out, I'd only have myself to blame.

After that first, difficult, session together, Ian continued to support me as I sought this new life. He signed me off work and kept on doing so over the subsequent months. This gave me the space I needed to sort out my affairs and lay the foundations for the future.

In reality, no one could have been more underqualified than me for this venture; all the ticks were in the wrong boxes. I knew next to nothing about the charitable or development sectors and had no real insight into the needs of children. Moreover, I had never even been to Asia, let alone Nepal. Running a charity is an uphill challenge and Nepal is a chaotic operating environment under any circumstances. But the seed had germinated and was being watered by my faith in God and my total confidence that I could, in some way, tackle the terrible injustice of Esther's death through making a success of this charity.

Underpinning everything was a growing spiritual metamorphosis that, in the first month after Esther's death, was bringing me ever closer to God. It just wasn't possible for me to believe that her death was the end. Although Esther had rejected God with such vehemence, by contrast, I was moving towards Him. This carried me through. If I had believed then that her death was the end, that I would never see her again and that there was no divine purpose, it would have been as unbearable as her childlessness had been for her. I was discovering the Bible as a source of comfort. In the midst of many obscure, archaic and sometimes ridiculous writings there are jewels like the Book of Job, beautifully written and with an authenticity that resonates across the centuries.

Other books were useful too, especially the writings of my fellow Northern Irishman C S Lewis. I re-read books I remembered from my youth such as *Mere Christianity* and *Surprised by Joy*. I enjoyed these primarily for the beauty of Lewis's expression and the clarity of his voice rather than the religious content. Like attending church, his writing took me to another place. And by coincidence other people, unaware of my interest and independent of one another, posted me two further books that were linked to Lewis. One was his own *A Grief Observed* and the other *A Severe Mercy* by Sheldon Vanauken. In A *Severe Mercy*, Lewis analysed his emotions in the wake of the death of his wife Joy Gresham from cancer after only three years of happy marriage. It led him to challenge his faith with a brutal honesty but, like me, he ended up sticking with it. I took valuable guidance from his viewing grief as being a case of self-pity as much as anything else. I accepted this analysis and in that sense I have never 'grieved' for Esther. I refused to be passive and surrender to malignant sadness.

The other question I had to ask myself – just as Lewis did – was would I bring Esther back, were it possible? The answer, as it had been for him, had to be an emphatic 'no'. After all the suffering she'd endured, I had to understand her pain and respect the yearning to be free of it and find peace. I would shoulder the burden of tragic loss now and move forward with it. In many respects when she died, I died too, but I died into a different life and a new beginning.

One bright Sunday morning in February I decided to go to church. I hadn't been to any church in well over a year and it was my first attendance at All Saints Church in Crondall, just outside Church Crookham. Esther and I used to enjoy it out of hours. We'd call by after a local walk to admire its Norman architecture, stained glass and intriguing memorials or just to savour its tranquillity. Now, it offered a haven of timeless beauty where I could switch off from the world and escape for an hour from life's daily grim realities. I slipped unnoticed into the back row to become observe the colourful sermon of the flamboyant vicar, Paul Rich. This former Army padre's florid style made for fine entertainment, and I left church feeling brighter for the experience.

I had hoped to remain anonymous but unfortunately a member of the congregation spotted me as I entered church on the following Sunday. She emerged from the shadows of the porch with a hearty welcome and an invitation to help with taking up the offering. I stuttered out a polite refusal but felt uncomfortable in doing so. The greeting was repeated on the next couple of Sundays; I knew she meant well and was merely trying to be welcoming, but all I wanted was to be left in peace. Eventually the weekly joust became too tiresome and I stopped attending altogether.

My sense of God's presence – albeit a frustratingly enigmatic one – grew not from reading the Bible, or frequenting church, but from the coincidences that had resumed after twelve years of silence. At first these occurrences were minor, so small they could pass unnoticed and hardly worthy of mention. However, the frequency of these modest happenings – and, in due course, the scale of them - convinced me *something* was going on. Cumulatively these little coincidences provided me with the sense of being on the right path, that I should maintain my course, wherever it might be taking me.

While all this was happening, I was still searching for clues that would help me understand Esther better and get my head around her death. I realised belatedly that there were huge gaps in my knowledge about her life before we met as she had been reticent about going there.

To find out more about those missing years I turned to a document that had lain on a bookshelf, untouched and undiscussed, throughout our time together. As Esther's dissertation for her second diploma in social work, it was called *'Dingen Die Niet Voorbij Gaan'* which means 'Things that don't pass' and had been published in Holland as part of a collection of essays. She'd subtitled it 'anti-Semitism, discrimination, persecution, racism'. Written at the end of her time with the Jewish Social Work organisation (JMW), it distilled her experiences and offered guidance on understanding Holocaust survivors and their management.

Armed with a massive Dutch dictionary and in the stillness of our house, I worked through the text, discovering the wide range of cases that she'd had to manage. There were of course the survivors from the camps and death marches themselves, but also those who had lived under the strain of spending five years in hiding. The first group would experience unspeakable horrors while the second had known an unrelenting tension. All suffered from flashbacks and nightmares but in addition they were tortured by survival guilt or a crushing sense of isolation after they realised that none of their peers or family members had returned.

It was ironic that, at the same time I was consulting Ian Palmer to avoid PTSD, I should have been concurrently working through this powerful therapeutic handbook. Aside from his basic advice, Ian had suggested on one occasion that to support my recovery I should consider trying to write a letter to Esther and to share my thoughts and emotions with her. That I leave the letter a couple of days before writing Esther's imagined response. This technique falls under a form of psychotherapy called 'Gestalt', that I had never heard of before. But I was to hear of it again later that same day, as I resumed my translation task. For Esther outlined her use of Gestalt in managing another category of clients that she termed 'war children': adult clients who had anger issues when they were left, or abandoned, with Gentile families by parents who were deported to their deaths.

Esther wrote in her book that these clients could be helped and managed by two Jewish concepts. The first, '*Nesjomme*', is the Yiddish word for 'soul', enshrining the sentiments of love, warmth, devotion and empathy. Nesjomme was appropriate for those who had gone beyond the point of rehabilitation. The best that could be done for such people, wrote Esther, was to offer what she described as a metaphorical 'thick woollen blanket'. The second is a Hebrew term, '*Tsedekah*', which these days is loosely translated as 'charity'. Esther applied a deeper interpretation based on traditional Jewish teachings in which Tsedekah is a blend of compassion and justice – compassion from the giver, and justice for the receiver.

I went to see Ian Palmer for the final time just after completing the translation. He seemed interested to hear what I had learned about Esther and of how the plans for my future charity were unfolding. As we parted, he shook my hand and said:

'You know, through all our conversations I've got the impression you've been handed a torch to carry forward.'

That was exactly how it felt. I would take Tsedekah to Nepal, delivering compassion and justice in Esther's name.

The following day I resigned from the Army.

S even year old Subhash was excited beyond words when his father, Krishna, told him that the two of them would be going on a trip to India. He had never before travelled more than a few miles from his home in a village near the town of Hetauda, south Nepal. Krishna explained that this would be a very special, once in a lifetime, holiday. They would be going on a pilgrimage to a place called Bodh Gaya in the northern Indian State of Bihar.

Bodh Gaya was the holiest site in Buddhism, the place where Lord Buddha had achieved his spiritual awakening. After years of contemplating human suffering he had found his *'nirvana'* – 'enlightenment'. Subhash didn't fully understand what this was all about but his father had told him that after meditating under a special tree for a long time Lord Buddha had become a better person, rejecting selfish and material things. This peepal tree was now called *'Bodhi'*, the tree of enlightenment, and it was still there to visit and worship.

Subhash knew this holy tree very well as there was one in the centre of his own village. It was growing alongside a Banyan tree, representing husband and wife, sacred also to their Hindu neighbours. He envied the trees a little as his mother had died a year previously and although his father had coped life had been tough for a single parent, even with the support of relatives. Villagers would congregate by the trees, sitting on stone benches to chat or pray. The Hindus wrapped sacred threads around the trunks while the Buddhists would hang prayer flags. But now Subhash would be getting to see the original Bodhi. Maybe he would be able to pick up one of its dead heart-shaped leaves off the ground as a souvenir. It was bad luck to cut a living one from the tree and he wouldn't be tempting fate.

Bodh Gaya was stunning, like nothing Subhash had ever seen before. There was an enormous statue of Lord Buddha that had a look of eternal peace on its face. He gazed at the massive brick Mahabodhi temple that was covered in intricate carvings, surrounded by stone railings that kept people from getting too close. His father told him that this was almost 2,000 years old and had been built on the exact spot where Lord Buddha had found nirvana. Nearby was the Bodhi tree itself. Subhash felt a little disappointed when Krishna revealed that this wasn't the original tree as trees don't live that long but it was for sure a direct descendent. Sadly, Subhash could see no leaves on the ground; the monks kept this hallowed ground well swept.

As they were standing there an elderly monk came over to speak with them. He told them all about the history of the site and shared more details on the life of Lord Buddha. The monk had a very kind face. Later, over a cup of tea, he said that he came from Tibet. Friends had taken him across snow-clad mountains to escape the Chinese when he had been a little older that Subhash. On reaching Dharamsala he had joined a monastery  where he had enjoyed a full education and lots of fun with the other children. Now he was living a very full, spiritual, life not missing anything of the material world. It was the best decision he could possibly have taken. He joked that he had so much to thank the Chinese for.

Then he leant over the table and asked Krishna if he could share a secret. These days his monastery was struggling to find new child monks from Tibet itself and it was accepting Nepalese children who had mongoloid features and could pass for Tibetans. This was important as Tibetan monasteries had to continue to be major attractions for visiting wealthy foreigners who loved all things Tibetan. Would he consider sending Subhash to be trained to become a lama, a decent person with a good heart? If he wanted to join with some friends then he was sure that the monastery could accommodate them and allow other lucky children to realise their destiny.

Krishna said that he would discuss it with some of his neighbours and get back to him. The monk gave him his number; Subhash noticed that he had a very smart mobile phone.

A fortnight later the monk came to their village to collect 20 children. Like Krishna, their parents had several sons and these were the little brothers who wanted to escape poverty and the hopeless education at home. Subhash and his friends would be going to a monastery that was just a few hours' drive from the wealth of Bangalore.

56

Upon arriving, Subhash's initial impression was very positive – this seemed like one great big party. There were around ninety other shaven-headed children in training, most of them Nepali. Each day they had to learn maths, English and Tibetan, but even if classes did run all day, this was still a pleasant change from the dull little village school back home. At the start they were treated very well and given good food. Although they knew that they wouldn't be allowed to go home for many years, they were still permitted to phone their parents. Best of all was Sunday, a day-off when they could go swimming.

Then, after three or four months, monastery life began to change. Their teacher started beating them for the most minor of misdemeanours. Even if they were caught speaking Nepali. At their village school the teacher used to hit them with a cane and that was considered normal. Here the monks were beating with wires and even iron rods. Subhash and another boy called Chering decided they would do as others had done before them and run away. They weren't sure to where and they knew they couldn't go home as this would bring shame upon their families, but anywhere had to be better than the monastery. So, one Sunday they slipped away and caught a bus to Bangalore. During the bus trip Chering was unusually quiet. After a while he revealed that the previous night, he had been attacked in his room by one of the older boys. He didn't want to describe the dirty thing that had happened.

In the vastness of Bangalore, they planned to spend their first night sleeping at the railway station where there were little nooks and crannies to hide. However, an NGO woman picked them up and said that she would take them to a safe place. The children's shelter didn't look very welcoming with its barred gate and windows. This seemed more like a prison. There were lots of other boys there some of whom were quite menacing. He and Chering stayed close as they were shown to a shabby dormitory where they had to share a bed.

Next morning the NGO woman took them to meet the refuge manager. He asked them why they had run away and they told him about the violence they had experienced. Chering showed him scars and burn marks on his back and legs. As he was doing so, a knock came to the door and there stood one of the senior monks who had come to retrieve them. The manager gave the two of them a dressing down for attempting to spoil the good name of the monastery and handed them over to the monk with a smile. Back at the monastery the beating they received made them feel like they were being flayed alive.

One week later, undeterred, they ran away again. This time they didn't stop in Bangalore but slipped onto a train that was heading to Delhi. They managed to dodge the conductor by hiding in the toilets. Subhash thought that this was no way to see India as they watched the sleepers fly past through the hole in the floor. In Delhi they jumped off the train and almost straight into the arms of the police. No questions asked, the police took them to Phulbari children's shelter. Subhash shuddered at the sight of barbed wire along the top of the perimeter wall and the mean-looking security guard. This place looked even worse than the Bangalore shelter.

Inside, they met the manager. After a few days they discovered to their cost why the other children nicknamed him *Malee* or 'gardener'. He delivered his frequent beatings with a thick rose stem, the thorns at one end wrapped in a cloth that formed a handle.

6.   Coast to Coast

The young man was sitting in the back row of the courtroom, notebook in hand, pen poised. The heart-breaking story of Esther's death was about to enter the public domain through the inquest. I was aghast. For example, not even our close family had known of our IVF attempts. If I'd realised that the Coroner's court would be held in open session, I'd have offered fewer details of our private life in my police statement.

In fairness the Coroner handled the hearing professionally and with sensitivity. He did his best to develop a rapport with me but I couldn't reciprocate. I wasn't in the mood and throughout the hearing I kept my replies brief so as not to reveal any further information. But by then it was too late. He reviewed my statement and the post-mortem findings. I hated the thought of how the pathologist must have savaged her body. Nevertheless, the autopsy established that the breast lump that had compounded Esther's worries in November had been benign. I expect she believed that was a further punishment from God although she'd said nothing like that to me at the time.

After hearing the evidence, the Coroner reached the verdict of suicide. He closed by saying:

'Having children had been Esther's reason for living but became her reason for dying.' He shuffled his papers, tapping them on the table into a neat sheaf. 'I have to say that this has to be one of the saddest cases over which I have had to preside.'

That evening the doorbell rang. I guessed who it might be but opened the door nonetheless. The reporter held up his identity card.

'Good evening, Colonel Holmes. I'm so sorry to trouble you at this time, but I was at today's inquest and am wondering if you might be willing to answer a few questions? Perhaps you'd like to pay a tribute to your wife?'

I felt it important to remain calm.

'I've nothing further to add to my statements but I do have one thing to say to you. If you'd felt one ten thousandth of the pain that I'd experienced in the past month you would not have had the temerity to come to my doorstep. Now please go away and show me the courtesy of not coming back.'

He raised his palms to me and left without demur, but by then the genie was out of the bottle.

The following day I returned to the Court to collect the death certificate. It showed the cause of death as being hanging with the stark conclusion 'Esther Geralda Louise Holmes killed herself.' This content wasn't anything to dwell upon. I tucked the certificate into my inside pocket and went home.

No sooner was I back than Anne, my next-door neighbour, called by. She appeared flustered.

'Philip, there are newspaper reporters nosing around. They're asking questions about you and Esther and trying to find you. One of them asked which woman on the estate had been closest to Esther. I told them nothing at all. I chased away a photographer who was taking pictures of your house. I'm so sorry. This is the last thing you need. '

An hour later a journalist from a national tabloid came to the door. Determined to remain calm and not treat her to any display of emotion, I asked her to leave. I was courteous but firm. She did so but returned afterwards to put a note through my letterbox. She wrote that if I changed my mind, I could use her mobile number and that the pages of her paper remained open. She is still awaiting my call.

Feeling hounded and vulnerable, I began to avoid answering the door or being seen at a window. It was outrageous that I should feel like hiding even though I had done nothing wrong. Nevertheless, I could keep a sense of proportion. Unpleasant as all this was, I reminded myself that the intrusion was nothing compared to the 4th of January. I'd manage. The next day headlines such as 'Army officer's wife hangs herself in married quarters' bayed at me from the national papers. Esther and I were in the news big time and my period of steady, reconstructive seclusion had come to an end.

I felt compelled to protest this irruption into my privacy and the behaviour of this particular journalist. The only option in those days was to write to the now defunct Press Complaints Commission. Esther was at my shoulder as I scripted the letter, just like how she'd use to check out my formal letters, the lawyer within her ensuring that they were measured and objective. My main complaint related to breach of privacy and harassment.

In its defence to the PCC the journalist's paper wrote that she had described me as being 'angry and upset' with her. After I challenged this untruth, she amended her comment to my having been 'unwelcoming'; I couldn't disagree with this adjective. During the exchange I pointed out that under the press code of conduct it was not permissible for a journalist to return to a bereaved person's home if they have been asked once to go away. Her persistence, albeit by letter, represented harassment. The Commission rejected my complaint. I discovered later that it upheld less than 1% of complaints.

Two weeks later, still bruised by the press intrusion, still immersed in practical tasks, still firmly resisting the emotional chaos that accompanies bereavement, I boarded the ferry to Holland. I was taking the car with me this time as I needed to clear Esther's flat and also get around to visiting a few people who had been important to Esther but hadn't had the opportunity to attend her funeral. It was a chilly late February morning, and my breath swirled around me as I leant out over the deck. It struck me as I looked at the grey sea below how it was almost exactly 12 years since I had last been on a cross channel ferry. I'd gone across to celebrate my 27th birthday with Esther but when she opened the door of her flat in Groningen there had been little sign of joy on her face. She looked like she'd seen a ghost. She brought me inside with hardly a word and showed me the television pictures of the ferry I had just left lying on its side in Zeebrugge harbour. I had been on the final crossing of the Herald of Free Enterprise. On its return journey it had capsized and almost 200 people had perished. Such is the random, unjust, nature of death yet no doubt many survivors would have flattered themselves by thanking God for being spared.

Hans was top of my list for a visit. He'd been Esther's immediate superior in the mid-nineties before being summarily dismissed and transferred to another department. Amongst his colleagues she alone had been brave enough to speak out on his behalf. She hadn't disputed the rationale behind the decision. Rather, she'd objected to a flawed dismissal process in which he had been denied the basic right to defend himself and given no prior warnings. Without any thought for her own position she'd marched into a meeting of senior management to confront them with her views. I learned afterwards how she had delivered a measured ten-minute rebuke in Hans' defence. This witness reported how she'd spoken with controlled outrage, not a word out of place. He'd said that after Esther left the room everyone was 'shaking in their boots'.

Later, in her shared office she challenged her peers to do likewise:

'It's your duty not only as Hans' colleagues but also as members of the legal profession to fight against injustice,' she'd declared.

They were unmoved. One of them, Ellie, countered:

'Esther, you know as well as we do that Hans wasn't the easiest of men, with that short fuse and fiery temper of his.' There were nods of agreement from her colleagues. 'This is a situation that he has entirely brought upon himself.'

This was just about the worst response she could have made to Esther who hit back:

'This was what people said in 1940 as the Nazis deported their Jewish neighbours. It was easier to condemn the Jews than to blame themselves for their cowardice and disloyalty.'

'That was then, this is now,' Ellie replied and busied herself at her computer. As Esther glanced around the room, she could see that everyone else's heads were down too.

This was my first meeting with Hans and he was far from being an ogre. We spent an intimate hour together over a cup of tea while I told him everything that had happened. After I had finished, he sat back in his chair and closed his eyes for a few moments, as if in prayer. Then he said:

'Thank you for taking the time to come to see me. Esther was a remarkable colleague and I'll never forget what she did for me, or tried to do. But in the end a kind of justice has happened. Last week I too was appointed to the judiciary.' He glanced out of the window for a moment before continuing. 'The strange thing is that throughout that selection process I felt that Esther was very close.'

I wondered if Esther had been fighting for justice even *after* her death.

My major practical task in Holland was to close down Esther's beloved pied-à-terre in Leeuwarden. It was sad for me to reflect upon how she'd held onto this as a lifeline to a profession and world she could still call her own. This had been part of her identity that she couldn't bear to shed. She'd clung to it even after realising she could no longer travel or return to her former work. With a typical sense of style, she'd chosen to rent a flat in the loveliest part of the town, the *'Grote Kerk Straat'*[3]. We'd both loved the street's grandeur with its cobbles and distinctive old buildings bearing dates going back into the eighteenth century. Famous

---

[3] 'Large Church Street'

and infamous alike once lived on this street. Next door stood the home of the renowned graphic artist M C Escher. Further along the street lay the birthplace of the doomed courtesan Mata Hari, shot for spying for the Germans in the First World War. A stone's throw away leaned the iconic 'Oldehove', a sixteenth century church tower upon which work was suspended after it started to sag. It has survived the centuries although it now has a greater tilt than the Tower of Pisa. As I looked at it again, I remembered how she'd clowned around in front of it, imitating its lean for a photo.

On my way to the flat I paused by the poignant Holocaust memorial in the little square at one end of Grote Kerk Straat. It stood next to the former Jewish School. A wall plaque refers to Genesis 37:30. Desolate in its simplicity, it reads 'The child is no longer'. A second inscription lists the 'absentee' children whom the Nazis rounded up and deported between 1942 and 1943. From the 3,000 Jews taken away by the SS a mere 100 souls had returned. Most striking is a column symbolising the Jewish mezuzah, the tiny metal cylinder containing a sacred parchment that is attached to the doorpost of every Jewish home. Although ours would never be consecrated by a rabbi, we'd still placed one on our doorpost wherever we lived.

It wouldn't take long to pack up the remainder of the flat. She'd already transferred the major items to our home in England. There were really just the bare essentials for cooking and some cupboards to clear out. I didn't want to rush it so I made myself a cup of tea and sat on the sofa bed to reflect for a few minutes. Leeuwarden held nothing but wonderful memories of my visits there to break up Esther's commuting routine. She would meet me off the train with girl-like enthusiasm, offering me a lift to the flat on the back of her bicycle. I'd decline and instead we'd walk through town, she wheeling her bike and full of chat. She was proud to introduce her husband to any friend or colleague we met on the way and I'd attempt some pleasantries in Dutch.

But now I had to draw a final line under that magical little part of our life. The sadness, the emptiness became profound. At the rear of the flat I looked down from her bedroom window upon what I guessed must have been an ancient mortuary building. On its wall a stone plaque depicted a skull with the Roman legal ruling *'Mors Omnia Solvit'* – 'Death dissolves everything'. Not for me it wouldn't.

I was still looking for clues but found nothing of note in the flat beyond a further stockpile of tablets. This added to my suspicion that she'd developed an addiction. I made an appointment to see her Dutch doctor. He was adamant that Esther had been suffering from depression but I remained unconvinced. It seemed to me that she'd just needed a rest, a sabbatical. The most revealing information came from the medical notes that the practice handed over to me. From her being diagnosed as depressive on New Year's Day 1998 I followed a chequered drug history, a cocktail of Seroxat with other supporting drugs. Along the way she had complained of a painful dry mouth in July and severe stabbing headaches in September. A note in October recorded that she'd collected all her medication, presumably in one large batch, with the annotation 'Suicidal??? I don't know'. Then in November the notes stated the practice had taken a desperate phone call from England. She'd said that she'd burnt her boats in Holland and was having increasingly morbid thoughts. I'd known nothing of this exchange. The notes ended with a record of Esther's suicide a week after her death.

The flat emptied and handed over, I flew back to UK feeling low. By then the first responses to my letter to friends were coming in and these tributes lifted my spirits. Our art tutor at Candili, Patrick Cullen, commented:

'I keep thinking about little things at Candili during those brief ten days, when I made her and your acquaintance. I remember being impressed with her assuredness – she seemed to know more than most what she wanted from that holiday and, I thought, from life in general. The same single-mindedness characterised her painting in which she was admirably persevering with results that had a distinctive charm about them. I felt she was capable of producing something rather good in time. Of course, I had no inkling of the longing and disappointment that was consuming her. It seems all the more remarkable that she was able to join in, delight in the beauty of the place and work so hard at her paintings.'

A Dutch friend wrote:

'I knew Esther from the time we were reading Law together in Groningen. My husband and I came to know her as a socially aware woman, always available for other people. Someone who had an ear for people's stories, for your problems and your feelings. Someone you could share your experiences with. But not only that, she was also able and willing to think with you, to help you, to advise and make you look at things in a different way. She was so helpful.'

She continued:

'...Sadly, I frequently heard about her life not being easy. People around her, no matter if they were family or work colleagues, could deeply hurt her. I have never been able to understand that. Why is it that someone can cause pain to one who cares so much about other people?'

One of Esther's British friends wrote:

'Esther spoke many times about the plight of underprivileged children, particularly in China, and of her feelings of despair for their situation. She said that there was growing concern amongst the Jewish community about the problem and that she was following publications on the matter with great interest. I cannot begin to imagine what she would feel to know that you will obviously be making a huge difference for many similar children, an issue inherent in her soul. I wish you all the luck in the world with such a fitting and precious memorial [founding a children's charity] to a truly beautiful and altruistic lady.'

Another:

'Dear Philip, "if only…". I have thought often about that. As you wrote, very many of her family and friends must have pondered over it too. But Esther was tenacious: if she wanted something, she went for it with all her heart. We must respect that.'

Most of all I was moved by the letter from my brother Willie. He had found just the right tone a month after the death and following his initial reaction on the phone:

'I am so glad that I only have happy memories of Esther. She had an incredibly strong and confident personality and I always found her so friendly and kind when we met, which sadly was not often enough. I particularly enjoyed visiting both of you at Florence Court and have pleasant memories of chatting to her as we walked in the snow. It is tragic that such a situation can never happen again but the memories of her will live as long as I do. Her death was, I think, the greatest, most profound shock of my life, but I know that it was nothing compared with what you experienced. Claire and I really felt for you in your sorrow and you have been very much in our thoughts and prayers. We continue to pray for your future fulfilment in life. We are sure that whatever you decide to do, you have the determination to make a success of it.'

As the year progressed, I found myself spending an increasing amount of time in preparing for my future work and ever less in closing down Esther's affairs. Whatever its faults, the Army excels at preparing its personnel for civilian life through offering a free choice in resettlement training. I chose three courses; one in desktop publishing, another called

'Working for a Charity' and finally a Nepali language course. These proved to be sound choices. The Esther Benjamins Trust in its formative years would rely upon me as its factotum and this included my designing all its literature. The charity course, with its balance of theory and internship, helped tick one of the boxes on my CV that had been glaringly empty. And the language training at the Gurkha Education Centre in Church Crookham was where I met a future key figure, the senior instructor, Captain Suresh Pun.

Softly spoken, with his short stature, receding hairline, modest moustache and round spectacles he resembled a gentle academic rather than the stereotypical fierce Gurkha. Unlike his junior instructors who delivered lessons in a didactic military manner, Suresh was laid back, his teaching subtle and good-humoured.

Maybe part of the reason for his easy demeanour was that, although still only in his early forties, he was at the end of his Army career. The Gurkhas operate an 'up or out' policy, whereby a soldier or officer who isn't going to get promoted has to leave; Suresh had reached his ceiling. So, he was looking for an employment opportunity and, curious to hear my plans, invited me around to his place for a drink.

Over a whiskey Suresh told me a little about himself and the Gurkhas. He had been born in Hong Kong, his father also a Gurkha officer. He was a Magar, one of Nepal's mongoloid ethnic minority groups that originated in the hills. The British Army had traditionally recruited from these tough tribes, but these days many of the recruits

actually came from Nepal's towns and cities. They were perhaps 'softer' than their forebears but still had to get through a very exacting selection process with only a couple out of every hundred applicants making the grade. It was an honour just to join the Army but to be promoted all the way to becoming an officer was a matter of great personal achievement. Suresh passed me over an ornate kukri, the foot-long Gurkha knife.

'The Army presented me with this on the day of my commissioning. Without doubt it was the happiest day of my life. My father was beside himself with pride.'

I fingered the edge of the blade.

'You shouldn't have taken that from its scabbard, you know. Our tradition is that it can't be re-sheathed without drawing blood.'

I heard his hysterical little laugh for the first time.

'Unless, that is, it's a ceremonial kukri.'

He told me how the legend that is the Gurkhas had all began back in 1815 when the British had invaded Nepal in a bid to expand the Raj. They won the battle but took such a hiding that they made the inspired decision to recruit Nepalis to fight for them rather than against. He continued:

'The future of the Gurkhas was guaranteed after they remained loyal during the Indian Mutiny.'

'Loyalty is probably the one sentiment that I value the most,' I replied.

He giggled.

'It was very easy to be loyal as we Nepalis don't like or trust Indians very much. We say that one dead Indian could outfox ten live Nepalis. And they treat my people like second class citizens. In the Kathmandu shops you'll see packets of biscuits that have been imported from India that are labelled "only for sale in Nepal" because they are poor quality factory rejects.'

Another whiskey poured, the conversation progressed from matters military and international relations to talk about social issues in Nepal. He admitted to knowing less about these than he should, as he had spent most of his life living out of the country. But he assured me that there were plenty of children in need who could benefit from a children's home. He talked in general terms about the discrimination that was endemic in Nepal, of how children were condemned at birth if they were born into lower castes from which there could be no escape. Or if they were born girls. Society even discriminated against children on the grounds of sins committed in previous lives, which is why they returned to life disabled.

'The way people see it, they're getting their just deserts,' and then, after a sip of whiskey, 'views that they're taught by the Brahmins in Nepal. They're a scourge upon us.'

Suresh was now speaking with passion, his eyes flashing as he rose to a subject that grated with him. As I listened to him I sensed that this impressive man could well be, quite literally, a godsend.

I made him an offer. I'd run the charity from the UK if he'd manage the project as my man in Nepal. We would collaborate towards setting up the children's home that would become the focus for the substitute family that I wanted to create for Esther. As part of the deal - and to save money - he could work from home and we'd base the project in his local area. This was the town of Bhairahawa that lay just 3km away from the Indian border in the mid-west Terai. He agreed without any hesitation – we could sort out the detail later.

I was so pleased to have overcome the stumbling block of not knowing Nepal and having someone who spoke the language. I could rely upon him to set things up for me while I concentrated on finding the funds to bring our plans to fruition. Although we had different nationalities, we shared the common culture of having both been in the military so that should make communication easier and he'd have the organisational skills. Also, I presumed that with his expatriate background and military values, he'd be untainted by Nepal's endemic corruption.

I walked home that evening with a spring in my step and Suresh's parting words still in my ear:

'I dreamt that a chance like this would come along so that I could put something back into my country. So many of my peers have left the Army to pursue money, but what happiness does that bring? Philip, I didn't just dream; I prayed for this opportunity.'

A few days later the Working for a Charity course tutor handed me a CV. She told me that it had just arrived in the post, sent in speculatively by someone who was looking for a job. She showed his work experience in the development sector in Nepal, including some very senior appointments with major charities that I recognised. Perhaps it would be useful for me to speak with him? I e-mailed him and Edward invited me to visit him at home for afternoon tea.

Edward's appearance didn't tally with his CV. He was very laid back, dressed in a cardigan that had seen better days and wearing checked bedroom slippers. Maybe Nepal had had this effect on him. In an initial exchange of pleasantries, I mentioned my connection with Suresh. He gave a wry smile and said:

'Ah, the Magars. They're the Scots of Nepal. Hearts of gold and drink whiskey like it's going out of fashion. I'm sorry to make such sweeping generalisations, but in my 20 years of living there for some reason generalisations seem to be valid. The thing about a Magar is that he'll approach a task with gushing enthusiasm but has a tendency to take his eye off the ball. By contrast, a Gurung tends to be a much better worker. He'll be steadier, overcome challenges and see a task through to the finish.'

Naturally, I wasn't in a position to comment and hoped this applied just to homespun Nepalis rather than to Gurkha officers. We moved on to my dream of setting up a children's home in Esther's memory. I didn't get very far before he interjected with:

'What did a children's home ever do for anyone?'

'I like the idea because even though the number of children who stand to benefit will probably be quite small, at least I can use my limited resources to do a small job well,' I replied. 'I don't want my investment to get "lost" within a bigger picture and I'll have a very tangible memorial to Esther. I'll be giving her, giving us, the family that she yearned for.'

I could see that he didn't share my viewpoint at all but he now tried a less confrontational approach:

'Philip, as an Irishman you'll probably have heard the old joke about the tourist in rural Ireland who asked for directions. The local replied that it would be better not to start from here. Just be careful of settling upon the solution to a problem before you've even analysed it.'

In my head I knew he had a point. As a dentist I wouldn't have thrown myself into a treatment plan before I had reached a diagnosis. The trouble was my heart was telling me otherwise. He continued:

'I hear what you say about getting a clear and tangible return on investment but equally you don't want to waste your money by barking up the wrong tree. Children's homes or orphanages are actually very expensive propositions in terms of the amount of money that's spent per child. And for what? Institutional care. Big deal! Who wants to grow up in an orphanage? More tea, vicar? You'd better get used to drinking lots of this stuff.'

He poured us a second cup of tea with a little smirk. I guessed that my future tea in Nepal wouldn't be served in floral bone china, the quaint kind that I recalled from the 1960's.

'One of the biggest drawbacks with institutional care is how a children's home dislocates children from the extended family that's ultimately their insurance policy for life. You might be lucky and have well-educated children leaving your home, but they'll struggle to find work because they don't have family contacts or a local network.'

I conveyed Edward's reservations to Neal Gillespie when he looked in on me again the following week.

'He's right. I'd be very careful with your money. So many foreigners get involved in Nepal by setting up orphanages, for all kinds of noble reasons. But the place is littered with failed building projects and those people leave the country fleeced and disenchanted.'

In spite of these words of caution, I held to the idea, probably emboldened by Suresh's enthusiasm. One evening he took me to meet Kiran, a former Gurkha who had joined the Army with Suresh but left before him to open a restaurant as his second career. He was a Worldly Wiseman who had worked internationally including in Nepal itself. Kiran was a sharp operator, an example of the ambitious money-chasing type Suresh had referred to in our earlier conversation. After hearing our intentions over some samosas, Kiran offered his advice:

'You should aim to buy some land and build your children's home ground up. Once it's done, it's done and in the long term you'll save a fortune on rental. You won't be able to do this directly as foreigners aren't allowed to own capital assets in Nepal. Suresh will have to set up an NGO for the purchase and for future project activities.'

He took out a piece of paper and made a quick calculation. He cleared his throat.

'I think that for around £10,000 you'll probably find a decent site in Bhairahawa. But you should factor in a further ten percent that has to go under the table. That's custom and practice in capital projects in Nepal.'

I knew that Suresh and I would have to find a way around that way of doing business.

Soon afterwards Suresh retired from the Army and returned to Nepal, preparing the ground for the visit we agreed I would make later in the year. For my part, as an afterthought, I decided that as I didn't own a house in UK I might just as well base myself in Holland and run the charity from there. With the lower cost of living in Holland I could make my modest pension stretch further and it would be a great pleasure to live in Leeuwarden with all its associations and happy memories. I found out that Esther's flat was still available to rent and reclaimed it immediately.

Having removed the last of the flat contents to England I would have to send them straight back. It was my turn to cause chaos. I loaded all of our antiques onto a van and drove them to Christie's auction house in London; these items meant nothing to be now and only stood to get in the way. The house clearers did the rest and after handing over our Army quarter I left for Holland. Opening the flat door in Leeuwarden I announced to the empty hallway:

'I'm back!'

As I nailed our mezuzah to the doorpost, I resolved that I'd spent enough time on the back foot; the fight was on.

In June I decided to share my dream with the national papers. This might seem like a puzzling decision after my indignation at how the media had barged into my private life just a few months earlier. But this would be a story that really was worth telling; the launch of a children's charity in the wake of personal tragedy. I approached The Mail on Sunday, the UK's most widely read Sunday paper, which led to a meeting with the very cool senior journalist Sarah Oliver. Her questions were penetrating.

'Why aren't you wearing a wedding ring, Philip?'

'I'm not married,' I replied. 'I took the ring off the day after Esther's death. I was determined to confront reality. I felt that if I was to survive, or overcome what happened to me, that was the best way of moving forward.'

She scribbled in shorthand.

'And what would you say you most missed about her?'

There were many lovely things I might have mentioned but Sarah looked surprised with my answer:

'Her capacity to correct me and especially in the past few months I've felt at times like I needed a guiding hand. Esther's wisdom, common sense and directness complemented the love she showed me and kept me from straying off-piste. She countered my mercurial tendencies.'

In the final article Sarah wrote:

'As he sits in the sunshine of an English summer, he has about him an air of calm which seems utterly at odds with both the tragedy he has suffered and the tumultuous year he faces. It is, it would seem the calm that comes from an unshakeable sense of purpose and a keen self-knowledge. He is a man who has faced the very worst hurt of life and survived and grown stronger from it. You do not envy him but there is much to admire.'

In fact, I couldn't have felt less calm as I chatted with someone from the press, but it looks like I concealed it well. She continued:

'He was born and brought up in a small village north of Belfast and retains that odd mix of volatility and philosophy that characterises many Ulstermen.'

I couldn't really dispute that comment.

My 'retirement' followed in August. For the first time in seventeen years I was free. No longer constrained by the Army's leave allowance, I could fulfil a longstanding ambition of tackling England's 'Coast to Coast' long distance path at my own pace. Mapped out by the late great veteran walker Alfred Wainwright, it runs across north England from St Bee's Head on the west coast to Robin Hood's Bay on the east. Over its 192 miles it passes through three very different English national parks – the Lake District, the Yorkshire Dales and the North York Moors. This would offer a perfect mind-clearing opportunity at the end of my Army days and for that matter after the hard graft of the previous seven months. And the journey crossed stunning areas Esther and I knew well from our many weekend walks and holidays. I was more than ready to clear my head for a couple of weeks.

I took with me a paperback that Angela Taylor had given me a few months previously. Angela's husband Hugh, an artillery officer, had been the only close friend I'd called to the house on the day of Esther's death. I knew that I could count on him to be calm and discreet and indeed he'd been brilliant. Later that month as I was waiting for my train on the concourse at Waterloo railway station, I sensed there was someone there I knew. Looking around, I saw Angela. We had a quick conversation during which I discussed my nascent interest in Nepal. As we parted, she said she'd lend me a book that might come in useful as background reading on the country. It was called 'Don't let the goats eat the loquat trees' by an American author called Tom Hale. It arrived in the post soon afterwards but I'd been too busy to even dip into it. At last I would now have the space in my life to read it and with my visit to Nepal imminent this would be very timely.

Before setting out on the trek I spent a couple of days with old friends Norma and Dermot Digges at their 'Secret Garden' guest house in Leyburn, North Yorkshire. I only had time to read the first few chapters of Angela's book, but I was immediately astounded by a parallel experience.

Essentially, Hale described his moment of epiphany when as a new young doctor he felt the inexorable call to go to Nepal. Like me, he had never been before but accepted the challenge. Then friends and acquaintances started supporting him, sending him items and smoothing his path.

Norma was a bookworm and I showed it to her:

'You must read this book some time. This writer's experience so mirrors my own. After answering the call everything fell into place for him.'

She laughed.

'Yes, by the sounds of it you've acted as a kind of catalyst. It seems to me like you've opened the valve of a car tyre and there's been a huge release of air. Long may it continue!'

The custom on the Coast to Coast walk is to aim to paddle in both the Irish and North Seas. After dipping my boots in the sea at St Bee's Head I set off eastwards, the prevailing wind to my back. My plan was to carry all I needed in a rucksack, staying either with friends, in bed and breakfast accommodation or in a tent that I could pitch near to a suitable pub.

But just a few days into the trek my plan was unravelling. The inclines of the Lake District and the rucksack had taken their toll on my joints. My left knee was swollen and I had twisted my right ankle. I found myself slogging up a hillside path, uttering 'ouch, ouch' with each step. Then I realised something strange had happened. By coincidence I was on that same track I had urged Esther to climb on our final holiday against her bitter

protests. It's understandable how people can try to stay close to loved ones after their death by holding onto their possessions and treasuring various mementoes at home. Yet here I was in the midst of the unexpected on a remote track and feeling her spirit right beside me.

The next day I accepted that I'd left the Army and didn't have to rough it by shouldering a rucksack across England. I started using a

Sherpa van service that transferred my bag ahead each day to the next overnight stop. The journey became enjoyable as my joints recovered. The sense of pilgrimage continued as after crossing the Pennines I entered the Yorkshire Dales. We had adored this area through our weekend rambles when we lived in Catterick Garrison. The route even passed right by the Frenchgate cul de sac in Richmond at the end of which lay the registry office where we'd taken our vows. Wainwright encouraged walkers on his route to 'stand and stare' and I paused there for a while to look up the cobbled street with its Georgian houses and old lampposts. I reflected on the happy day my old friend Mike Boardman had escorted Esther up that street to stand by my side. It remained a happy day in spite of what had happened.

Ten days into the trek I stopped for the night in a tiny village on the North Yorkshire moors. It was an isolated spot with only a few houses and a pub. After pitching my tent in the pub's back garden, I went into the bar for an early evening dinner. It was empty. Just then an elderly man walked in and asked if he might join me. Alan was also completing the Coast to Coast although he had been doing it by sections over a series of weekends. During our conversation it transpired that he was the Chairman of Trustees of a UK charity that translates the Bible into central Asian languages. I told him about how Nepal was exerting a tidal pull upon me and outlined my plans, while admitting to knowing next to nothing about the country. Alan had a suggestion:

'If you like I can put you in contact with one of my best friends from university days. He lived in Nepal for many years and there's not much about the country that he doesn't know. He's called Tom Hale.'

Goosebumps ran up and down my arms.

'Alan, I'm reading his book.'

The chances of this meeting in a remote place while reading such an obscure book had to be miniscule.

The next morning Alan's daughter joined us for the final two days of trekking. Alice was in her late twenties and had been a successful human resources professional who was now adrift. She was struggling to find a direction and meaning after losing her husband, Geoff, a few months before. On the way to Robin Hood's Bay we talked at length and compared experiences. After a couple of miles, I noticed that Alan was holding back a little to give us the privacy we needed.

'My problem is that I can't focus on work anymore,' she said, 'HR seems to be of very little importance. I find myself whiling away the time. Sometimes I count paper clips in a box.'

We paused at a field gate and looked across to the far hillside. The heather had now turned purple, postcard-perfect and fragrant on the early morning breeze off the moor. In the near distance a kestrel hovered quite close to the ground, wings flickering as it fixed the unfortunate beneath it with deadly eye. After some moments it swooped and was gone.

'Death is so indiscriminate in the animal kingdom,' I said, 'but for humanity it seems to be more targeted. It's the best who are taken from us in their prime. This makes no sense.'

We carried on. I liked Alice very much and found her easy to converse with but I was nevertheless cautious in my comments. She was clearly in a different place from me and much more fragile.

'People are quick to tell you that they know how you feel but they can't really empathise unless they've had an identical experience,' she said.

'Yes,' I replied, 'and circumstances vary so much even if there appears to be a similarity. For instance, on the face of it we've both been widowed through tragedy while still being very young. But one fundamental difference is that Esther chose to die, Geoff didn't.'

Our walking poles fell into harmony as their tips sprang across the yielding turf.

'In spite of such differences, I believe the important thing is to respond if you can. You know, a couple of days after Esther's death I went to see my local GP. I needed some sleeping tablets for a couple of nights to help me get through that week. Thankfully I haven't needed anything since. When I told him what had happened he put his head in his hands. I asked him what the matter was and he said that he'd lost his teenage daughter to suicide three months before. She'd been unable to come to terms with his wife's murder that had happened two years previously. He'd returned to work but he told me that he was now just going through the motions. He said that all the beauty had gone out of his life and he would look at a rose and see it only as being a flower. As I looked at this poor guy, I could see that he was languishing in a time warp.'

'Not everyone can respond,' Alice said. 'I guess you need to have a certain strength of character. And a faith helps.'

'True,' I answered, 'but you also need to have the space in your life to be able to react. I think the problem was that this doctor had other dependent children and he was responsible to them as both a breadwinner and a father. He couldn't change his life radically. I'd no such family commitments so have been able to realign myself into a totally different direction.'

I guessed that she was in a similar situation and by her silence could see that my comments were striking a chord.

After we completed the walk Alice and I had a final drink together in Robin Hood's Bay before going our separate ways. We stayed in sporadic contact and in 2002 she wrote to me to say that she had changed her life too and moved to work in Nepal with a Christian development charity. She lived there for a few years and we met up a couple of times in Kathmandu before she returned to UK to become the HR Director at one of the biggest international charities. It seemed that this time I had been a supporting actor, a catalyst, in someone else's story, helping her change direction into the sector.

The public response to the Mail on Sunday article was modest but it was nonetheless helpful for two reasons. The first was an approach from Rose, a corporate fundraiser with experience at several major British charities. Rose offered to help me structure my funding proposals and provide free consultancy on the daily operation of a charity. I'd have been lost without this initial guidance. The second was a pledge of support from a Councillor Ann Watters who lived in Kirkcaldy in Fife, Scotland. The doughty Ann coaxed her local West End Congregational Church and its charismatic Minister, Revd Willie McNaughton, into adopting the charity. They did so primarily by placing a collection plate at the door of the church so that each Sunday church members could drop in a few coins as they left. Their donations build up to approximately £1,500 annually. Each year since 2000 I have made a pilgrimage to visit this loyal congregation, receive a cheque and report back in person. The funds have been invaluable but so also have been the moral support, loyalty and friendship I've received.

The Esther Benjamins Trust became a registered charity in September 1999. I appointed a group of Trustees, selecting individuals who had known Esther and her values and who had been supportive to me after her loss. These included stalwarts like John Sharp, Chris Collinson and Neal Gillespie. The Trust had some money in the bank and now I needed an operational plan. In November I made my first trip to Nepal, brimming with confidence and optimism, unaware of the mother of all rollercoasters that lay ahead.

Before I left, I had one final duty to fulfil to Esther and that was to check out her headstone. She had given me a clear directive that her grave should be left so that it required no maintenance or return visits. That's what she had done with her father's grave, covering it in stone chippings, so that she'd had no need to go back to it or think of its upkeep. 'Thank God, he isn't there', she'd say. I planned to place a flat slab of basalt on top of Esther's grave with raised brass lettering that would survive the extremes of weather in north Holland. Then a problem arose in that the rabbi objected to the wording 'wife of Lt Col Philip Holmes' since we hadn't been married under Jewish law. He wouldn't recognise Esther as my wife in life or in death, a further insult to humanity after his initial attempt to exclude her body from the cemetery.

Behind his back a Dutch friend of ours arranged for my wording to be translated into Hebrew and for the slab to be sited without the rabbi's permission. He said that if the rabbi didn't like it, he could lift it himself.

Esther's old friend Frouk drove me to the cemetery in her little car. She was full of conversation.

'You know,' she said in her precise English, 'the problem with old people is that we don't understand young people. And we don't want to understand them. When I was 70, I found a volunteer job in a hospital so that I could interact with them. I came to enjoy their sense of humour and to respect their ideals.'

As we drew up at the cemetery gates, she hit me with a non-sequitur.

'Can you forgive her?'

I didn't have to consider my answer.

'Frouk, there's nothing to forgive. I was the last person on this earth that she wanted to hurt. It was because she loved me so very much that she wanted to set me free and let me start afresh. How can I hold any grudge against her for that?'

The headstone was perfect, my choice of epitaph: 'Her life was Tsedekah.'

We each placed a pebble on the slab to record our visit and left.

U nbeknownst to me, someone else in 1999 was planning to set up a children's home in response to personal loss. Dr Peramangalam Porinju (PP) Job, the self-styled 'India's Billy Graham', was a Man on a Mission.

Originally from Kerala, south India, Dr Job had taken up the challenge of spreading his version of the Gospel to non-Christian nations within South Asia. This was his contribution towards fulfilling 'The Great Commission' from Jesus Christ that the Word be spread to all nations after which He would return to earth. Dr Job's target nations were ones in which the Church was allegedly persecuted, including Nepal.

To help get the message across he'd held rallies and even set up his own printing press which he claimed published annually three million items of Christian literature in 37 languages. These included some of his own books. He could only conduct his calling with the support and adulation of a clique of international fundamentalist evangelists. Foreigners can be very quick to put fairly mundane people from South Asia onto pedestals, project their own values onto them and throw money at their cause.

Reading around Dr Job's life story it's hard to distinguish fact from fantasy. One source describes how he rose from an impoverished childhood selling peanuts and soda on a stall. Another identified him as being the third of four sons of a vet. In a TV interview he claimed that his Christian ministry began at the age of three when he started preaching to other children. That was nine years before Jesus. In one of his books he described how as a young man he was the sole survivor of 13 people who'd been bitten by a rabid dog. He described how this miraculous deliverance only followed a feverish episode that reduced him to going onto all fours and howling like a dog before losing consciousness. God had bestowed His providence on him while the lives of the other twelve unfortunates hadn't mattered.

In June 1999 as Dr Job was on his way to the airport to attend a Christian conference, he suffered a minor head wound from a smashed windscreen. Dr Job alleged that Hindu fanatics, enraged at his ministry, had pelted his car with stones. He wrote that he had been hit by a 'rock'. A doctor, who fortuitously happened to be travelling in the car with him, bandaged the wound and rushed him to hospital.

One of Dr Job's journalist friends attributed this incident to having been nothing more than a shattered windscreen but Dr Job asserted that this had been an attempt on his life. While he was 'recovering' in hospital from his ordeal he learned that the younger of his two sons, Michael, had been killed – 'martyred' - in a hit and run traffic accident at Dehradun, north India. Dr Job alleged that this was a murder conducted by Hindu extremists frustrated at their failure to kill his father. This allegation was never proven but of course the roads in the Indian subcontinent are inherently dangerous places.

Dr Job's response to his loss was to set up a girls' home in Michael's memory. At God's instruction he chose to build his facility on a 50-acre site at Coimbatore in India's deep south. This donated land was arid and had no water supply, yet one of Dr Job's online testimonials proclaimed how the site had since miraculously developed an ample supply of fresh water. The truth of the matter was revealed in one of Dr Job's own books. Through a friendly contact at the Coimbatore water authority, his Centre was able to tap into a mains water supply that happened to run through the site. This meant that while Coimbatore residents endured regular water restrictions, Dr Job's campus enjoyed a continuous supply of stolen water.

The Michael Job Centre would be part of a Christian proselytising agenda. Dr Job wanted to raise a generation of girls who could follow in his footsteps. He declared that they would be travelling around the world with a college degree in one hand and a Bible in the other, sharing the gospel. He wrote that, like Paul, a tentmaker, they would make their own money by hard work while preaching the gospel.

But where would Dr Job find the orphan girls that God had promised him as daughters to replace his lost son?

Part 2

Patan Durbar Square, Nepal

'Synchronicity is an ever-present reality for those who have eyes to see.'

- Carl Jung, *Synchronicity: An Acausal Connecting Principle*

7.   The yam between two boulders

I t is especially worth remembering that time hardly ever means money in Nepal. For the average Nepali, time is an abstract philosophical concept.'

On the flight into Kathmandu I was reading '*A Simple Guide to Nepal*' by Sunil Jha. As part of my background reading a tourist handbook seemed as good a starting point as any. He continued:

'You may find that letters are left unanswered, decisions are delayed, opportunities missed, appointments postponed at the eleventh hour, people responsible are absent or difficult to find.'

Esther used to tease me about my impatience and now, more fired up than ever, I was launching myself full sail into this backwater. Would Nepal be my nemesis rather than my chance to triumph over tragedy?

Actually, there can be no 'simple guide' to Nepal. It's even a struggle to find it on a map. This little slither of landlocked country, population around thirty million, reclines in semi slumber between the restive bedfellows of India and China. Or, as the first king of Nepal, Prithvi Shah, described it more lyrically in the eighteenth century, 'a delicate yam between two boulders.' These days Nepalis venerate King Prithvi for having conquered the nation by uniting disparate, warring tribes under his crown. In portraits he is characterised standing with one finger raised to symbolise the  national unity he forged. The intrinsic strength he created meant Nepal could remain independent throughout the colonial era.

The passenger on my right had been sipping whiskey, to my mind a bit early on a morning flight. He was also looking rather incongruous in a grey pin striped suit that, like him, had seen better days. With his comb-over, slightly pronounced lower lip and loose jowls he reminded me a little of a school teacher I'd despised back in the 1970s. I wasn't at all sure that I wanted to chat with him. But eventually he struck up the conversation:

'Good book?'

'Very informative, thanks,' I replied, 'but then again with my knowledge of Nepal any guidebook, however small, is going to teach me a lot. This is actually my first visit. What about you?'

'Oh, I live in Kathmandu,' he replied, 'I took early retirement when I was 55 and decided to settle over here. In my earlier days I was a clerk in the Gurkha camp at Dharan and fell in love with the country.'

'I used to be an Army dentist but I guess that was after your time. So, how's your life in Nepal?' I asked.

'Well, an old geezer like me commands more respect in Kathmandu than I would do in London. Back home I would be stacking the shelves in a supermarket to supplement my pension, but in Nepal I can live like a king. And the booze is cheap.'

He took off his little round glasses and wiped them with a cloth handkerchief.

'I think because of my advanced years and general decrepit appearance the local people expect me to be a font of wisdom, but I keep my thoughts to myself. I've learned that in life if you keep your mouth shut then others might think you're clever even if you're not. It's still hard to hold your tongue though when you see some of the terrible things going on around you.'

He downed the remainder of his whiskey in one and pressed the overhead button to summon a stewardess. He continued:

'But when it comes down to it, Nepalis don't appreciate foreigners arriving in their country and presuming to tell them what to do, however well-intentioned that might be. They'd prefer to sort things out for themselves, in their own cack-handed way, at their own leisurely pace, taking the craziest decisions that beggar belief.'

For no apparent reason he began to laugh.

'Since this is your first visit to Nepal you won't have experienced the delights of an Asian squat toilet. Basically, it's a rectangle of porcelain over which you hover and try to hit the hole in the middle. The flush can be nothing more than a bucket of water and you can forget about toilet paper. That's what your left hand is for.'

'I'd heard about that bit,' I said. 'Someone told me that's the reason why it's considered rude to offer someone something with your left hand.'

'Correct,' he said. 'But I tell you this because the Indians say that a Nepali person will go for a crap and afterwards go looking for water to flush it away with. The joke is that Nepalis lack any capacity for forward planning. Not that they've anything to crow about themselves.'

His laughter resumed.

'I bet it doesn't tell you that in your guidebook; there's much more to this country than meets the eye. And people's true thoughts are concealed by smiles. That's part of their upbringing. They become expert at telling you bad news with a grin.'

I laughed.

'Maybe you should write an alternative guide book. No holds barred.'

He cleared his throat and his denture wobbled.

'No chance. One thing I've learned is that when you think you've got your head around Nepal then you know that you really have gone bonkers. I won't confess to that through writing a book.'

He was more receptive to my plans than Edward had been.

'Yes, there are a lot of children's homes in Nepal, most so filthy that they're unfit for a dog, let alone children. However, some of them work really well. I knew a bloke from the Pay Corps in Dharan called Tom Hughes who set up a very good one. There are a lot of young people walking around Dharan now who have taken his surname. He became their father to all intents and purposes.'

This was just the kind of story I wanted to hear; I was at the mercy of confirmation bias. He ordered a large whiskey from the stewardess.

'But be wary, my friend. This is a very predatory society and watch out for the tricky Brahmin who'll part you from your money quicker than you can say orphanage. Take your time, don't aim too high and just remember that you won't save the world.'

He tore a piece of paper from the back of the in-flight magazine and scribbled down his number. I detected a slight tremor.

'My name's Billy. If you ever need my dubious advice, you'll find me most evenings propping up the bar in The Everest in Thamel. That's the main tourist area in Kathmandu. If I'm not around the barman will know where to find me. He's as good as next of kin these days.

Most of the other passengers were young Nepali men who seemed to be unusually excited and garrulous. The noise levels were increasing in inverse proportion to the proximity to Nepal. They too had been enjoying the refreshments. Billy told me that these were migrant workers on their way home from Qatar. He said that thousands of unskilled labourers were working in harsh conditions in the Gulf States and Malaysia in the absence of any employment being available in Nepal. In fact the working conditions were so dreadful that suicide rates were high and others just died from overwork and heat exhaustion. This was akin to slave labour.

As soon as the plane touched the tarmac these young men were on their feet scrambling for bags in overhead lockers. Apoplectic cabin staff tried to get them to resume their seats with limited success.

'Bloody typical,' said Billy, 'they treat the plane just like it's a Nepali bus.'

His laughter brought on a paroxysm of coughing.

This sight offered a foretaste of the scrum that lay ahead. Billy and I became separated in the chaos of the baggage hall where the staff and porters gave all the appearance of being new to their jobs. But thankfully my trusty rucksack had made it through in one piece.

My relief was short-lived as I exchanged the frying pan of the baggage hall for the fire of the wall of pushy taxi drivers that confronted me outside. I was just about to retreat inside to compose myself when I spotted Suresh's grin in the midst of the mayhem. We embraced before jumping into a taxi to enter the organised chaos of Kathmandu.

Before long, I sensed his unease, possibly even some insecurity; if anything, Suresh appeared subdued. He must have realised that I had arrived with high expectations of him but he was a stranger in this city and this society too. Man and boy he'd lived a world away from the intrigues of his homeland that are worthy of fifteenth century Florence. He'd talked the talk in the UK but the time had come for him to deliver and he risked losing face.

His only support network comprised other former Army veterans, but they weren't movers and shakers. We met up with a few of them but it turned out they had little to offer beyond expressions of goodwill and admiration. With lofty words they'd commend Suresh for how his plans exhibited 'dharma', a Hindu concept of spiritual behaviour that enshrines duty, virtue and doing the right thing by one's fellow man. That was all fine and dandy but praise alone wouldn't find us a project.

87

In those first few days we nosed around Kathmandu, unsure of our goal. We visited some of the big names like UNICEF to sound them out. No one we spoke to was thrilled at the prospect of our opening a children's home in a land already teeming with them.

After those non-productive initial enquiries in Kathmandu, we left for Bhairahawa. This meant a ten-hour hair-raising journey along a bumpy road with hairpin bends and crazy drivers. Before we set off Suresh offered life-saving guidance:

'If we're involved in a collision, run for it.'

I looked at him askance.

'No, I'm serious. This is what bus drivers do if they have an accident. Their vehicles are often overloaded and poorly maintained and 'mishaps' are very common. After an incident a mob can form from nowhere either seeking compensation or, if there's been a fatality, vengeance. The vehicle may be torched and if they catch the driver will give him a hiding, maybe even kill him. There's another side to the coin. I've heard it said that if no one's looking a driver might well "finish off" an injured victim to avoid liability for long-term care costs.'

Suresh's remark suggested that I was in a country where different ground rules applied. This land would be no genteel Shangri-La.

'There's something else. If you are spotted in the vehicle, we will certainly take the blame and the compensation claim will be even higher. White people are always rich.'

'What about the police?' I asked.

'They're no help. Congenitally inept and corrupt, from what I've seen. If they're on the scene of a two-car collision they don't try to establish fault. Instead they demand that the person driving the bigger car compensates the other driver as he can better afford it.'

The morning after we arrived in Bhairahawa we set off into town on Suresh's motorbike. He needed to pick up some goat meat for the evening curry. I was quite surprised as this vibrant border town looked more Indian than Nepali. We stopped for a tea in the main street, not far from the Hotel Glasgow with its sign depicting Tower Bridge in London. This was my first opportunity to observe this very foreign world that was so different even from Kathmandu. Two male police constables strolled by, walking hand in hand. On the opposite side we could see a Sadhu[4] with a long beard and dressed in saffron, staff in hand, going from shop to shop collecting donations in a little tin bucket.

---

[4] A Hindu holy man

Within the space of a few minutes we had seen just about every form of road transport imaginable from water buffalo or oxen-drawn carts to rickshaws, to vintage tractors, their canopies richly bedecked in tinsel, to the omnipresent motorbikes. There were trucks painted garishly in primary colours, transporting freight to and from the border. These had obscure hand-painted slogans on their tailgates such as 'sweet memory' and 'no time for love'. I couldn't help but notice the discordant juxtaposition of the Star of David and the swastika hand-painted on the back of one of them. Suresh explained that these were both auspicious Hindu symbols; no truck driver should be without them.

With this bedazzling mix of transport came the sounds of horns, rattling ox-bells and the cries of street merchants, their bicycles laden with wares ranging from heaps of mangoes to strings of carp to assorted items of ironmongery. We could smell dal (lentils) and onions cooking for someone's lunch to the accompanying hiss of an invisible pressure cooker. A woman in a sari squatted by the pavement turning corn cobs over coals, their rich aroma tainted by the acrid smoke of a roadside fire just a few metres away; apparently this was the local solution for domestic waste disposal. A pointy-eared skinny piebald dog hovered outside an open-fronted meat shop, its hopeful gaze met by the sightless eyes of two pig heads on public display to passers-by and flies alike. A child threw a stone at the dog and it scarpered to re-join its fellows in a pack that was investigating a rubbish pile on nearby waste ground.

His shopping duties completed, Suresh took me for a sightseeing trip into the surrounding countryside. It was getting very hot so I found it pleasant to be his pillion passenger. Unlike Bhairahawa this scenery was sedate and pastoral, almost with a mediaeval feel to it. We stopped now and again to watch very weather-beaten men, or more often women, till the land with hand tools. It was hard to imagine that just fifty years before, these same organised fields had been jungle and swamp. Once they'd drained the marshland and brought the endemic malaria under control, hill people, who included Suresh's forebears, had moved into this new fertile area. They bought land from the indigenous *Tharu* community at knock-down prices. Or it might have been given to the immigrants in return for political favours. Unfortunately, it has to be said that the comparatively wealthy interlopers lorded it over the Tharu and the sizeable ethnic Indian population that straddles the open border. Their large villas arose like overbearing icebergs amidst a placid green sea of paddy fields, towering like playground bullies over the simple mud huts of the poorer echelons of society. This was not a situation to be

89

proud of and, from my knowledge of the origins of the Troubles of Northern Ireland, surely fertile ground for future strife.

Returning home, we stopped by a wayside temple dedicated to the elephant-headed Hindu deity Ganesh. The brass idol was boxed in on three sides by what looked like bathroom tiles, a bell dangling to the left, an oil lamp and smoking incense stick to the right. The idol itself had been smeared in red dye and some marigold leaves lay scattered at its feet.

'People will come here every day to offer Pooja[5],' explained Suresh, 'leaving their mark and ringing the bell when they've finished. Hindu people believe that Ganesh can overcome obstacles. I can't quite work that one out though as others believe that an obstacle won't be overcome if it's part of your destiny.'

Sitting astride his motorbike, he reflected for a few moments.

'The thing that I wonder about too is, if we're right about praying to all these gods, how come this country is in such a dreadful mess?'

'Maybe if people spent their time trying to sort out their problems for themselves rather than wasting it in praying for deliverance then we'd all be better off,' I replied.

He nodded and we continued on our way.

Back at the house Suresh had visibly relaxed; here in Bhairahawa he was lord of his own little manor. Early one morning, as we were sitting on his first-floor balcony surveying the activities in the fields his wife joined us. She gave him a coffee and then knelt, touched his feet with her head, said some words and left.

'What was that all about?' I asked.

He gave one of his trademark little anarchic giggles.

'In a Nepali household the husband is god to his wife; she has just apologised for perhaps having been inadvertently in contact with my body last night while we slept and without asking my prior permission. It's not all bad in the Hindu faith, you know!'

---

[5] Prayer

Small wonder he felt more confident and in control after having been such a small minnow in the big pond of Kathmandu. With Suresh at ease we began to discuss project ideas but we kept foundering on the rock of our ignorance of child-related issues in Nepal. Moreover, we'd put ourselves into a planning straitjacket with the solution of a children's home devised before defining the problem. We were having to reverse plan and work out how a facility as self-limiting and small as an orphanage could be made useful given the huge number of potential 'needy children' across the country. With so many falling into that category, how might we select say twenty or thirty of them as worthy beneficiaries over the rest? We had absolutely no idea.

Then one afternoon as I was relaxing over a cup of tea, I picked up a copy of the previous day's Kathmandu Post that happened to be lying on Suresh's coffee table. I was expecting to scan what is usually a very light piece of reading but the leader story brought me up short. The banner headline read: 'Minors starved, cramped and abused in jail.' Underneath a picture showed three boys squatting in a cell with the caption: 'Hard core criminals? - It's said children are greatest gifts from God to mankind. But with many such innocent children languishing in jail for no fault of their own a serious question can be raised about their future.'

The article focussed on the plight of two boys, aged seven and eight, who had been held inside Kathmandu Central Jail with their mother for the past four years. Their father and elder sister were imprisoned elsewhere. They were two of the hundred or so children under the age of 14 who were in prison. These would have included young Ramesh Badi. The journalist reported that they had been jailed because there was no one else to look after them. She described conditions as being congested with meagre prison rations and no educational provision beyond some teaching provided by an NGO worker. Worse still, several boys claimed they had been sexually abused.

This report would be a game-changer. With my newfound sense of the metaphysical I was convinced that my future project had found me. Or, more accurately, that I was being steered in a particular direction. Helping children in desperate need fitted with Esther's aspirations but besides that she had also been a close supporter of Amnesty International. Therefore, the issue of innocent, vulnerable children in jail had to be the cause I'd been seeking. And it offered me the opportunity to tackle a well-defined contemporary problem that no one else was addressing. A hundred children would be a lot to try to help with the charity's limited means, but at least we could make an impact on such a finite figure.

We decided we'd spend a few days in Kathmandu before I flew home and consult with the NGO from the report. It was the 'Prisoners' Assistance Mission' (PAM) and the journalist had mentioned a field worker called Indira Rana Magar.

At the PAM office Suresh and I met its Chairman, Sukanya Waiba. Indira was there too. Even if she was kept in the background, I could see that she was a very striking young woman with high, prominent cheek bones and sharp eyes. As Suresh explained our interest a bewildered Waiba stopped him in his tracks.

'Why are you speaking Nepali like a foreigner?' she demanded in English.

Suresh shifted in his seat. She'd just told my former language instructor that he couldn't speak his own language. Suresh had lost face in front of me and this didn't endear her to him. He resumed the conversation in English. It was nothing personal, but for the first time I began to wonder if Suresh was the find I'd imagined him to be. Just then the speech made by Suresh's last boss at his Army leaving party sprang to mind. He had joked how I ought to have recruited someone who actually *knew* Nepal. Afterwards Suresh had smouldered with anger for the jest had contained more than a ring of truth.

Eventually Waiba closed what became a frosty meeting by saying that we were most welcome to visit their 'Nestling Home' to meet the children. Indira would be very happy to host us and to answer any questions we might have about the prisons.

With that, we extricated Indira from Waiba's domineering presence and repaired to a nearby café where we ordered lemon sodas. I could see the immediate rapport between Suresh and Indira; they were both Magars and that made all the difference. She spoke with passion about the prisons, so much so that we had to interject from time to time to get her to slow down. It was this same passion that had unfortunately recently caused the breakup of her marriage. Her husband had given her an ultimatum; it was either her work or him. Her answer was self-evident. Now she went everywhere hand-in-hand with her little daughter, including into the prisons.

'The prisons in this country are destroying families and punishing innocent children,' she began. 'When someone is remanded in custody it can take years for the case to come to trial. That's too long to be without a breadwinner and it's not easy for his wife to find a job, or to manage it if she has young children.'

She paused to open a window and release a fly that had been distracting us.

'Very often the wife remarries as soon as possible, just to avoid having to beg. The woman's new husband will most likely not want to take in her children.' She nudged Suresh. 'As you know, *dai*[6], stepchildren are very unwelcome in Nepalese families.'

'It used to be the same in England in Victorian times,' I said to Suresh. 'Charles Dickens wrote about this in Nicholas Nickleby. In those days stepsons were packed off to dreadful "boarding schools" in some faraway place. Out of sight, out of mind.'

Indira continued in full flow, her eyes dancing between Suresh and me:

'This all means the unwanted children face the dreadful choice of either going onto the streets or joining their father in the prison.'

Suresh's brow furrowed.

'Surely there is another option. In this country the social support revolves around large extended families. Can't children just stay with relatives? Rather than you taking children into a children's home, wouldn't it be more cost effective to support families?'

She shook her head.

'The problem is that there's a huge amount of stigma around imprisonment and families will conceal that they have a relative in jail. Looking after his children admits a kind of shared guilt.'

This was shocking for me, but also quite outrageous.

'Indira, are you telling me that a man can spend several years in prison pending trial – with or without his children - be found not guilty and then released to find he's lost his family in the meantime?'

'This happens all the time,' she replied.

Then she looked at her watch and a big smile spread across her face, wrinkling her nose.

'Shall we go and meet some children? They'll just be getting back from school around now.'

It was a short walk down an earth track to the PAM Nestling Home. On the way we stopped by at a little shop to buy lemonade, coca cola and bags of sweets.

---

[6] The Nepali word for 'big brother', a term of respect and endearment

As we approached the home, I asked Indira a question that had been nagging at me:

'You've only mentioned men going to prison. What about women?'

She paused to wipe her daughter's nose without a hankie, displaying a deft finger and thumb, twist of the wrist and flick worthy of a magician. Suresh winked at me.

'In Nepal we throw away what an Englishman wraps up and stores in his pocket.'

Indira seemed to miss his comment and continued.

'Philip, it's so easy for an innocent woman to be imprisoned. In our culture a son is vital for inheritance and also for religious ceremonies, including conducting the last rites. If a wife doesn't produce a son, she's very vulnerable. Abortion is illegal in Nepal and a husband or, more likely, a mother in law can denounce a woman after a miscarriage and then she's in jail. After that the husband is free to re-marry and try again.'

This really did seem to be my destined project, a response to childlessness that had such ramifications in both Hinduism and Judaism.

The PAM Nestling Home consisted of a high blockhouse that towered over a tiny dirt playground, not a blade of grass in sight. A drooping clothes line laden with little pairs of trousers and dresses was the only indication that this was indeed a children's home. Just by the entrance a couple of kids peeped out through a bamboo fence at the approaching strangers. But no sooner were we through the gate than we were being mobbed by around 30 boys and girls, Indira being the star attraction.

A little girl called Jamuna was quick to take my hand though, keen to tell me something in Nepali that I couldn't understand. My digital camera proved to be more of an ice-breaker than the drinks and sweets. The kids never tired of posing and then dashing to see how they looked on my screen, pointing and laughing to one another. Jamuna had left the group but returned carrying a black and white passport type photo of a serious man who seemed to have almost bouffant hair.

'This is her father,' Indira explained, 'they sent him and his wife to jail on a human trafficking charge about a month ago. She's missing them terribly but, *ke garne*?'

This was the first time I would come across the expression *'ke garne?'* It means 'what can you do?' and is used a lot in Nepal when people are out of ideas or accept the need to surrender to destiny.

Jamuna tucked the picture away and a radio cassette player was produced from nowhere. While some scratchy Hindi dance music blasted out, house mothers produced plastic cups and distributed the lemonade and sweets. One of them brought me a cup of excruciatingly sweet tea. Then a circle formed with Jamuna dancing in the centre as everyone clapped. The circle gradually thinned as the spectators joined Jamuna one by one. Then it was Suresh and Indira's turn before Jamuna came over to draw me into the melee. I dislike dancing even more than I hate sweet tea but there was no choice with either option. I entered the dance with all the ability a footless Northern Irish Presbyterian could muster.

In spite of my reluctance I found it deeply touching to look around at the apparent unbridled joy, the delight in simple things that these children exhibited in spite of what they had so recently endured. Children like these were nothing short of inspirational.

Before parting from Indira, I asked what I could do to help. Straight away she named three girls and four boys who were in desperate need of being released from jail. Her face creased up in delight when I told her that if PAM had the spare capacity at their home, I would fund their keep. It was as easy for me as that. The thought of children in jail was anathema to me and this 'contracting out' arrangement offered a cost-effective quick solution compared with the time we'd require to set up our own home. My impatience was making its presence felt. Indira assured me that the release process would be straightforward as these innocent children had become an administrative burden for the prison. As for the children's parents, they would be happy to have someone look after them. She was certain she could make the necessary arrangements overnight. We agreed to meet by the main gate of the Central Jail at 11 a.m. the next morning.

'You're great,' she said as we parted.

'No,' I replied with a smile, 'God is great.'

As it happened Suresh and I were staying in a cheap little hotel in Thamel. He was off colour that evening, attributing that to something he'd eaten, and excused himself in favour of an early night. I was still elated from that day's experience and felt ready for a drink. I set off into the heady streets of Thamel in search of The Everest. It took me a couple of passes before I found a very inauspicious entrance that took me down a dark corridor towards a narrow flight of stairs that led to the first floor.

Upstairs it was abuzz with young people, the walls covered in graffiti that I could make out in spite of the low light. I spotted my target, an elderly figure in a grey suit slumped on a stool at the bar. He was swirling a glass of whiskey absent-mindedly. In spite of the suit he looked rather unkempt.

'Hello Billy,' I announced. 'Remember me?'

He turned a watery eye that flickered into recognition.

'Well, if it isn't the Colonel. How's it going?'

It had been three weeks since the flight into Kathmandu and I'd been on a steep, but fascinating, learning curve. There was so much to tell him. He ordered us both whiskeys and I gave him a potted account of all that I'd seen and done in the interim, leading up to that day's memorable visit to PAM and its Nestling Home. I told him of my amusement at Suresh's advice to run for it in the event of a road accident.

'Sadly, he's right,' he replied. 'But, you know, that's Nepal in microcosm. From what I've seen, just like the driver, many people at all levels within society have an unwillingness to accept responsibility for their actions or failings.'

Warming to his subject, he swigged some whiskey.

'These range from the teachers who don't turn up to their work to the politicians who blame one another rather than admitting to indecision or lack of leadership. Sometimes it feels as if you're witnessing the pathetic behaviour, the crazy decision-making, of irresponsible children or drunks who can't think things through.'

I guessed that at least in respect of the latter Billy was well-placed to comment. But I was curious to hear his take on Suresh's uncomfortable meeting with Sukanya Waiba. I had been amazed that she had been so cool towards someone whom I believed had gained such kudos from having been a British Army officer.

'I'm not in the least bit surprised,' he said. 'In Nepal former Gurkhas command little respect outside of their own castes and villages. In fact, quite the opposite. The British and Indian armies recruit their Gurkhas·from ethnic groups that are lower in the caste pecking order than the *Brahmins*, *Chettris* and *Newaris*. We used to call them NBC[7]'s in the Army and they are the closed shop that runs Nepal these days. Moreover, with so very few applicants being accepted into the Army Gurkhas are the subject of a great deal of jealousy, a sentiment endemic in Nepal.'

---

[7] In the Army NBC actually refers to nuclear, biological and chemical warfare.

His denture shifted, causing him to slur his words in Churchillian fashion. I struggled to keep my face straight.

'Local people might perceive Gurkha veterans as being *dhani* – that means "rich" - because of the comparative wealth they accumulated during their military service underpinned by a secure pension. You or I might expect that with all the experience they had gained overseas and in the Army, they'd be highly employable in a second career after returning to Nepal. But this isn't the case. Instead many see them as already having had their golden opportunity in life and undeserving of the further good fortune of a top-flight job. That's why so many of them choose to continue to work abroad.'

Before I could fully digest this statement, he hit me with even greater food for thought:

'Why do you think those kids today were so excited?' he asked.

'I've absolutely no idea,' I confessed, 'unless staying happy in the face of adversity is a national characteristic.'

'Nope,' he said, 'I don't believe it's that and you weren't witnessing genuine happiness. I am no child psychologist but my guess is that those children feel lost and unloved. NGOs claim to set up what they call "family-style homes" that are nothing more than institutions. They appoint staff whom they call 'house mothers' but who're doing a job without offering any kind of individual affection. Given the numbers involved there's little else they can do, even if they wanted to. Those children you saw today were craving for meaningful adult contact and they were hoping that you could deliver on that. Maybe they even thought that their saviour had arrived.' He chortled with his chesty laughter.

Some minutes later Billy arose unsteadily to head to the toilet and with a handshake I bade him goodnight. I told him that I would be leaving Nepal the following evening but I promised that I would call by on my next visit.

Walking back to the hotel, I thought again about little Jamuna and that treasured picture. I wondered if she too would grow up with the same kind of irrational anger and rejection issues that Esther had described in the 'war children' she'd worked with as adults. Tragically, I was powerless to do anything to help Jamuna as she was totally the victim of circumstances. These were the failings of her parents, if they were guilty, or of the flawed Nepali justice system if they were innocent. Billy's inebriated comments on the children's home scenario had been sobering in the extreme. I had no choice but to support flawed

97

institutional care, it being the only alternative to children being in jail, denied their rights and in free association with dangerous criminals.

The next morning at 11 a.m. seven little children walked out of Kathmandu Central Jail with a radiant Indira in their midst. It was the 4th December 1999, eleven months to the day after Esther's death. Standing by the prison gates, I was overwhelmed by the magnitude and power of my achievement. To reach this point I'd drawn upon all my reserves of resolve, determination and energy, tapping into an inner strength that I hadn't known existed - or that came from somewhere else. With this triumph the year's pendulum had swung from one apogee to the other. I had fulfilled my pledge to rekindle her light and done so much faster than I could have expected. More than that, I'd come as close as I could to realising her New Year's Eve wish for me to have a 'good 1999'. After how the year started it was never going to be *good* but for sure it had been productive and eventful, taking me to unexpected places geographically, emotionally and spiritually. And now our first children stood before me.

There was something else. I sensed how Esther would have reacted had she been there on this poignant occasion. She'd have nudged me and with a mischievous twinkle in her eye said 'Let's go for a drink to celebrate'. But she wasn't there, only a gaping void by my side that no friend could fill. At that moment, alone and in a strange land, I missed her as at no other time that year.

The dam of my composure that had held firm all year began to crack and I had to walk away from the happy scene, overwhelmed and heart-broken. In the seclusion of a small backstreet I burst into tears.

8.   Gates of Bronze

The Esther Benjamins Trust may have been conceived in UK, had part of its gestation in Holland but it was born in an unexpected place: Hong Kong.

Friends of mine in Hong Kong, Ronnie and Carol Ford, responded to my letter telling them of Esther's death to say that they would stage an exhibition of Ronnie's art in a local gallery as a charity fundraiser. Maybe I would like to attend? I jumped at the chance; aside from the importance of reciprocating interest, Hong Kong had been a potential Army posting for me that I would have loved to have seen. But being stationed there hadn't been feasible because of Esther's work commitments.

The show was a great success, helped along by lovely coverage in *The Hong Kong Standard*, the smaller of the two English language broadsheets in Hong Kong. The article was entitled 'The Children Came Later'. I could only stay for a few days but after my return to Holland I was e mailed by Fionnuala McHugh, a freelance journalist with the larger English daily, *The South China Morning Post*. She also had a long history of writing for the UK's largest broadsheet, *The Daily Telegraph*.

Normally - and especially in advance of making an expensive trip from Hong Kong to Nepal – a freelancer would seek a commission from the paper first. But Fionnuala has a sixth sense for a strong story and took a chance by paying her own way. More than that, on the strength of her personal knowledge of the Features Editor at the Telegraph and the strong British angle, she managed to persuade a photographer friend, Graham Uden, to join her, also at his own expense. I agreed to meet them in Kathmandu for the release of a few more children from jail.

Fionnuala and Graham joined me on my next trip to Nepal in April 2000. Meeting them the morning after their arrival, I could see immediately that this was a very unlikely duo. I warmed to them for differing reasons. Fionnuala and I had the natural affinity for one another that Northern Irish people seem to have when they meet up abroad. There was also something quite intriguing about this former convent girl, a Cambridge-educated barrister turned journalist. She was elfin, quick-witted and clearly *very* clever, teetotal unlike her travelling companion. Shaven-headed Graham, who bristled cameras and associated gizmos, was a Jack-the-Lad figure, seemingly wed to clubbing in Hong Kong when he wasn't travelling the globe to take on edgy photographic assignments. He dressed for the part wearing harnesses and a collection of pouches worthy of a frontline soldier. Indeed, from our initial chats it emerged that he admired the military and relished taking his chances in hot spots around the world. Before long he was referring to me as 'Colonel H' with my reciprocating as 'Sergeant U'. Already he was addressing the prim Fionnuala as 'Miss McCoo', she listening with an indulgent smile as he tried without success to startle her with tales of his nocturnal excesses in seedy Wan Chai.

Despite their differences, they worked in powerful combination, the common denominators being that they were consummate professionals, masters of their respective arts. And in how they were both stirred by the spirit of what they came to witness in Kathmandu. For all his fooling around, I noticed Graham discreetly wiping an eye as I shared with Fionnuala some of the detail of how I had lost Esther.

Naturally they wanted to see inside the prisons for themselves and we used Indira Rana Magar's good influence to get us into Kathmandu Central Jail the following morning. We arrived early and sat on a wall outside the prison, watching the world go by as I told Fionnuala more about Esther, her professional background, how happy we'd been as a couple and how it had all unravelled for us. In front of us a man passed a live chicken through the prison gate while a parakeet fidgeted on a guard's shoulder. Some hill women, dressed in tartan shawls and with gold ear and nose rings squatted on the other side of the road, one of them smoking a very pungent cigarette in the cool early morning air.

'My thinking has been very, very clear since day one,' I said to her. 'After Esther's death it seemed like everyone else was flapping around me. In many ways it feels like there's a pattern unfolding before me, a kind of destiny.'

Fionnuala was writing only scant notes, details like names and dates. I guessed that she was committing most of her observations and impressions to memory.

'Through this work I will be setting up a living memorial to Esther, one that will stand the test of time. That said I've a personal dream of one day unveiling a brass plaque on the children's home I'll open in her name at Bhairahawa. I already know the inscription.'

I had found the passage from Isaiah 45 as I sat in Crondall church one Sunday and could recite it from memory:

'Thus says the Lord to Cyrus his anointed,
Cyrus whom he has taken by the hand

101

to subdue nations before him
and undo the might of kings;
before whom gates shall be opened
and no doors be shut:
I will go before you
and level the swelling hills;
I will break down gates of bronze
and hack through iron bars.
I will give you treasures from dark vaults,
hoarded in secret places,
that you may know that I am the Lord,
Israel's God who calls you by name.'

My voice breaking a little, I explained:

'Nothing ever stopped Esther until childlessness became Gates of Bronze that she couldn't overcome. I'm determined to break these down too. The strange thing is that I chose these words before finding out about the issue of prison children. So, the allusion to iron bars, dark vaults and secret places has been uncanny to say the least.'

The assistant governor arrived at 11.30 and took us inside. By rights I should have been pleased at the conditions within. The atmosphere was benign with the inmates lounging around playing cards, strumming guitars or busying themselves in a well-equipped prison workshop. But I was mortified as this was far from being the misery and squalor I'd expected and as described in the original Kathmandu Post report. Indira showed us around with typical enthusiasm. Fionnuala was recording all in her quaint little Chinese notebook while on the periphery the affable Graham brought the photographic best out of convicts, snapping images with his winning grin.

Whatever crimes the inmates may or may not have perpetrated, there was at least one person in the prison that day who had committed a cardinal offence. Me. I was scolding myself that I had overlooked the Army adage of 'time spent in reconnaissance is never wasted' and instead gone in blind. Indeed, this was my first ever visit to a Nepalese prison.

Yes, there were children there. Fionnuala later wrote how they would 'bob in and out of view, disturbing and incongruous, like flashes from the wrong film'. I offered her general comments about the breaches of child rights, such as the lack of education and freedom, and the impropriety of children in free association with criminals. Nevertheless, my remarks felt hollow and defensive. Undoubtedly many kids on the outside were much worse off. I looked up at the blue sky and asked myself if this had all been a huge mistake. I felt like a total fraud. By what authority could this former British Army dentist, who knew next to nothing about Nepal, childcare or prison issues, be giving interviews on these matters? Surely there had to be someone better placed than me to act as a spokesman, as a child rights activist? Maybe I was in the wrong spot altogether. Should I return to the UK and the safe haven of dentistry, doing something that was in line with my qualifications? Perhaps I needed to apologise to those friends like Ronnie and Carol who had shown such early solidarity to a misguided widower who'd dared to dream. To someone who had put faith in coincidences that were in reality nothing more than that.

Just then I saw one of Fionnuala's 'flashes from the wrong film' that quelled my doubts. Instantly, I found myself cast back in time to a month before Esther's death. She'd come to bed one evening and noticed the book *If This Is a Man* lying on my bedside table. This is the powerful account by Italian Jew Primo Levi of his incarceration at Auschwitz and one of the most moving books I've ever read. The front cover carried an unsettling picture of shaven-headed men in camp uniform gazing desolate out at the reader. Their faces had lost all hope. She'd asked me to turn the book face down as she could no longer cope with such imagery.

Now, a little over a year later, as I looked away from the cluster of Fionnuala, Graham, Indira and curious prisoners I noticed a little boy haunting the margin of our group. He had a shaven head and a pyjama top with vertical green stripes. The boy's uncomprehending stare gave me all the confirmation I needed that, yes, beyond any shadow of a doubt I was standing in precisely the right place.

As we left the jail Fionnuala turned to me:

103

'Did you see anything inside there that echoed any other situation?' she asked.

'That boy in the pyjama top,' I replied. 'That was sharp-eyed of you.'

The prison authorities freed three boys that day and Fionnuala and Graham returned to Hong Kong satisfied with their assignment. Their report made cover story in the South China Morning Post's Sunday magazine, Graham's picture of a female warder holding up a crying baby to the headline 'Cry Freedom'. Fionnuala had refused to give me sight of her write-up, let alone copy approval, before publication. But I'd been right to trust her as it was beautiful, stirring and at times humorous. Here was a story she described as being 'about imprisonment and liberation - and how freedom of the spirit can be found in distant, unexpected places.' Her piece ended with my vision for commemorating Esther.

The feature sparked major interest in Hong Kong, including from the wealthy Kadoorie Foundation, who invited me for a meeting. Then Fionnuala's gamble paid off when it was accepted by the Daily Telegraph. In what represented an enviable fillip for my new charity it was published as the cover story in the 'Weekend' section of the Saturday paper in July 2000. This meant a readership of around three million. I think the very sensitive Fionnuala was mortified at the change in headline to read 'A Hope in Hell' that drew on the linkage between suicide and going to Hell. Actually, I wasn't bothered for I realised headlines were beyond her control (or knowledge) and if Esther was in Hell there was little hope for the rest of us. In any case the quality of the report in word and image more than compensated for any crassness in the choice of title.

It is very difficult to work out what I might term the 'charitable return' from this one article but it was immense. The immediate public response in the form of the mailbag that arrived at my flat in Holland made for an unforgettable sight. Piles of letters and donations covered my sitting-room table. The messages were so touching. Within those first correspondents two had lost family members to suicide on the same day as Esther. Another sent a donation with a letter expressing gratitude to the Gurkhas for freeing her from a Japanese POW camp in 1945.

In a ripple effect, the article sparked other media interest. On the Monday morning after Fionnuala's article was published TV producer Bev Waymark joined her team meeting that planned the week ahead for the afternoon show *Open House with Gloria Hunniford*. As usual, she and her colleagues had been trawling the previous weekend's papers for eye-catching human-interest stories for their magazine programme. Bev was championing my story but it wasn't a hard one to sell. Everyone agreed that she should find out more with a view to inviting me to the studios to be interviewed by Gloria.

The interview went well in more ways than one. Later that week I phoned Bev to invite her out for dinner. Ostensibly this was in response to her offer to volunteer for the charity although I had other thoughts. After twenty years in TV she'd told me that she was ready for something different. She was passionate for children and dreamt of being in a situation where, in her words, she could help 'scoop them up'. That dinner date launched our professional and personal relationship. Only this time around I was the one who was living in Holland and my new girlfriend was in England.

While love was taking root - and in contrast to my charity's dream start - the project work in Nepal had taken a downturn. In June Suresh e-mailed me to say that the internal tensions and jealousies that we'd detected within PAM had boiled over leading to Indira Rana Magar's resignation. With her departure we lost the reference point we'd so admired within that organisation and we, least of all Suresh, didn't want to work directly with Sukanya Waiba. We reverted to the original plan of setting up our own jail children's refuge in Bhairahawa which Suresh could supervise himself. Indira declined his offer to join the local team, preferring to go it alone and found her own NGO.

This decision coincided with a seminal visit by Suresh to a rural jail at Tansen in Nepal's mid-west. He had gone there in June merely to accompany a British researcher, expecting to see a situation similar to what we'd found inside Kathmandu Central Jail. However even as they approached the prison, they sensed that this might be a different scenario. Descending the hillside path that led to the prison, they could see armed guards patrolling the jail's forbidding walls and watchtowers. The jailer greeted them at the main gate. He appeared friendly enough and spent three hours showing them around.

The scenes inside resembled the very conditions described in The Kathmandu Post article. It was grossly overcrowded with the prison holding 162 prisoners against a capacity of 100. The old buildings were terribly dilapidated with their thin corrugated roofs rusty and full of holes. The jailer showed them one of the eight accommodation blocks in the male prison that had been abandoned after the roof had collapsed;

subsequent flooding had turned even the upstairs floor into a sea of mud. All the living areas were dark and poorly ventilated with the inmates having to live, sleep and cook in the same room. A single standpipe served the whole prison as did one open toilet that had no drainage system or septic tank. Forty-four of the prisoners were women although only sixteen of them had been convicted of anything. Included in their number were ten mothers who were looking after fifteen children aged between one month and six years old. The baby had been born inside the jail in these atrocious circumstances and without any professional medical assistance. All the children showed the signs of chronic illnesses and malnutrition.

As a gut reaction Suresh wanted to remove the children to a safe place immediately but that wasn't possible. He'd require some time both to deal with the inevitable bureaucracy and to prepare our own refuge. The best he could do before he left was to give the jailer two thousand rupees (about £15) to buy some food for the children. There was no way of confirming that it was ever spent on that purpose.

Suresh wrote the next day to describe the visit and beg my support.

'I will never forget what I saw yesterday,' he wrote, 'the children's swollen bellies, their coughs and runny noses, the pleading eyes of their parents. I am ashamed that this situation exists in my country in the year 2000.'

Stark as his message read, I felt encouraged. For the first time he seemed to be self-motivated rather than requiring me to coax him along. He appeared to be taking the lead now and this local ownership of the issue was exactly what I wanted to nurture. No doubt he'd also come to feel the setting up of a small refuge to be well within his capacity. He would also be able to do this within the comfort zone of his own patch in Bhairahawa.

Suresh's immediate objective was to have a facility in place to free four of the Tansen children whose parents were happy to take a chance on Suresh. For these prisoners would have to trust this stranger with a limited command of Nepali. For all they knew he could well be a trafficker. After all, some of the inmates came from that background themselves and were well aware of the deception that was the hallmark of their sordid profession.

Shortly afterwards, Suresh found a rental property just along the way from his own home that could accommodate around twenty children. This would become our first 'White House' refuge. He appointed the initial staff members to his new autonomous NGO which was called the Nepal Child Welfare Foundation (NCWF). Most of these employees turned out to be his relations but such recruitment practice is common in Nepal where jobs are scarce and given family pressure to look after *aphno manche*[8]. Moreover, an employer perceives relatives as being more trustworthy than strangers. Up to a point I can understand this mentality as the Nepal workplace is a particularly vicious one. Nonetheless nepotism of course is intrinsically unfair and leads to the recruitment of underqualified employees. And naturally family members can just as easily blackmail you and betray you too. For instance, the refuge manager was Suresh's brother-in-law, a pleasant man but eventually dismissed for alcohol abuse. Likewise, Suresh appointed a committee that he felt he could rely upon or that would at least toe the line. It included himself as Chairman, his wife, two former Gurkhas and two other local people from his own ethnic group. This was a false advantage as the committee was thin to non-existent on experience, ability and willingness to challenge the Chairman. In short, his personnel selection made for conflicts of interest and poor governance.

Concurrently - and building on the experience of the productive media coverage of the Daily Telegraph - I'd lined up interest from the popular UK tabloid, *The Mirror*. The proposal to the Mirror was basically to repeat what we'd done for the Telegraph in allowing coverage of a prison release. The story nearly didn't happen. In advance of the rescue Suresh had returned to the prison several times to prepare the way but sensed a cooling in the jailer's enthusiasm. Perhaps he'd expected to see this NGO producing more money. As we drove to the jail with journalist Gill Swain Suresh murmured to me that he expected the jailer wouldn't be there in a bid to sabotage our efforts. Sure enough he was nowhere to be found. He'd abandoned the prison to the charge of a lowly clerk who couldn't authorise the admission of a journalist let alone release dependent children.

We went to the top, with Suresh and I going to meet the local Chief District Officer (CDO), the senior civil servant within the District. We wanted him to use his authority to intervene but he spent hours avoiding us too. I was learning first-hand how right Sunil Jha's guidebook had been in observing 'people responsible are absent or difficult to find.' Finally, he emerged from his office to meet us. Suresh showed him his identification card and said:

---

[8] 'one's own people'

'CDO sahib, there are little children inside the jail who shouldn't be there and I'd like to take them to our children's home. There seems to be no good reason why they can't be freed as they aren't offenders. All we need is the parents' agreement and they're begging us to take their children.'

During the exchange I could see how Suresh was making limited eye contact with the CDO, unsure of himself and probably also of his command of Nepali as he addressed a homespun Brahmin whose Nepali would for sure be perfect. He continued:

'We have international journalists with us and if we go away empty-handed, we'll all lose face and it'll reflect badly on Nepal and its humanitarian record.'

The CDO was unmoved. 'This is a Prison Department matter; I can't become involved,' he said, offering the disarming smile that I had read about. 'Perhaps you could return tomorrow?'

We gave up and left, frustrated. A return tomorrow wasn't possible given Gill's prior commitments elsewhere and, in any case, it felt like we were simply being strung along. There would be no public releases. Once again, I found myself offering platitudes such as how this incident reflected the challenges we faced. The best that could be achieved that day was to photograph desperate parents and their forlorn children clutching the bars of the prison gate as they implored us to help.

In the end we returned to Kathmandu where Gill's photographer took pictures of the PAM Nestling Home children. These combined with the Tansen ones gave them enough for a story. As a matter of fact, the day after our visit the prison authorities released the children but the jailor had been successful in thwarting our media initiative. Or so he thought. Gill's report appeared as a two-part feature in The Mirror but, more importantly, was syndicated to *Pronto* magazine in Spain and *Gente* magazine in Italy. A wealthy Italian philanthropist read The Gente article, resulting in her Foundation making a major grant towards our work.

At a return visit to Tansen the appearance and wellbeing of the four boys reassured the parents of the remaining children. They relented and handed over their children to Suresh too. We also picked up two further boys, Akash and Suraj. They had been sleeping rough outside Tansen jail, going by day to the gates of the prison to get food that their mother passed through the bars. By the end of the year we'd removed all the dependent children from the environs of Tansen jail, their care funded by supporters turned child sponsors. We'd reached another major milestone.

In September we admitted the first three girls to our refuge. But I, for one, was suspicious. The inmates had presented two of the girls, Sharmila and Mona, to Suresh as being siblings although they looked markedly different. The mother lied that they were half-sisters but it emerged some time afterwards that they weren't related at all. Sharmila's and Mona's parents were friends but only Sharmila's father was in jail. Adults would send children such as Mona into Kathmandu jail as a cynical ploy to have them 'rescued' by organisations like PAM. I found it hard to comprehend the lengths that adults would go to in order to get children admitted to a children's home – even sending them into free association with murderers inside jail.

To avoid such deception, we decided to focus our future efforts solely on provincial jails that were firmly off the tourist trail. The first of these was at Bhojpur which lies in the picturesque hills of east Nepal. We became involved there after reading about a boy called Jithang in the local papers. The article nicknamed him 'Jail Bahadur'. *Bahadur*, meaning 'warrior', is a common middle name in Nepal. Most people would find this very unfunny but Nepal can be a cruel place when it comes to mocking the vulnerable.

Jithang had been conceived and born inside Bhojpur jail after his father had gained access to the women's section. After that Jithang spent the first five years of his life inside prison. Bhojpur is so remote that his first taste of the outside world had to be an internal flight to Kathmandu. The remoteness of provincial jails presented not just a rescue challenge but also created difficulties in maintaining family links; return visits could be a nightmare. Nepalis seem to have a genetic predisposition towards travel sickness which isn't helped by the quality of the roads and vehicles. A seven-hour road journey with vomiting little children is not an enticing prospect. It would be impractical, unkind and not financially viable to revisit places like Bhojpur.

The coincidences that had peppered my life since (and even before) Esther's death, like little cosmic double-takes, continued as I pursued the charity's goals. On one trip to Nepal I was aiming to bring some children, including Ramesh, out of Tulsipur jail in the far west and rescue some more from Kathmandu Central Jail. Beforehand the British television *Esther Rantzen* programme had asked me to document the visit through a video diary. Pleading a tight budget, the Producer had equipped me with a camera and a series of questions that he wanted me to ask of myself on film as part of a video diary. One of these questions invited me to share my thoughts as I awaited child releases.

As I sat outside Tulsipur, perhaps predictably, I told the camera how I thought of Esther and of the inspiration that she had been for me. That was used in the final film but the remark I'd made after that was edited out. For I had added how I was also thinking of a family member who two months previously had made a very generous donation towards the charity as my birthday present. I thanked him on camera, and assured him that I was having a great belated birthday. Minutes later five children emerged through the prison gates. One boy was wearing a pullover that read 'Happy Birthday'.

In Kathmandu I accompanied Indira to the Central Jail to release six children. On the way there Indira was as delightfully garrulous as ever.

'The children are so excited at getting out today,' she said. 'There are two boys there, Kumar Basnet and Bhejendra Pun, whom you'll really like. They're very polite and I think also very clever. They'll do so well at school, given the chance.'

At the prison, she introduced me to the children and their fathers. Through Indira, Kumar's father was able to tell me how relieved he was that Kumar wouldn't be sharing his sentence. He promised me that Kumar would respond to this opportunity by behaving impeccably and working hard at school.

As we drove off in the taxi Kumar put his head out the window; I'd assumed that he wanted a last look at the prison but in fact he was facing forwards. The breeze on his face was a simple sensation of freedom that prison life had denied him. But I was touched to note that even on this most exciting of days, both Kumar and Bhejendra were showing such attentiveness to the four younger children. Although unrelated, they were acting as big brothers.

The final TV programme broadcast me paraphrasing a verse from the Talmud that states 'he who saves one person saves the world'. I said that thus far in my jail rescue programme I had saved 24 worlds. This reminded me of Billy's cautionary advice about not expecting to save the world. How wrong he had been.

So it was that, after I had completed the filming assignment, I dropped by The Everest on my last evening to catch up with this very eccentric old chap. Sure enough, there he was sitting at the bar. He'd shed his jacket because it was getting warmer as the monsoon approached. I tapped him on the shoulder:

'Haven't you moved from here all this time?'

He peered at me over his glasses.

'Ah, it's you,' he replied, 'I've been reading a lot about you in the local papers.' He hailed the barman. 'Dan, get this man a drink – and give him some money! He's doing great work for Nepal. How's your children's home coming along?'

'We've made a good start,' I answered.

'Not been ripped off yet?' he asked with a rather sardonic smile.

'No, I trust Suresh. Cheers.' I tapped his glass.

He sighed. 'It's early days. Take my word for it, you can't trust anyone in Nepal and sooner or later even the best of 'em will let you down. The trouble with foreigners coming here is that they leave their brains at home.'

'For instance?' I asked.

'I know of a children's home, not a mile from here, where the overseas donor even gave the home manager his own bankcard. That allowed him to withdraw money whenever he needed it directly from the charity's bank account in the USA using an ATM machine in Kathmandu. And the donor was a very clever attorney; he'd never have dreamt of giving someone his bankcard back in the States.'

'And did he become unstuck?'

'Ha! The donor's living in blissful ignorance in Florida. Meanwhile his contact in Nepal is riding a Harley with a flashy gold chain around his neck and a big watch. He's recruited his relations as child carers. Even the children are the guy's relatives. Talk about a win-win situation for him!'

I thought for a moment about the slight unease I'd felt over the nepotism involved in Suresh's staff recruitment.

'Don't worry; I remembered to pack my brain. You seem to know a lot about children's homes,' I ventured.

'Oh, I visit two or three in my spare time, take them in bundles of pencils for the kids, exercise books, sometimes a sack of rice, that kind of thing. That's my little charitable contribution, if you like. But I'm very selective as I've heard so many horror stories about the bad ones. The thing is that parents are a soft touch for conmen who can get children so easily. Parents still perceive their kids to be better off inside children's homes where they'll be looked after for free by foreigners and they'll lie and cheat to get them admitted.'

As I started telling him about Sharmila and Mona, an unusual looking Nepali guy strode into the bar and high-fived some of his mates who were sitting in the corner. He was dressed in a sharp suit that seemed to clash with hair that was tied back in a long pony tail.

'See that chap?' Billy said in an uncharacteristically hushed voice. 'He's also in the orphan business. Calls himself "The Apostle" and he's one of the biggest crooks in Kathmandu. He's gone from being a trekking guide to becoming a big shot who owns land in the hills on the edge of the valley. Guess where his money has come from? A children's home scam.'

I glanced over at The Apostle who had now sat down, a waiter taking a drinks order for all of them.

'Tell me more,' I said.

'Well, it's a classic piece of entrapment,' he said. 'People like him take kids off vulnerable poor people with high promises of education, free food and accommodation. Then they keep them in deliberately disgusting conditions where they're presented as orphans, which they're not. The bait set, they wait for a chump like you or me to come along with more money than good sense.'

A loud collective laugh came from the corner. I could see that the waiter was distributing cocktails while Apostle rolled a cigarette.

'Visitors to Nepal with their brains left at home?' I suggested.

'You've got it,' he said. 'You know the place he set up in Kathmandu was so appalling that the district authority even shut him down. It was that bad. But six months later he was back in business again in the adjacent district. And then his fortune changed. One day, he ambushed an elderly couple of American tourists in the street outside of here. He begged them to come and see his orphans who were very sick and dying.'

'Hard to refuse, I suppose.'

'The couple duly obliged and were shaken by what he showed them. They resolved that 'something had to be done' and when they went back to The States started raising money from their friends. I think they even set up a charity to support him.

'But surely that can't bring in so much money?' I asked.

'You'd be surprised. Just like the geezer on the Harley, the Apostle tells his donors that he's a fellow Christian, a kind of Good Samaritan, and Christian donors would give you their last penny in Jesu's name. I think he's also become a Rotarian so that he can milk that lot too.' He cast a backward nod towards the corner. 'If they could see that pile of shit over there now.'

The group in the corner was now smoking and a distinctive sticky, sweet smell wafted across. Reggae was blasting out as one of the Apostle's pals topped up the graffiti on the wall.

Billy continued:

'The donors all assume that Apostle is solely relying upon them – or more importantly the children are counting upon them, but that isn't the case at all. He'll have supporters all around the world not knowing of one another's existence.'

'Where did the land ownership come in? Was that him investing his ill-gotten gains?' I asked.

'Colonel, I thought you told me you'd packed your brain?' He wiped his chin with his hanky and suppressed a laugh. 'No, no, it's much more subtle than that. Apostle pulled the classic trick of telling his donors that paying rentals was a waste of money. And besides that the landlord had hiked the rental and they needed to move, disrupting the children's education and so on. The solution he offered was to invest in the future and buy land in a nice scenic location where there's lots of fresh air. He told the donor that it was important to keep the government's greedy hands off the assets and the only sure way of doing that was to buy the land in the name of a private individual.'

'His own,' I suggested.

'Yeah, that's what he did, purchasing land through an Australian Christian organisation and then he dropped them.'

'But can't the authorities do anything?' I asked.

'He'll be able to pay them off handsomely and move on to the next stage of his business plan. Probably getting some fool to build an orphanage on that land that he'll offer to them out of his generosity. They won't realise that anything that is built in Nepal becomes owned by the person to whom the land belongs. After the building's been completed, he can throw the kids out and re-role the facility into becoming a very nice bijou hotel in the hills above Kathmandu.'

By this stage I was wishing I'd met Billy so much earlier. This man was a mine of information even if his wisdom was highly depressing in content.

'And what of the parents? Can't they pull their children out once they realise they've been tricked?'

'No chance. Apostle will scare them off by saying that he's invested in their children's futures and if they want them back then they must reimburse him the investment. Poor people can't do that and if they persist, he can afford to set the police on them.'

I'd heard just about enough for one evening, thanked Billy and left early, also as I had an early morning flight the next day. Back in my room I lay awake for a long time, pestered by a mosquito whose persistence mirrored my hearing Billy's sobering words over and over again. But I wasn't thinking about Apostle. I was being troubled by one little throwaway comment:

'Sooner or later even the best of them will let you down.'

In November 2001 the Government of Nepal marked International Children's Day by outlawing the jailing of dependent children over the age of three.

It is impossible to link my activities to this ruling as cause and effect. Nevertheless, I like to think that the negative worldwide publicity had influenced the Nepali authorities into taking action. For feature articles about my work with the prison children had appeared as widely afield as in *The Boston Globe*, *De Telegraaf* in Holland and *The Melbourne Herald Sun*. It's hard to imagine that embassies abroad weren't relaying these adverse reports back to Nepal.

Whatever the case, I saw this as being the end of the project as there was no longer a cause to champion. It was a major landmark and, unlike after the first releases, I had someone to join me in celebration. On the 4th January 2002, the third anniversary of Esther's death, Bev was by my side as I unveiled my memorial plaque to Esther at the White House in Bhairahawa. The Gates of Bronze were yielding. Determined that this would be a happy occasion, we held a children's party afterwards for the refuge children, these treasures we'd found in dark vaults. The lead dancer was Ramesh Badi.

9.   Alpha and Omega

Those first three years had passed with unbelievable speed and been more productive than I could ever have imagined. Had I spent the time in suspended animation I would have had nothing to show for the navel-gazing. In large part I could put this success down to how I had rationalised Esther's death and found a place for it. Yet underneath it all my conclusions from 1999 didn't quite add up.

For one thing I wasn't convinced that she'd been a depressive. Throughout all the time I'd known her up until her final year she'd only ever been positive, outgoing and energetic. She had been the person who would urge others to 'keep trying' in the midst of adversity. Moreover, one major residual imponderable continued to niggle at me. How could she have left me - the one person she so adored - to be traumatised by the hideous scene in our hallway? Why had she made our house potentially uninhabitable for me? Couldn't she have, say, gone into the nearby woods to end her life there and be found by someone else?

A possible answer came in 2002 when the BBC's *Panorama* current affairs series challenged GlaxoSmithKline's assertions that Seroxat was safe and non-addictive. In an episode called 'The Secrets of Seroxat' the programme highlighted researchers' allegations that the drug was potentially harmful. Worse still, it offered some evidence suggesting that normally well-balanced people had perpetrated acts of extreme violence while taking Seroxat. These included killing family members and themselves in a vicious manner. GlaxoSmithKline had lost major lawsuits in both the USA and Australia following bizarre murders and associated suicides.

The expert witness who appeared in the programme was psychiatrist Dr (now Professor) David Healy. He was the then Director of the North Wales department of psychological medicine and the UK's leading authority on antidepressants. I wrote to him to find out more.

His prompt reply was both startling and disturbing. He told me that he'd based his conclusions upon his investigation of GlaxoSmithKline archives going back to the 1980s and on his own in-house research. It is normally difficult to attribute cause of suicide to being the effect of an anti-depressive. Therefore, Dr Healy had conducted a study in which he

116

gave a similar drug to Seroxat to 20 healthy volunteers recruited from staff members at his psychiatric clinic. He sent me his research findings that revealed two of his volunteers had displayed general side effects that I had seen also in Esther. These were insomnia, nightmares, severe headaches, agitation, hyperactivity, dry mouth and mood swings. One volunteer had lost her inhibitions and unnerved a colleague by telling him intimate details of her life. Both experienced violent suicidal ideations. Significantly, his volunteers reported that their fantasies arose without any thought of the consequences to their partners or families. One considered throwing herself in front of a car while the other 'visualised hanging herself from a beam in the bedroom ceiling'. For the first time Esther's ruthless violence and apparent disregard for me made sense.

In response, I compiled all the documents I had for Dr Healy, sending him Esther's clinical notes and even her secret letter to me. I included background information that showed her innate strength of character. There was a letter of reference written by a consultant psychologist who had supervised Esther in the mid-1970s when she had worked in a clinic for girls with learning difficulties. Describing a chaotic, archaic working environment that lacked any leadership, he wrote:

'I was full of amazement for the way in which Ms Benjamins handled herself during this difficult time. She did this intelligently with perseverance, resolve and objectivity. She alone stayed standing where colleagues had succumbed under the pressure. I was struck by the special way she managed challenging situations: she spoke directly, face to face, giving the girls such a place in her life that they advanced emotionally. This is a quality not given to many. Work, study, marriage and hobbies: where many might withdraw, Ms Benjamins manages to combine everything. In respect of qualities such as decisiveness, analytical capacity, immunity to stress and a robust work tempo, she commands these in great measure.' In conclusion he summed her up as being, 'Someone who has an enriching influence on the lives of others.'

Yet within a matter of months of that reference being penned Esther had lost her way and buckled. I shared with Dr Healy other episodes from 1998 that mirrored his findings. Like the day in July when she'd gone shopping with our doctor friend Margaret. I returned from work to find the hall floor covered in purchases. Esther was on an uncharacteristic high as she showed off her spoils, modelling new clothes. I'd commented with irony that she should have bought a hat while she was at it. 'I did!' she exclaimed, vanishing off into the sitting

117

room to reappear sporting a broad-brimmed hat. That evening Margaret phoned me to apologise that she'd been unable to curtail her spending. She laughed as she told me how even though she loved shopping she'd needed a stiff drink after returning home. Sometime afterwards Margaret added that the trip had been unduly prolonged because Esther had been having intimate personal conversations with sales staff. That was out of keeping with her deeply engrained sense of privacy.

On a subsequent shopping spree another friend had witnessed similar frenetic behaviour. She'd remarked after Esther's death 'I don't know what she was "on" at the time'. She'd been on fire. Now I realised that Esther's doctor doubling her dose of Seroxat a month before she died might well have fanned the flames and tipped her into oblivion. Especially given her decisive personality type and how she wasn't frightened of anything, including death itself.

Dr Healy's conclusion after reviewing my material was that Esther's death was 'probably' related to the Seroxat. However, he could not say so unequivocally because of the added factor of childlessness.

I took the matter no further beyond preparing a written submission for the UK's Committee on the Safety of Medicines. The Seroxat debate trundled on throughout the decade with GSK conducting damage limitation. The company has since acknowledged the heightened risk of suicide in young people and the dangers of withdrawing from the drug. GSK no longer presents the medication as being 'safe' and more detailed warnings are available in the patient information leaflets.

One thing was for sure. Although I may have made the wrong analysis in deciding that Esther's death had been a matter of 'choice' I'd been right not to hold any resentment against her for what she'd done. Pity had been absolutely the correct response. That conclusion reached, it was time to resume my onward journey.

Just as it had been with Esther, my relationship with Bev grew in spite of geographical separation. In another echo of the past, we discovered a shared passion for remote places. Where Esther and I had relished exploring the Scottish Highlands, Hebrides and Orkney, Bev introduced me to the gorgeous Scilly Isles. And when she came to see me in Holland, I took her to the Friesian islands off-season, cycling through Esther's beloved Schiermonnikoog and dinky Vlieland at their windswept best. And, of course, we travelled together to the far reaches of Nepal to visit the kids in Bhairahawa and trek in the Annapurnas. Bev was a natural with the children at the White House refuge. They swarmed about her full of curiosity. The little girls were intrigued to meet 'Philip Daddy's' girlfriend, as they tried to get their tongues around her name. B's and V's are interchangeable in Nepali-speak and they would call her 'Baberley'.

For Bev, one bright-eyed, chubby-cheeked and very jolly small boy always stood out from the throng. He was the dancer, Ramesh Badi, now aged seven. More than any other child he'd taken to the refuge, loving every aspect of it and especially enjoying party time. Nonetheless there was a lurking sadness in his life as his younger brother, Sameer, remained inside prison, still too young to be separated from his mother. His vulnerable older sister, Anju, stayed at her uncle's home.

Bev accepted the need for Sameer to stay in prison for now but couldn't understand why he hadn't brought Anju to join her brother, saving her from the sordid fate of Badi girls. When she asked Suresh what could be done, his answer had been 'all in good time'.

This apparent cop-out was anathema for someone who produced live television programmes where opportunities were seized and everything had to be achieved by yesterday. But Suresh had no intention of rescuing this girl and he wouldn't be 'told' to do so by me, let alone a woman visitor. All Bev could do was to sponsor the monthly care costs of Ramesh and hope for the best for his two siblings.

In fact, there might have been a plausible explanation for the local inertia. For from what I would see time and again in the future, many Nepali children are at the mercy of the unhealthy attitudes of parents including their financial greed. Prostitution wasn't just allowing Badi families to survive; some of them were prospering from the practice. For this perverse reason the Badi community prizes its girls for the income they can generate. Surprisingly, a new mother may cry at having given birth to a son. Had Suresh rescued Anju her father could well have turned up in due course to claim loss of earnings and demand compensation. Chances are that as a convicted murderer he wouldn't have been the nicest of characters either. He could easily have badmouthed Suresh to the media for exploiting his daughter for his own nefarious purposes, such as by raising money from wealthy foreigners through child sponsorship. This was potentially a no-win situation.

Heaven knows what became of his sister but it's easy to guess. For every success we'd score in Nepal there'd be one or two failures, often many more.

Our early work in the next town along, Butwal, certainly had been a success. We'd been intrigued by the street children issue that was there on our doorstep. There are two ways of going about assessing the need and possible uptake of support. You can conduct a survey, meeting with children and other stakeholders within the community to hear their views. Or you can do what we did, and set up a contact centre in the town and see what comes through the door. We went for the second option, establishing a night shelter in a rented building where street kids could at least sleep safely at night. But a group of thirteen boys, including Dinesh, were having none of that. They moved into the shelter and decided that this had become their new home.

To our surprise, they behaved themselves well and took part in the non-formal education that we laid on as a way of enticing them back into mainstream education. We could see that we had some real characters on our hands and if we could rehabilitate Dinesh and his friends after the traumas of the streets, they had a chance of becoming great young people. Time would tell. The failure rate with rehabilitating street children is sadly very high.

After returning from that salutary trip Bev and I drew a line under separation. I was a little sorry to pack up the flat in Holland for the final time but I was satisfied that at least I was doing so on my own terms. This would be a structured move into the future rather retreating under a cloud of sadness. Bev and I bought a house together in southwest London and soon afterwards she accepted my marriage proposal. I had found the right partner at just about every level, the only difference being our differing religious backgrounds. Or, more accurately, Bev's absence of one.

We discussed various venues for the wedding but in the end, there was one clear preferred choice: All Saints Church in Crondall. This was a church that meant something to me although I knew it would be a challenge to get permission from its vicar, the Revd Paul Rich. He was well used to fending off wedding hopefuls from London who set their sights on taking over this sleepy village and picturesque church for the day. The forthright Paul wasn't one to indulge such shallow sentiments and was protective of his parishioners' privacy and sensibilities. I'd have to convince him that I was both a local boy - of sorts - and that All Saints had been special to me in the weeks after Esther's death.

A phone call was sufficient for that but he insisted that we would have to pass through the hoops in attending five prenuptial classes with him. As we approached the manse, I asked Bev to leave the talking to me since I had a better insight into religious matters. A ruddy-faced Paul greeted us with a broad grin:

'Hello Patrick and Bev. Do come in and let's have a nice glass of chilled Sancerre.'

It was ten in the morning but we felt it prudent to go with the flow. I accepted my name change without comment and we agreed his offer of wine with apparent alacrity. Then, glasses in hand, we sat in his study while Paul gave forth on the sacrament of marriage.

'This isn't something to be tried out for a while. When you two stand at the altar you'll be making an unconditional and solemn commitment before God, to which everyone will be witness.'

He handed each of us a copy of the Anglican Alternative Service Book and referred us to the marriage service section and began to dissect it line by line. He read:

'Marriage is given that husband and wife may comfort and help each other, living faithfully together in need and in plenty, in sorrow and in joy.' He paused. 'Note the reference to husband and wife. I don't go for all this gay marriage nonsense; this sacrament is for a man and a woman.'

Picking up on Bev's sidelong glance I knew that I couldn't let that one pass.

'Paul, I think you should be aware that we'll have two gay couples amongst our wedding guests.'

He took this remark in his good-humoured stride.

'Oh, that's nothing,' he replied. 'You know I've three peers of the realm in my congregation. That means each Sunday I preach to three Lords.'

He returned to his original reading, his flow unchecked.

'Do you see also the reference to "in sorrow and in joy"? I believe that's significant for, from what I've seen, you can't fully appreciate the joy until you've first experienced sorrow.'

He was speaking with authority as he too had known the pain of losing a wife followed by joy rediscovered through a second marriage.

Paul's final session with us was rounded off with supper – he's a keen chef. During this meal he remarked that on the day of the wedding he wanted us to look upon him as a father, someone to rely upon when the nerves were jangling. Underneath Paul's bluster lay the warmest of hearts.

On the morning of the wedding Neal Gillespie bounced onto the scene, ready to act as an usher. Fresh back from a tour of duty as the Army's senior medical officer in Kabul, this was the raffish Neal of old. In contrast with three and a half years before when he'd been so subdued and moved in a Dorking pub, that day he was once again full of stories and his trademark black humour. He handed over a present of an Afghan rug he'd brought back with him.

'I hope you like it. It took 20 children a week to make that, working round the clock. I got a good deal on it though.'

He then excused himself in the direction of the village pub while my Best Man, former 'minder' John Sharp, and I set off for the church. As we arrived Paul greeted us brandishing a bottle of best Sauvignon Blanc that we could enjoy behind the scenes in the vestry while the guests took their seats in the church.

Paul had no time for the custom of the bride being late; he insisted that Bev would be there spot on time and she arrived on cue. As she walked up the aisle on her father's arm, she wore a band of white pearls she'd commissioned from a London jeweller. As an afterthought she'd phoned the designer to ask that a single blue stone be incorporated as the traditional 'something blue' ingredient. The jeweller replied that the band had already been made but that the craftsman had been astounded that he'd added a blue stone inadvertently. No such 'mistake' had ever happened before. Bizarre things were happening in our lives - just as they had before Esther and I had married.

Paul opened the service by welcoming those from other faiths who had joined us. These included one Jewish couple, for whom this was Rosh Hashanah, the Jewish New Year. This led to his mentioning the Alpha and the Omega, the beginning and the end from the Book of Revelation. Whilst acknowledging that it was more common to use these words at a funeral service, he said that from his knowledge of the background to the wedding they were apposite to this happy occasion.

In choosing the lessons I had eschewed the usual readings that seemed so austere and frankly unromantic. Old friends of mine, Jules and Ewen McColl, read a blend of The Song of Solomon and Proverbs. I had attended their wedding three months after Esther died and Jules was now heavily pregnant with their first child. Ewen opened with Proverbs:

'Let your fountain, the wife of your youth,
be blessed, rejoice in her,
a lovely doe, a graceful hind, let her be your companion;
you will at all times be bathed in her love,

and her love will continually wrap you round.
Wherever you turn, she will guide you;
when you lie in bed she will watch over you
and when you wake she will talk with you.'

Jules' response was from the Song of Solomon:
'I am my beloved's his longing is all for me.
Come, my beloved, let us go out into the fields
to lie among the henna-bushes
let us go early to the vineyards
and see if the vine has budded or its blossom opened
if the pomegranates are in flower.
There I will give you my love,
when the mandrakes give their perfume,
and all rare fruits are ready at our door,
fruits new and old
which I have in store for you, my love.'

And finally again, Ewen:
'Wear me as a seal upon your heart,
as a seal upon your arm;
for love is strong as death,
passion cruel as the grave;
it blazes up like blazing fire,
fiercer than any flame.
Many waters cannot quench love,
no flood can sweep it away;
if a man were to offer for love
the whole wealth of his house,
it would be utterly scorned.'

My reception speech presented the challenge of setting the right tone since some of Esther's old friends were present on this day of celebration. My words needed to be just as poignant as those after the funeral, albeit lighter. I observed how so many at the reception, including me, had already known such personal sorrows that we could thoroughly enjoy this day.

I chose to reflect on the words from the marriage service that Paul had read earlier that day: '....for love is strong as death, passion cruel as the grave'. I shared my view that love was actually *stronger* than death. The evidence for that lay in how love had triumphed after Esther's death both in the work of the Trust and in how I stood before them re-married.

By this stage many guests were in tears, but there was more to come with video greetings from the refuge children. The film showed excited boys and girls on the refuge balcony, waving to the camera below and calling 'Happy Wedding'. Ramesh Badi gave a personal, self-conscious, greeting to 'Auntie Bev' and 'Philip Daddy'. Then the children danced in celebration with Ramesh, as ever, at the forefront.

A few days after the wedding Bev stumbled upon a newspaper cutting in an old purse, a horoscope from the Daily Mail. She doesn't believe in astrology (nor do I) so she was surprised she'd kept it, doubly so as it didn't predict anything of any note. Then she noticed the date on the clipping: *The 4th January 1999*.

Part 3

Lion statue
Bhaktapur Durbar Square
Nepal

'Success is the ability to go from failure to failure without losing your enthusiasm.'

- Winston Churchill

10.   Circus Children

At The Esther Benjamins Trust Trustees' meeting of January 2003 the Trustees had to consider the challenging findings of research we had commissioned in 2002.

The story began at the start of that year when Suresh attended a regional Rotary conference in Calcutta. His trip came at a time when I was looking for a new project in the wake of the ruling on prison children in Nepal. I asked him to keep his ear to the ground for a possible new cause and I thought the conference might be a useful forum for ideas. Sure enough, while he was there a fellow delegate mentioned that there was a circus in the area that had Nepali child performers. His informant suspected that physical and sexual abuse was going on as he added that the circus made 'private arrangements' for after the show.

Suresh didn't have time to visit the circus to assess the situation for himself but he relayed the comment back to me in the UK. I trawled the internet for further information but drew a blank. I was riveted but could only find mention of the work of organisations like *People for the Ethical Treatment of Animals* (PETA) whose campaigning had resulted in a ban on the use of wild animals in Indian circuses. I wrote to leading PETA activist Maneka Gandhi who suggested that I approach *Bachpan Bachao Andolan*[9] (BBA) for advice. I went to Delhi to consult BBA and a few other NGOs directly.

No one that I spoke to in Delhi during that May visit seemed to know much about circus children. It was certainly common knowledge that the circus industry was going into eclipse. This was particularly the case in urban areas where an increasingly sophisticated middle class had come to view the circus as passé and sought more contemporary forms of entertainment. Circuses still attracted audiences in rural areas but this was only economically viable for the smallest circuses.

The owners of large circuses were in a financial squeeze. They had to meet the operational costs of a company of up to two hundred people, soaring charges for land rental or the need to bribe the opportunistic authorities from diminishing revenues. To make matters worse, thanks to the attentions of Maneka and her colleagues, they could no longer use wild animals in their acts. The owners' solution to

---

[9] 'Save the Childhood Movement'

both problems was to slash overheads by treating performers as slaves and to present under-dressed little girls as the new key attraction. With their lighter complexions – a sign of beauty in the South Asian region – and exotic mongoloid appearances, Nepali children made for physically attractive performers. As foreigners they were also easy to exploit. While traditional forms of entertainment went into decline, little Nepali girls were paying the price with their bodies.

Before I called at the BBA office, the Director of another NGO had tipped me off that, like many regional NGOs, BBA was a very hierarchical organisation with its Founder, Kailash Satyarthi[10], very much the key person. Unfortunately, at the BBA office I found Kailash to be out of the country. He was clearly a figure of some standing internationally. A picture on the wall showed him posing alongside Bill Clinton.

Instead, I met with his affable son, Bhuwan Ribhu, and some other senior staff members. It soon transpired that while BBA was also aware of the circus children issue, they had no hard data to offer. Therefore, on the spot, I commissioned BBA to conduct a five month long undercover survey of around 30 Indian circuses. They'd start the survey in August with researchers posing as university students or journalists rather than as NGO workers. I wanted them to quantify the scale and nature of the use of child performers, establish their geographical origins and find out how the circuses were procuring them.

The research was both very dangerous and a logistical nightmare. In those days the Indian circus industry was still quite large with circuses scattered all over the country. Moreover, circuses made for difficult targets as they moved around a great deal, frequented remote areas and often changed their names. Their name-changing behaviour was a ploy to dupe the public into revisiting a circus thinking that they'd be seeing a different show. Being a peripatetic chameleon is also a good way to conceal trafficking victims; relatives might believe their daughter was with the xyz circus when she'd actually be with the abc circus in a totally different part of India. Most challenging was that following the animal rights activists' clandestine interests, circus owners were on their guard. And some of them were very dangerous men, hardened criminals for whom life was cheap.

We'd accepted that the research was always going to be inevitably flawed in that the researchers wouldn't have free access to all

---

[10] Satyarthi is an assumed name meaning 'Seeker of Truth'. His real name is Kailash Sharma.

the children. They'd be doing well to get to speak with them at all in such a suspicious, secretive environment. It would take a lot of time and visits to build any rapport with circus owners. Rather than collecting data through conventional questionnaires the researchers needed to adopt a very casual conversational approach (or approaches). This required a great deal of rehearsal, play-acting and memorising of the questions they wanted answering. On top of that inside the circuses the children would not be available to speak openly as there would always be a circus staff member listening in. Sometimes evidence could only be collected by attending shows and conducting a head count of child performers. The researchers told me how they'd been bored witless sitting through the same old acts again and again, but sufficient of a picture emerged to allow them to compile the final report.

The document I presented to the Trustees was a catalogue of abuse. The researchers had found 230 children under the age of 14 with just over 80% of them girls. The average age was 11 but the youngest was only five. The circuses liked to procure girls this young as their bodies were still flexible enough to train them as gymnasts. Just about all of the children were ethnic Nepali, with half coming from Nepal itself and the other half from northeast India where there is a large ethnic Nepali population. The latter is a throwback to the days of the Raj when the British imported Nepali labourers to become the workforce in the tea plantations of Darjeeling and Assam. All of the Nepali children came from the central south and southeast Nepal. The towns of Hetauda in Makwanpur District and Biratnagar in Morang District were recruitment hotspots. Most of the Indian ethnic Nepali children originated in West Bengal, its main town Siliguri and, to a lesser extent, Bihar.

Child traffickers, acting as latter-day Pied Pipers, were operating with impunity in impoverished rural districts as they recruited new performers. Once at the circuses the lives of the children could be summarised in three words – captivity, danger and violence. They were bound to the circuses for periods of ten to fifteen years by a combination of fake contracts and a high perimeter fence that barred any escape. Although many of the acts were ground-based and fairly safe, others were highly dangerous. These might involve the use of fire and swords or aerial acts without any safety nets. The circus trainers were quick to deliver beatings for the most minor misdemeanour, with attempts at escape from dreadful living and working conditions attracting the most vicious assaults. Given the nature of the research with children unable to speak openly, it was difficult to confirm the suggestion of sexual abuse but at least one teenager had managed to communicate through body language that she was being abused. Certainly, there was a very strong sexual dimension with the children being made to perform in revealing costumes.

I was comfortable that the report contained enough information for the Trustees to make an informed decision. But I had also ensured that it would have an emotional impact by interspersing the narrative with the child interviewees' own words and with pictures. The cover photo was of a boy clown, probably a dwarf, but a child nonetheless. He was wearing what looked like a pink onesie, with red spots, and a matching pink bonnet. Greasepaint had been applied to chin, cheeks and around the eyes to brighten up the boy's face, but that didn't conceal the misery. His empty expression reminded me again of the prisoners' faces from the cover of Primo Levi's book.

In presenting the report to the Trustees I felt that I needed to add some context:

'For me, this charity is all about commemorating Esther and perpetuating her values, advancing the causes that she cared about. We've already done that very successfully with the prison children issue, but here's a situation that's even more relevant, given Esther's passion about the Holocaust. Clearly, what we read in this report cannot parallel those horrors, but there are some echoes; children in a foreign land in captivity who are being brutalised and exploited.

'The question for us now is do we content ourselves with having funded this original research that exposes a largely previously unknown subject or do we do something about it? I say we intervene. Esther would not have looked away while children are suffering and, in my view, we can't do that either.'

I guessed from the body language and demeanour of the Chairman, Clifford Irish, and of Trustee John Sharp that I could rely upon their tacit agreement, if only out of loyalty to me. But another Trustee, Neal Gillespie, just as loyal, had a different viewpoint and he could always be counted on as a friend who spoke his mind. Clearing his throat and with a slight grimace that I recognised as foreshadowing potentially unpalatable candour, he began:

'Here's what I think. This is a very useful report but we should not become further involved. It's just too dangerous. We risk getting on the wrong side of ruthless traffickers and from what we read the circus owners are obviously very violent people. Bringing children out of prison doesn't affect anyone's business interests but not so with this undertaking. Once they realise that we're damaging their assets then they'll come back at us hard. And you can't look to Athe Nepali or Indian police to offer any protection – they are too inept or corrupt. This is way beyond our capacity and if we carry on, we'll quickly find ourselves out of our depth. Someone could get killed and we'll be responsible.'

Another Trustee, Patrick Folkes, spoke up:

'I agree with Neal. This will be no picnic. Couldn't we just settle for expanding our project work with street children? We've already made a very positive start in setting up a night shelter. How about setting up a few more at other locations?'

Just as I felt that I was losing the argument, the final Trustee, Bina Patel, had something to say:

'I'm with Philip on this one. I know what Neal means about risks and he's absolutely right about the difficulties of working in India. But look at what people like Gandhi and Mandela achieved in the past through being willing to take a risk, including of their own lives. In my opinion, as a charity we should place ourselves in the frontline of all of this and be proud to do so.'

Neal and Patrick acquiesced before Bina's impassioned intervention. We had a project. After the meeting I gave Bina a big hug of gratitude. Without her input at that pivotal moment this report would have collected dust and children would have been condemned to remain in slavery.

Actually, at that stage we were not in a position to intervene in any case. First off, BBA wanted to give the better circuses a chance to change their ways and go child-free by consent and negotiation, rather than going straight to confrontation. Secondly, we needed to expand our refuge capacity so that it could accommodate returnees, not to mention finding a lot more funds to cover their care costs, educational and training needs. And, most importantly, I had to get Suresh fully on board. Straight after the Board meeting, I went to Nepal to discuss the way ahead with him.

On my first evening back in Kathmandu – and before travelling to see Suresh in Bhairahawa the following day – I decided to ignore the jetlag and call by The Everest. I hadn't seen Billy in ages. To my amazement he wasn't there. A couple of young Nepali guys were occupying his usual spot at the bar.

'Is Billy around?' I asked.

They fell about laughing. After a minute or two, one of them composed himself:

'Billy doesn't get out much these days.'

The other guy chipped in:

'He's developing a striped suntan. He wants to look like a tiger.'

That set them off again.

'What's this about, Dan?' I asked the barman. He put down the glass that he'd been polishing and looked off into the distance.

'Billy's inside Central Jail. Last week the police caught him in the act with a little boy in his room. I think they'd a tip-off. It seems one of the orphanages that he was visiting allowed him to take children out for the day. For treats.'

The laughter at the end of the bar reached a new peak.

'Some treats!' called the first guy as he mimicked fellatio with his beer bottle. I couldn't share their mirth; Nepalis seem to find some things hilarious that we don't and vice versa. Feeling shaken with this ghastly news and disgusted by the antics of the two jokers at the end of the bar, I left without ordering.

Over breakfast the next morning I was reprimanding myself for being so badly caught out. I recalled how while on my Working for a Charity course I'd had an exchange on the subject of child protection with a senior worker from a national children's charity. She had cautioned me with words that now weighed on me like lead: 'You'll never be smarter than a paedophile.' And there I had been laughing and drinking with one who had worked his way into my confidence without really trying. I should have trusted my first impression on the plane that this wasn't someone I wanted to engage with. My only crumb of comfort was that our childcare facility in Bhairahawa had been well beyond Billy's grubby reach.

But I knew that almost certainly I had an immediate problem to contend with as most likely there'd be a few kids inside the Jail and they'd be in free association with Billy. For although the law had changed there remained a loophole that allowed a Jailer to still admit children in extremis. But allowing children to be in the company of a paedophile was one of those unthinking, mind-bogglingly crazy decisions that Billy himself had warned me about. I called up Indira.

'Yes, Philip dai, there are four new children in the Jail. They went in the day before yesterday.'

1. Captain Holmes in Belize, 1987

2. Esther, aged 20, wearing her Star of David penda

3. Esther in her beloved
Hoge der A, Groningen,
north Holland

4. Before our wedding
reception in Groningen,
August 1988

5. Inside Kathmandu Central Jail, March 2000

6. Cry Freedom

7. The shaven-headed boy in the striped pyjama top

8. Releasing prison children with Indira Rana Magar. A boy has one last look back at the jail

10. Children being freed from Tulsipur Jail, west Nepal. The boy's pullover reads "Happy Birthday"

9. The first seven children released from prison in Esther's name

11. Nepalese child performers (slaves) inside Indian circuses

12. Wedding day, September 2002

13. Bhairahawa street life

14. The new arrivals in Bhairahawa with their first dog, Bryher, and puppy, Agnes

15. Bev enjoying an art session with refuge kids

16. Refuge children going on an outing, with Kumar Basnet in the lead

17. The menacing figure of Fateh Khan surrounded by tiny Nepalese circus performers

18. Praying for deliverance - a Christian shrine inside an Indian circus

19. Emaciated girls inside The New Raj Kamal Circus

20. Circus deception: A girl poses for a picture purporting to show her having a good time. The downcast eyes and toy still in its cellophane wrapping says it all

21. Unicycle training inside the New Raj Kamal Circus

22. Trapeze training without a safety net

23. Rescued New Raj Kamal Circus girls learning mosaic techniques at the workshop in Philip's home

24. My own mosaic art work at Martin Cheek's course in Candili

25. An unforgettable chess game on Necker Island

26. Esther with the Cupid statue in the grounds of Chenies Manor

27. The police on parade before the raid on the Raj Mahal Circus

28. The police arrive at the circus

29. Our team is confident on the way to the circus. Nandita is on the left, Shailaja on the right

30. Nandita dominates the ring of the Raj Mahal Circus

31. Fateh Khan's brother, Siraj, (second right) attempting to save his Circus

32. Wed to the Circus: For these Nepalese former circus performers our visit had come too late

33. A girl calls a previously freed friend using Shailaja's mobile, confirming that it is safe to leave

34. Meeting the American performer at the Circus. She was totally unaware of the other girls' true circumstances

35. Overwhelmed with emotion, girls walk free

36. The "contract" that spelt 20 years of slavery

37. A released girl shows hands scarred by cauterisation with molten wax

38. A surrogate father's blessing at the refuge on the main day of the Dashain festival

39. Meeting Kenyan and Russian performers inside The Great Prabhath Circus

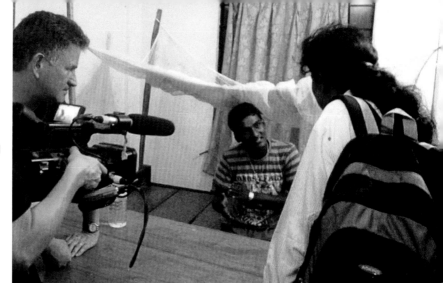

40. Shailaja, at last, gets the chance to confront alleged rapist Mithun Chaudhari

41. Shailaja remonstrating with a police officer outside The Great Apollo Circus

42. 'We've rescued the children!' Renu claims success as they snatch the children from us. Bhaskar Karki on the left

GIRLS OF PERSECUTED AND MARTYRED CHRISTIANS

MICHAEL JOB CENTRE, NEAR SULUR BOAT LAKE, COIMBATORE-641103, INDIA

rt by >> **Name**,Permanent Number,DOB   **1** 2 3 4 5 6 7 8 9 10 11 12 13 14 15 16 17 18 19 20 21 [Next >>]

ABBEY	ABIGAIL	AGATHA	AGNES	ALCIRA	ALICE
ALLISON	ALMIKA	AMANDA	AMBER	AMELIA	AMMU
AMY CAR MICHAEL	ANAMICA	ANCY RAJENDRAN	ANDREA	ANEENA	ANGELA
ANISHA	ANITA	ANJALA	ANNA	ANNA BELLA	ANNETT

43. 'Chosen by God':
    Dr PP Job

44. Dr and Mrs Job with Richard
    and Sabina Wurmbrand

45. Fraud on the Michael Job
    Centre website: *'Girls of
    persecuted and martyred
    Christians'*, all with new
    identities, awaiting sponsors

46. One of the
    monstrous buildings at
    The Michael Job Centre

47. The Nepalese girls whom we rescued from The Michael Job Centre with Shangmo, the mother who accompanied us on the trip. The girls have a far from typical appearance for trafficking victims

48. Dutch evangelists Jan Bor (left) and Abwin Buteijn enjoying Nepalese cuisine with self-confessed child trafficker DB Phadera

49. DB Phadera (right) having tea with former Nepal Prime Minister, Madhav Kumar Nepal (left). DB is a prominent supporter of MK Nepal's political party.

50. Aman Tamang, one of the first five children rescued from the Indian circuses, performing with Renu Ghalan in contemporary circus show "As a Tiger in the Jungle"

51. With Shailaja - ready for the next big success

52. The Holmes family back in Europe

This was a 'ke garne' moment for me. I didn't want to resume rescuing children from Central Jail given that they might be there on a spurious basis. Nevertheless, I needed to act quickly. Then I had an idea. I asked Indira to meet me at The Prison Management Department.

Indira introduced me to the official whom she dealt with on child welfare matters. I suspected he was some way down the Department's food chain. He took notes as we explained the problem to him. He paused at one point to clarify the spelling of 'paedophile'. It looked to me like it was the first time he'd heard the word. Then I presented him with a simple solution.

'Would it be possible to move this guy to a jail where there are no children?'

The official considered the suggestion for a moment.

'Yes, we can do that. We can transfer him to the jail at Dillibazar. No children are allowed in there. I'll give the instruction straight away.'

I thanked him copiously and left, just making it in time to the airport to catch my internal flight to Bhairahawa. I never heard of Billy again.

That afternoon Suresh and I had tea on his balcony. It was good to be back with what had become to feel like family. Indeed, Suresh had told me that I was now *pariwar*[11]. We were watching a noisy gaggle of mynah birds that had just landed in the paddy field below when there was a thump at the door. Suresh arose with a little giggle.

'I know who that will be. My new best friend, second only to you, Philip.'

He opened the door and out bounded a Tibetan Mastiff puppy. It was only six months old, but already huge with a great thick coat. Simba was his third dog, but his favourite and the only one that was allowed into the house.

'Isn't he splendid? And look at that bushy tail,' he said.

---

[11] 'Family'

134

'When I look at him, I think of one of our Nepalese sayings. It goes something like "you can put a dog's tail inside a piece of bamboo for ten years but when you take it off the tail will curl back up again". It's similar in meaning to a leopard not being able to change its spots. Great isn't it?'

He scooped Simba up in his arms and with the great dumb beast partly straddling his shoulder he performed a little waltz before releasing it on its way. Then he said something very strange that came from nowhere.

'The British officers love their Gurkhas. I love my dog, but it will never be my equal.'

'What do you mean?' I asked.

'Just what I've said,' he replied. 'We have this farcical arrangement in the Army where the Brigade of Gurkhas is dominated by British officers who've a kind of patronising attitude to their Nepalese counterparts. We're kept out of the most senior appointments as we're deemed incapable. It's a kind of institutional racism. Mind you, we are our own worst enemies as we engage in a little dance – like me just now with Simba – where the Nepalese fawn around the British and flatter their egos. It's a big game, a sham and I'm glad to be out of it.'

This spontaneous remark made me feel rather uncomfortable. It was uncharacteristically petulant and I remembered then a comment one of Suresh's peers had made to me in private during that first visit to Nepal. He'd obviously been very fond of Suresh but said that he had been quite outspoken within the regiment. If ever the Nepalese officers had an issue with the British officers it would always be Suresh who acted as the spokesman. The others kept their noses clean, probably acting out the little dance that Suresh had just described. Suresh's friend told me that as his senior he'd had to work really hard to get Suresh promoted because he'd upset some British officers along the way.

I elected not to take that exchange any further and turned the conversation towards the circus report. Suresh had of course seen the document and straight off he challenged me with the question:

'Philip, are you seriously proposing that just the two of us and the dog take on the whole Indian circus industry?'

Here he had a point. We were very under-resourced and inexperienced, but that hadn't put me off in the past and I, for one, had the drive.

'Yes, we will,' I replied, 'I'm sure I can find the resources we need for this and we've got off to such a strong start with all our media coverage. When this story breaks, I expect there'll be more of the same.'

'Oh well, bang goes my plan to be a "Grandfather Walton",' he answered. 'You've shifted the goalposts!'

He wasn't being unreasonable. Running a small children's home had been the basis I had recruited him on and now we stood to take on a programme, as yet unclear, that could take us the length and breadth of India. We would be entering very dangerous, uncharted waters.

I mollified him by suggesting that we start gently by setting up a field office at Hetauda in Makwanpur District, south Nepal. The circus researchers had identified this as being the main trafficking hotspot so we should plant our standard right in the middle of it all. We could appoint a small team that would be able to confirm and extend the circus research by meeting with families and returnees who would be able to speak openly about their experiences. Concurrently I could use some of the money I had raised to expand his residential care facilities and already we were eyeing a red brick building along the way that could become a 'Red House' to complement the White House. This would be very affordable. Suresh seemed content with that proposal for a way ahead.

After tea, Suresh invited me to join him for a visit to someone he'd been introduced to the previous week. She was called Shailaja and lived at a place called Manigram which was on the road between Bhairahawa and Butwal. He said that she was originally from Kerala in south India and seemed to be a good woman who was running a small children's home. Perhaps we could support her without too much outlay. He warned me that she was a little 'different.'

We arrived at the bungalow she lived in to find nobody around. The door was open though and we could see at a glance that it was basic in the extreme. And rather dark. We crossed the road to the little government school where we knew Shailaja was teaching. It was pretty shabby too. As it happened classes for the day were just ending and Shailaja emerged with a bright grin that was in marked contrast to her very drab clothes. It was already different to meet someone wearing a pullover and skirt rather than a sari. I guessed she was in her late twenties. She invited us over to her home for a cup of tea.

'How does a woman from Kerala find her way to Nepal?' I asked.

'That's a long story,' she replied, 'but I was with an order of Catholic sisters. You'll find a lot of priests and nuns from Kerala all over India and Nepal. Many become teachers and I was trained at college in Gorakhpur, just across the border from here.'

'Shouldn't you be dressed as a nun, then?' I teased.

'I left the order because they wanted to send me to teach in a middle-class private school. I told them that wasn't what I wanted to do as I had become a sister to help poor people. I found a job at the place across the way and that gives me enough to get by on.'

'But you're looking after some children on that salary as well?'

'Yes, I have eleven girls.'

Curious children, fresh back from school, were starting to cluster around her like a mother hen. I was starting to sense that I was in the presence of someone who was incredibly modest but very special. Like me she was a foreigner in this country, witness to her faith in a very practical grassroots way. The only difference was that she was an Indian and had chosen to live in a country where her nationality wasn't at all popular. I didn't understand this decision.

'How did you come by them?'

As she removed her brown woollen scarf, I noticed a broad scar straddling her neck and the side of her face. It looked like a burn.

'See, most of these children are unwanted stepchildren from very poor families. One or two of them have parents who are drunkards. People all around here know about me and they just drop children on me. They know that I can't refuse genuine cases.'

That self-effacing grin lit up her face again.

'But this is a huge commitment. Don't you worry about taking on so much? Forgive me for asking, but what would become of these kids if, heaven forbid, something happened to you?'

Shailaja was silent for a few moments, giving all the impression of this thought never having occurred to her. She was totally at ease living a hand to mouth existence and everyone was happy, especially the children.

'I have a faith and my work is my prayer. I know that I'll be fine, man.'

I needed time to digest this statement, so after taking a few pictures of the children I bade her farewell, promising that I would help her out as much as I could. As I left on the back of Suresh's motorbike she called:

'Please pray for me.'

Afterwards I suggested to Suresh that he drop her off a sack of rice every month. Perhaps we were answering her prayers.

137

This February visit to Nepal had been a productive one, with Suresh now seemingly on board for the circus project. It had become clear to me that he needed a lot of moral and practical support in the midst of his professional isolation and with the increased demands I was placing upon him. These four to six monthly visits served to recharge and inspire him; indeed, Suresh referred to me as his 'batteries'.

For me the trips to Nepal felt a bit like the plate spinning trick whereby a performer keeps multiple plates spinning on the ends of poles; like that performer I just had to give the poles regular tweaks and Suresh's organisation would be okay for a while longer. In my innocence I could congratulate myself on my fine-tuned leadership and return to UK with peace of mind.

The setting up of a field office in the provincial town of Hetauda proved to be a sound decision. Before long parents of circus children came to hear of our work and began visiting the office to seek our help in tracing and retrieving their children. We started to build up a 'Hetauda list' of missing girls and their last known whereabouts.

One day two men called in and asked to speak with Bishnu, our local coordinator. One of them was dressed like a peasant farmer, the other wearing a smart leather jacket and looking like he'd never done a day's work in his life. The first was the father of a circus girl, his companion described only as a friend of the family. They had with them a grainy picture from inside the circus showing an Indian man towering over a cluster of adolescent Nepali girls, the man's daughter being one of them. The guy in the leather jacket seemed to be quite pushy and did most of the talking. He began:

'This man is called Fateh Khan and he owns a number of big circuses in north India. He's a very bad person who procures girls and then tricks their parents. He doesn't send the money he promises.'

Bishnu turned to the parent, determined to hear from him directly.

'Why did you send your daughter to the circus? Didn't you know what was at stake?'

The other man interjected:

'This community has been sending girls to the circuses for the last twenty or thirty years. This man's own sister was a circus girl. It used to be a good opportunity for a girl and she'd make good money for herself and her family. But in the last few years this cheating has begun. I think the circuses are having a hard time and the girls are paying the price.'

Bishnu thought that the father was trying to catch his eye but for some reason seemed reluctant to speak for himself. His companion continued:

'Can you help us get this girl back? She's coming near to the end of her contract and her father, I mean the girl, is owed a lot of money. We are worried that Fateh Khan will marry her off to one of the circus staff and we'll never see her again.'

As he listened Bishnu began to wonder if there was an ulterior motive beyond the greed. His initial research had revealed that many of the circuses were Muslim-owned and a Nepali father wouldn't want his daughter to marry a Muslim at any price. Better to marry someone from the village, the arrangement underpinned with a good dowry. Bishnu took the girl's details and said that he would see what he could do and the two men left.

Later that day Bishnu spotted the father sitting alone in a tea shop.

'Why were you so quiet today?' he asked.

'I was frightened to say anything. The man I was with told me to let him do the talking. You see, he was the agent who took my daughter to the circus. He's a wicked man but he's annoyed as we've all been tricked and his business is being ruined. I tried to signal to you to be careful.'

The more that Bishnu heard, the more he realised what a very complicated picture he had to piece together. And the name Fateh Khan kept cropping up in his enquiries. He and his family stood accused of deceit and all kinds of violence. Khan's power extended well beyond the circus as he was also a big shot in the lawless northern Indian State of Uttar Pradesh (UP) where he enjoyed strong political support and wielded major financial clout. He protected himself by confining his circus activities to that part of India. It seemed that the circus project could not succeed without breaking this modern-day slave-master's power and that was a tall order.

Hetauda research also revealed that there was another source of circus performers that had been missed by the BBA study; bizarrely, young women who had returned to Nepal after completing their 'contracts' were returning to re-join the circus. This reflected the desperation of returnees who after they got back to Nepal would be stigmatised as 'dirty circus girls' and unable to find work. They reasoned that they would be treated better as most beatings were inflicted upon children during the training phase and at least, being older, they'd be fed and paid (after a fashion). But no girl would ever return to a Fateh Khan circus voluntarily.

Meanwhile in India, BBA was holding exploratory discussions with those circus owners who were willing to speak with them. The forum for the exchanges was the grandly-titled 'Indian Circus Federation' which represented 22 of the major circuses.

As these preliminary negotiations were underway, I was unsettled by a surprise development in Uttar Pradesh, northern India. In June an organisation called *Pravasi Nepali Mitra Manch* (PNMM) raided the Great Apollo Circus and freed a number of Nepali girl performers. This operation followed the escape of two girls who had immediately alleged sexual abuse and extremes of physical violence against the circus owners, brothers Haji Yunis and Haji Alim. Haji Alim had been committing rape on a daily basis inside his tent. We'd never heard of PNMM but they had clearly pulled off a major result with 44 performers rescued.

Our subsequent enquiries indicated that PNMM was a very small organisation of expatriate Nepalis with no resources. However, they had got lucky in an acutely dangerous situation. For this Muslim-run circus had been playing in the midst of a volatile Muslim community and it would have been all too easy for the circus owners to incite retaliation against their Hindu intruders[12].

During my next visit to Nepal in July some of the girls that PNMM had freed filed shyly into the Hetauda office. With the girls revealing their accounts of systematic rape I was struck by the magnitude of the task that lay ahead. There was a dearth of trauma management services In Nepal and many, if not most, counsellors were men who were based in Kathmandu.

I desperately needed someone with Esther's kind of skillset and experience. The sort of person who could at the very least offer the 'thick woollen blanket' that she had described in 'Dingen Die Niet Voorbij Gaan'. Children and teenagers were being confined and brutalised in another country, returning home with PTSD to be shunned and stigmatised by their parent communities. Esther had told me how some of her clients upon returning to Holland had been mocked by neighbours with comments like 'I thought Hitler had got you.' Not only would I have

---

[12] Religious riots in the same area in 2013 left sixty people dead.

to stop this trafficking but also manage survivors with the same compassion and tenderness as she had shown to her clients twenty-five years before. I was in no doubt that this was the torch that I was destined to carry forward in Esther's name.

In August 2003 Bhuwan was elated at being able to call together a number of circus owners for an 'All India Circus Conference'. He and his team were now able to reveal their interest and challenge the circuses with the information they had obtained through their undercover research. They knew that the 230 children they'd found would understate the scale of the problem, but they were taken aback when the circuses admitted that the true figure was closer to 500.

Amidst a blaze of media publicity, the Conference closed with the circuses promising to disclose the identities of all the children under the age of 14 and begin a phased release towards ultimately going child-free. This was too good to be true but, in his e-mails, Bhuwan was triumphant. The catch was that as a trade-off he'd offered to help the circuses develop and help move their shows into the 21st Century. I'd only had a flicker of such interest from the UK circus industry and Bhuwan had been highlighting these prospects.

I agreed with Suresh that for my final trip to Nepal in December 2003 we should host a visit from Bhuwan and two of his colleagues from BBA for face to face discussions. Bhuwan brought with him a guy known only as 'The Professor' as he was allegedly very clever and the softly spoken Unni who was originally from Kerala. All three had taken part in the original circus research and in subsequent negotiations with the Circus Federation.

The chemistry between us was generally very good although it was obvious that Bhuwan was the dominant presence within the visitors. He was as good-humoured as ever, drawing upon a healthy collection of anecdotes to keep the conversation flowing. The Professor may have been clever but didn't really have much to say for himself; I warmed to the softly spoken Unni straight away. He had a certain innocent charm about him, was clean-living and sincere, with a gentle smile.

I was proud to show them around our facilities. By the end of that year and thanks to grant funding we had not only a White House but also a Red House and a Blue House (extremes in colour are popular in Nepal). All of our kids were well cared for and genuinely happy. Moreover, at my instigation Suresh had been able to encourage Shailaja to close down her home and move with her children to stay at the Blue House. This was a much less fragile situation for her children and we

141

were bringing an energetic and genuine person into the organisation. She resigned her teaching appointment to become the chief carer at the Blue House, placing herself right in the frontline ready to receive the first returnees from India. She beamed at our guests, a very presentable person indeed.

At a meeting afterwards Bhuwan waxed lyrical about the prospects for the forthcoming releases.

'We'll be the talk of India for pulling off this outcome,' he declared, 'and all without a shot being fired.'

The Professor laughed.

'Do you remember the guy with the shotgun at the Amar Circus?'

'Oh yes, how could I forget?' he replied. 'That was one of our survey circuses, Philip. The owner pulled a gun on us on our second visit and said that if we came back a third time, he'd kill us even if it meant his going to jail. He said he didn't care.'

'Can we really expect owners like that to comply with a voluntary release process?' I asked. 'And what about the non-Federation circuses, including those owned by Fateh Khan? They're the worst circuses of all and haven't been part of this process. Also, I'm very uneasy about this process only applying to 14-year-olds and below. What of the girls like Maya whom you met who are older than that and being abused? Or the 15-year-old who's been inside the circus for ten years? Don't they matter?'

In response to my rhetoric Bhuwan dabbed his nose with his nasal inhaler stick.

'Philip-ji[13], don't concern yourself about that right now. We have to take this very slowly, one step at a time, and build some momentum. It'll be critical for the circus owners to see us reciprocate and offer some benefit to them. How are you getting along with that anyway?'

'Very early days, I'm afraid. I've had a good meeting with the Chief Executive of *Circus Space* in London. It's Europe's largest contemporary circus school. As it happens, just before my meeting they'd had an Indian circus owner visit them. He was in London for his honeymoon and called by pleading that they help him save his business, with its 200 employees. They're aware of what we are up to but nothing more than that at this stage. Wouldn't it be wonderful though if we could set up a circus training school in Nepal itself that could ensure trainees

---

[13] The suffix 'ji' indicates respect in India

receive an education and then as young adults go on proper contracted employment to decent circuses?'

'Yes, that's a tremendous vision,' Bhuwan replied, 'but for now it would be great if we could even organise a consultancy visit from Circus Space to meet some representatives from the Federation to show that there is some substance to our discussions. We need to dangle a real carrot before them.'

The meeting concluded with our agreeing to see what happened next with the imminent child releases. As a new operator in India I had to accept Bhuwan's advice to follow their measured approach. Even so, having met those brutalised returnees in Hetauda, underneath it all my patience was wearing thin.

11.   Raid and Rescue

On the Nepal border early one morning in January 2004, a nine year old boy called Aman was overjoyed as he tucked into a plate of *momos*[14] from a wayside vendor.

'This is the first Nepali food I've tasted in two years!' he exclaimed.

A full five months after the Indian Circus Federation's 'momentous' decision to go child-free, the circuses had freed nine children voluntarily, five of them Nepali nationals, including Aman. This was done with further media hyperbole at a second Indian circus conference hosted by BBA.

It was of course heart-warming for me to see pictures of these little boys and girls heading north by Indian train. Yet for all the brouhaha I remained unimpressed with such a modest result compared with the startling success PNMM had achieved. I had anticipated the release of 25 to 30 children, not nine. Besides, of the 19 circuses that had been represented at the August 2003 Conference only five had complied with producing the promised lists of children who were working for them.

BBA once again hailed this as a major breakthrough but their enthusiasm reminded me a little of the story of *The Emperor's New Clothes*. I told Bhuwan that after all this time and charitable investment I was underwhelmed. For me this voluntary release reeked of a publicity stunt and BBA might have inadvertently played into the hands of cunning and opportunistic circus owners. The circuses had gained positive publicity that they just didn't deserve. Where, I asked him, were the other 223 children that BBA had found during their research?

Our professional relationship was becoming strained. I told him that our Hetauda List of parents seeking children had already grown to 109 children and our credibility with expectant families was in jeopardy. The Hetauda office was receiving ten to twelve visits per day from family members eager for news of their children and of our progress. We risked being written off as just another Nepali NGO that was raising people's expectations while attracting funds for itself. These voluntary releases weren't meeting the scale of public demand and actually not one of the freed children had appeared on our list. Worst of all, after the PNMM

---

[14] Nepalese steamed dumplings.

action we'd been left in no doubt that sexual abuse was indeed endemic in the circuses. We couldn't wait any longer.

Eventually Bhuwan relented and agreed to shake the circuses up with a raid and rescue operation. It was time to apply the stick in advance of the carrot.

Our target circus was Ariti's circus, the Great Indian Circus, that was playing at this time in Kerala, Unni's home State. For us, though, this was a long way away both literally and metaphorically from where we had started out in Bhairahawa. Our initiative would be bold and dangerous. The date for the operation was set at 17th April 2004 as the team would need two or three months to prepare the way. This involved researching families in Makwanpur District, drawing up affidavits and finalising the reception needs of returnees.

Suresh sent me pictures of his staff collecting parents' thumbprints on affidavits, the same thumbs that had condemned the children into a wretched existence on illegal circus contracts. We decided that a couple of staff from the Hetauda office along with three parents of children from the circus would join a BBA team led by Unni for the long train journey south. Communications would be sparse and I was on tenterhooks as I awaited news.

The raid exceeded my expectations with 29 performers freed from slavery. It took them a long time to get back home though as they had to go via Delhi so that BBA could present their success to the national media. After that the children of course needed to spend some time with their families. It was two weeks before I could catch up with the group at our Hetauda office. I took Suresh along with me in the hope that exposing him directly to the experiences of the returnees would fire up his enthusiasm – rather like how he'd been inspired by the visit to Tansen jail at that time.

The sun was smiling on us as I entered the compound at the Hetauda office. There must have been sixty or seventy people gathered there, children and their families, dressed in their finest clothes. They could not have known me or imagined how thrilled this *gora*[15] was to witness their joy as they laughed and exchanged stories with one another.

In the midst of this celebration it was wonderful to see Unni again and to be able to congratulate him personally on his success. We sat down together in the office with Suresh and the head of the Hetauda

---

[15] The Nepali word for a white person

145

team, Bishnu, who had also gone on the rescue operation. I couldn't wait to hear their report first-hand.

'How was it?' I began.

'Scary,' answered Bishnu, with one of those enigmatic Nepalese smiles, 'We had to be so cautious.'

'Yes,' added Unni, 'We watched the circus for two days before we made our move. I could see that the circus was well embedded within the community. They'd been there for several weeks. I was very aware of how potentially we could stand out as strangers. We rotated the monitoring duties a little. One wrong move could have been fatal.'

'How did you get inside the circus?' Suresh asked.

'It was just like during the research,' Unni replied. 'On the second day we attended an afternoon performance – hopefully my last one of those ever. Afterwards I asked to meet with the owner, Malik, and managed to bluff him that I was a journalist who wanted to see behind the scenes to run a story. I am well practised at doing that and he bought it. That gave me a chance to see the lie of the land and gain an idea of the numbers involved.'

He shook his head and a pained look crossed his face.

'The thing I remembered most was the sense of fear and despair I'd seen on the girls' faces when they weren't performing. That evening I couldn't eat my dinner at the thought of how they were being abused and exploited. I decided that however intimidating this rescue might become I wouldn't be leaving without children.'

Just then, Ariti and another girl called Nisha dashed into the room. I'd noticed earlier how hyperactive they were, running around like the office was a playground. Suresh caught Ariti and quickly calmed her down. He was great at connecting with children and talking to them at their level:

'Is it good to be back in Hetauda then?'

'I had been praying for years that the gods would come to rescue me. I imagined that they'd sweep down from the sky to whisk me away.'

She turned a little pirouette with her arms outstretched like wings.

'And did they?'

'Not like that. But my rescuers are still my gods.' She smiled at Unni and Bishnu.

'When did you realise what was happening?'

146

'I was outside my tent doing my *dhobi*[16] when I heard a man whispering to me through the perimeter fence. I couldn't see him but he was speaking Nepali.'

'That was me,' interjected Bishnu. 'I decided to take a risk and prime the girls for our visit and reassure them. I told Ariti that I was from Hetauda and that I'd come to take her home. When we called back later she and the other girls had to cooperate with us as much as they could if they wanted to be free.'

'And what did you do, Ariti?' asked Suresh.

'There was nothing I could do. I didn't dare tell anyone as I would've been beaten if it was found out that I'd been speaking to someone from the outside. They would also beat us for speaking Nepali. And the older girls were very close to the circus staff. I couldn't trust them.'

She looked a little awkward at that admission. Her sister Muna was of course one of the older ones. Suresh excused her with a little nod and she dashed off outside with Nisha.

Unni continued:

'Later that morning we approached the circus formally to try to reason with Malik. Some of the older girls gathered around. At first it was civil enough but when Bishnu started speaking to the girls in Nepali the situation suddenly became very tense. A crowd seemed to assemble from nowhere and the threats began to fly, including from the girls themselves. "There's your answer"' Malik said to us. He turned to the girls with a sneer; "These men want to take you to a brothel in Mumbai, is that OK with you?"

'At that point we decided it was sensible to leave before things turned violent. During all of this the police just stood by as passive observers, but I think that their presence at least allowed us to get away from there without injury.'

'Unni, this sounds to me a bit like *Stockholm Syndrome* where captives side with their captors. There was a famous case of this back in the seventies when an American heiress called Pattie Hearst appeared to join her kidnappers. I think it's a kind of survival strategy in the face of abuse and threat to life,' I said.

'Very possibly,' Unni replied, 'as those girls were certainly terrified. But there was more to it than that. We'd taken one girl's father with us as we thought that this would make our task easier with the

---

[16] 'Laundry'

147

authorities and that when his daughter, Sushma, saw him she'd feel reassured. In fact, his presence had quite the opposite effect. On the way to Kerala I realised that her father was a pretty unsavoury sonofabitch who'd had no qualms about selling Sushma in the first place. When she saw him at the circus, she swore at him for what he'd done to her and demanded to know what his plans were to make more money from her. Malik's comments on a brothel didn't seem at all implausible to her.'

'That's when you called on the District Collector[17] for support?' I asked.

'Yes, we went straight to his office. We knew that Sanjeev Kaushik was a good man but we hadn't expected him to be quite so helpful. He stopped what he was doing and went with us in person to the circus. We had about 20 or so police officers with us and this time, with the Collector being there, they took firm action and sealed off the circus.'

'What time was that?' I asked.

'Around 4 p.m. Our arrival coincided with the end of the afternoon performance and the girls were still in their circus clothes. Everyone seemed surprised to see us back again with a bus parked up outside.

'The Collector didn't waste any time. He summoned the whole circus company into the main tent, introduced himself and vouched for our credentials. The girls had a simple choice. Those who wanted to leave should go to the left, those who wished to stay should move to the right. The whole selection process took no more than half an hour – and throughout Malik didn't dare say a word.'

'That's more than can be said for Sushma,' said Bishnu. 'She began screaming that she wouldn't go anywhere with her father but the Collector insisted that she must leave with him. Her father's say-so had to be final. Ke garne? We physically had to manhandle her onto the bus. She was quite hysterical.'

'That can't have been a very reassuring sight for the older girls,' I suggested.

'Didn't make much difference in my opinion,' said Bishnu. 'Most had already decided to stay where they were. It seems that many of them had become sexually involved with the circus staff and they

---

[17] A very powerful senior civil servant who is responsible for administration and revenue collection within an Indian State. He is sometimes termed the District Magistrate.

probably thought they'd nothing to return to in Nepal. They'd lost their virtue.'

'That's putting it mildly,' said Unni. 'Malik was raping the girls. On the way back to Nepal one of the boys, Santosh, told us that his task had been to take the girls to Malik's tent where he'd hear their cries for help, or them begging Malik not to do it.'

'Looks like Malik's got away with that,' Suresh commented.

'For now, yes,' Unni answered. 'We didn't know about his crimes at the time of the rescue but even if we had, we probably wouldn't or couldn't have done anything. The Collector was very keen to get us onto that bus and on the road to Nepal while we had the element of surprise and before trouble could flare. He was worried about the circus retaliating which is why he assigned us an armed guard all the way out of the State.'

We went outside for a stroll in the office grounds which had become a picnic site for the afternoon. It felt like a swarm of bees had descended upon the garden. Returnees and their families were enjoying samosas, onion bhajis and fizzy drinks. A cassette player was blasting out Nepali songs.

A toothless old man, dressed like a Buddhist monk, was thanking us again and again, raising his hands together in obeisance above his head every minute or two. His 15-year-old daughter, Urma, was amongst the returnees.

'God has helped me,' he declared through tears of joy.

'Urma might see things differently,' muttered Bishnu, ironically. 'Her act involved having to balance a sword vertically with the tip between her teeth, a flowerpot on the handle, while she climbed a stepladder. One slip and that sword would have gone right through her. She might resent God for having put her in that situation in the first place.'

'Yes,' said Unni, 'But the strange thing is that in the midst of dangerous acts and all those beatings all of them seemed to hate having to wear revealing costumes. They were ashamed.'

Suresh had drifted off after we'd gone outside but returned with his arm around a little girl who must have been about ten or eleven.

'Philip, as a former dentist you'll be interested to meet this one. Her name is Sunmaya.'

Sunmaya looked a little awkward, her lips pursed as she smiled.

'She doesn't like people to see her teeth. Please let uncle have a look,' Suresh said to her.

149

Sunmaya lifted her top lip to reveal that both of her central incisors were broken across the middle. The nerve in one of the two had clearly been exposed during the trauma.

'What happened?' I asked.

'She tells me that she went over the handlebars of her bicycle during a performance. Then straight after that she had to continue with the "Starkiss" act. It's one of the most dangerous in the circus. A girl has to grip a piece of cloth at the end of a rope and she's then spun around the big top maybe about 20 feet in the air. She becomes a kind of human fan. Sometimes the girl's hands will be tied behind her back. If she loses her grip, she dies.'

I could only imagine the agony and absolute terror that Sunmaya would have felt during those few horrific minutes. Suresh sent her off to re-join her mother who was squatting on the porch, her arms adorned with cheap red plastic bangles. She must have been forty but looked sixty; life was tough in the hills around Hetauda.

Before I left that day Bishnu introduced me to Hari. Just short of 18 he was the oldest of the returnees. He was quite a likeable lad, gangly and tousle-haired. Bishnu asked him to tell me about the discipline within the circus.

'It was beatings, beatings, beatings. For anything and everything. A girl would be beaten if she smiled too much in a performance or not enough. They had to learn to balance in more ways than one.'

He nodded in the direction of Nisha who was now chasing Ariti around a flower bed.

'Beatings came by day and by night. Just after that girl joined the circus, she was overheard crying in her sleep. Malik thrashed her with a latti.'

'Tell Philip-ji about the punishment for running away,' coaxed Bishnu.

'There weren't many runaways. A girl like Ariti would know that if she ran away the balance of her contract would be added to her sister's, so she was a kind of hostage. And anyway, where could they run to? A Nepalese child would be very obvious in south India and wouldn't have any money to get anywhere. Chances are she'd be caught by the police very quickly and returned to the circus owner who'd pay the cops well. After that there was a standard punishment of thrashing the soles of the child's feet with wires.'

'I meant you to tell him about how you were punished for trying to escape.'

150

Hari dropped his head, pained or ashamed by what he was about to say.

'After they caught me, I was taken into the middle of the wall of death, a circular wooden well used for motorbike stunt riding. There they stripped me naked in front of the whole company, boys and girls, who had to watch me from above. I was very embarrassed and humiliated. Then two of them beat me with canes while two others revved their motorbikes. The idea behind that was that the motorbike engines would drown my cries. But I took what was coming to me without making any noise or pleas for mercy. I was terrified but I wasn't going to show it.'

On the drive back to Bhairahawa that evening I tried to reconcile conflicting emotions; elation combined with profound sadness at what I had heard. I also felt vindicated in having pushed BBA into taking firm action but had I left this too long and been misguided? There was no way we could have negotiated with criminals like Malik. Now we would have to make up for lost time and press on with more of the same – 29 rescued in one raid was the kind of figure I'd had in mind.

There could be no going back. We were now at war with the circuses. My other nascent emotion was a longing to take part in the rescues myself. I didn't want to be exposed to these stirring events second hand and I certainly wasn't prepared to lead from behind, five thousand miles distant.

I was due to leave for Kathmandu and on to the UK the following day, but before leaving Bhairahawa I had time to call and see Shailaja who was now in charge of our Blue House reception facility for circus returnees. She had also been almost full time at the bedside of Sushma who'd had a psychotic episode after her forced removal from the circus. She'd been admitted to hospital in Bhairahawa but after a few days seemed to be retrieving her equilibrium.

'She knows she's safe now, man', Shailaja told me, 'And if we keep her father away, I'm sure she'll make a rapid recovery. It's the rest of the children who are a nightmare.'

'How's that?' I asked.

'See, generally speaking they're all very wound up. I thought at first that was just excitement at being free but that hasn't worn off. They are almost literally bouncing off the walls, doing somersaults on the concrete and sitting on first floor window sills, taunting me to come and get them. After the harsh discipline they're used to in the circus my words of correction mean nothing. They just laugh at me.'

151

I recalled how abnormally agitated Ariti and Nisha had been in Hetauda. She continued:

'These children have no fear of heights or of anything else that I can see. In the midst of these general behavioural problems there are individual cases who almost need one-to-one support. There is Santosh with his anger issues, furious at his family for having abandoned him to the circus and to all that trauma.

'Most difficult of all is Ariti. I think she has an odd sense of guilt combined with sorrow. You see, during the circus selection while she chose to go to the left her sister Muna went to the right, and is still in the circus. Ariti of course knows that her sister took the wrong decision and she's tormented by that thought. Sometimes I find her wandering on her own outside the house. She cries a lot.'

This had a strange resonance with the behaviour patterns Esther had described in her thesis. For example, the fury of the adults who'd felt abandoned and tricked, when as children they'd been left with Gentile families for their protection. And the 'survival guilt' that tormented others who questioned their right to a happy existence when family members had perished. Shailaja challenge was a similar one as she tried to help these children find their faith in humanity again and lead normal lives. Thankfully, she seemed to be a natural counsellor and I could see that with the correct professional support she was just the person for the task in hand. There was hope.

Shailaja took me on a tour of the Blue House, pointing out the little classroom that she had set up for the 12 children from the 29 that she was looking after. They sat at very low benches as their tutor coaxed them through an unenthusiastic recitation of the English alphabet. It was very obvious to both Shailaja and me that we needed to do so much more and without addressing the children's psychological issues we couldn't expect them to progress much beyond ABC. For me the letters that sprang to mind were PTSD; I was convinced that this was the provenance of Shailaja's child management challenges but we lacked the experience to deal with it.

I promised Shailaja that I would find her the specialist expertise she needed. But as I boarded the plane to leave Bhairahawa that afternoon I hadn't the first idea how to go about it. If she was so at sea in trying to manage these 12 kids how would she cope with another group who could be with her within a matter of a couple of months? Both of us needed faith while others around us, including Suresh, were beginning to take fright.

12.   A bad day at Gonda

News of the bold April rescue spread like wildfire through Makwanpur District. Soon afterwards a new group of parents came to the Hetauda office pleading for our help. They brought with them a number of photographs that showed their daughters apparently having a good time. One girl was visiting a tourist attraction, well-dressed in a colourful sari rather than in her usual threadbare smock. Another was of a girl posing with a cuddly toy. The clues to the reality weren't hard to spot in the second picture. For behind her lay the high sheet metal fence that enclosed the circus perimeter and her cuddly toy was clearly unused, still wrapped in cellophane. Most haunting of all was the girl's unsmiling face and downcast eyes. She couldn't fake it for the camera.

The parents begged us to rescue their daughters from The Great Roman Circus, Fateh Khan's main circus. The circus was playing at a place called Karnaliganj in Gonda District, just outside Lucknow. The parents told us how they had just been to this circus, no doubt primarily to obtain the money that had been promised to them, only to be turned away. During the visit they'd been shocked to find their daughters in a terrible state and tried to take them home. But Fateh Khan's son and circus owner, Raza, had refused, showing them the contracts that they had thumb-printed. Of course, they hadn't understood the content. Their daughters had become circus property. Khan had threatened them with violence if they didn't go away and he had been quick to draw his pistol.

Returning to Nepal empty-handed and feeling cheated, the families had gone to ask *Maiti Nepal* for help. Maiti Nepal is the Nepali NGO renowned internationally for its work against sex trafficking. Its Founder, Anuradha Koirala, is a national icon[18]. However, Maiti Nepal couldn't help the families as, in spite of its reputation, it didn't mount cross-border rescue operations. I suggested to Bhuwan that this should be their next target. If they could crack the tough nut of a Fateh Khan circus that would really concentrate the minds of circus owners across

---

[18] Anuradha Koirala was a CNN 'Hero of the Year' for 2010, receiving a cash prize of US$125,000, and won the 'Mother Teresa Award' for 2014. Her celebrity admirers have included Demi Moore in the USA while in the UK Prince Charles has sold some of his watercolours to support her work.

India. Bhuwan agreed and we set a target date of 15th June for the raid. He assured me that the operation would be a walkover. 'Consider it done,' he'd declared with typical self-confidence. I was less convinced.

It was around this time that a U.S. journalist, Angie, contacted me in the hope of joining a raid. I gave her a holding reply, making no mention of our imminent plans as I didn't want to compromise security. Also, I felt it was too risky, indeed irresponsible, to put a journalist into a potentially life-threatening situation at a stage when our circus operations were still in their infancy. However, I was unaware that Angie had also made parallel approaches to BBA who had welcomed her with open arms.

As for our contribution (apart from providing funds), Suresh, Bishnu and a couple of his staff members would go to Gonda in support with four family members to facilitate the girls' release. But on the day before the operation, Bhuwan told Suresh that they had received some intelligence information to suggest that the Nepali staff members might be at extreme danger if they were to join the rescue itself. He advised Suresh to remain safely at the hotel that they'd been using as their local base. Suresh took this guidance at face value and complied. This meant that the rescue would be solely a BBA operation.

The national and international media coverage that BBA had tried to coordinate unfortunately ended up backfiring to a certain extent. Writing in the highly respected *Nepali Times*, journalist Rameswor Bohara described the rescue as having been 'botched'. This seemed to be at variance with BBA's own communications and I was keen to analyse what had really happened during a rescue that could have turned out so much worse.

A couple of weeks afterwards I arranged to meet Angie at a pizzeria in Kathmandu so she could describe what she'd seen. She began:

'We entered the circus compound led by Kailash with the police alongside. There were lots of journalists and photographers. It looked as if we were fully expected. Circus staff and girls had gathered around with Raza Khan standing in front of them all.'

'That's not so surprising,' I said. 'Our research around Hetauda has shown that circuses have strong links with source villages in Nepal. As soon as field workers start asking questions you can bet that the circus will hear about it.'

Angie continued:

'At first the exchange was quite normal. Kailash explained that he'd come to rescue the girl performers who were being held against their will. Then, for no apparent reason, Kailash raised his voice and that seemed to provoke a response from the circus people. Raza Khan became angry and pointed a pistol at Kailash. Others produced iron bars and cricket bats; they'd obviously had these ready to hand.'

She broke off from the story to sip her red wine as she drew upon painful memories.

'Then the jostling began with even the girls joining in. Apparently, some BBA people had gone behind the scenes and intruded upon the girls as they were changing in their tents. The girls were screaming "How can we go back to the village? Who will pay us? Who's going to give us clothes? Everyone will call us whores!" They were also defending Raza Khan.'

Once again it occurred to me that Stockholm Syndrome was coming into play.

'What did the police do?' I asked.

'Not much. They just looked on. BBA later accused the local authorities and police of complicity with the circus. I don't know if that was the case or not, however another journalist overheard one senior police officer commenting that this is what NGO people could expect if they came to this part of Uttar Pradesh and provoke an incident.'

She fiddled with the flower in the vase on our table. I detected some annoyance.

'When the violence started everyone ran for it. I felt that we'd been abandoned in a situation of extreme danger with all our expensive cameras and equipment. We'd no choice but to run too. I've never been so frightened in my life as I ran down a road with that stick-wielding mob chasing us.'

'I saw the photograph of your photographer with her black eye,' I said.

'Yes, she was very unlucky or lucky, depending upon your point of view. When we ran the circus locked the gates behind us and Sarah was trapped inside. The circus people beat her up. They could easily have killed her. I only realised she wasn't with us after we'd gone some distance. I managed to persuade one of the policemen to go back with me to retrieve her. At the same time, they rescued a girl called Gita. She came forward spontaneously and accused Raza Khan of raping her.'

I'd seen the pictures of her too. These showed the girl standing alone in a plain smock, looking vulnerable, awkward and forlorn. I was shocked and furious by the way they had treated a possible rape victim, who should have been protected from such attention – especially since, in that society, a girl who has been raped is so stigmatised that she may even find herself banned from her village. The press intrusion into my private life now seemed so trifling by comparison.

As I listened to Angie's account of this mess-up that could easily have cost someone their life, I resisted the urge to say 'I told you so.'

After the raid BBA upped the ante with a news release to its international support base that offered a dramatic account of events, allegations, demands and a call to arms. They wrote:

'In this critical hour we urge the friends, allies, associates, well-wishers, patrons and civil society partners worldwide to rise to this occasion and mount pressure on the Government of India to punish the culprits and provide security to Satyarthi. We would appeal to everyone to show solidarity and put moral pressure on the Indian government including the President of India, Prime Minister and the Union Home Minister to take note of the seriousness of the matter and give Satyarthi 24 hours security since the local police has miserably failed to protect him. There is a grave threat to his life by the circus owners. Satyarthi was threatened to be killed on the spot and also to the extent that he would be followed to his home in Delhi where he would be eliminated. All this was said in the presence of the media, local police, administration and they could do nothing.'

Along with that, BBA provided the text of a message that they suggested should be faxed to the State and National authorities.

The half dozen or so police who were there on the 15th June stayed out of the situation but their boss, Superintendent of Police Amitabh Thakur, took action. Another good guy, he instructed the police to return to the circus the following day and find the missing girls. Upon arrival they were told that there were no girls at the circus and that there never had been any. It was a ludicrous stance and Raza Khan was taken into custody, becoming himself a hostage until his people returned the girls.

Kailash continued to agitate, embarking upon a 'fast onto death'. This is a symbolic weapon used commonly in India, following the example set by Gandhi. He staged this on behalf of the missing girls in front of the UP State Assembly in Lucknow. Gandhi's fasts usually lasted just a few days and never more than 21 before the authorities caved in and Kailash's gesture also followed in that tradition. He called it off after five days, citing failing health and apparently under police pressure.

Declaring that he had been receiving death threats from Raza Khan and his accomplices, Kailash withdrew to Delhi. From there he orchestrated media activity and launched high profile protests and rallies. Bollywood actress Nandita Das joined one of the marches.

In the end it was the belated intervention of the Nepal authorities and the Indian National Human Rights Commission that led to the handover of eleven girls nine days later. Even then there were still ten girls missing. The circus staff had hidden away the smallest children inside boxes on the day of the raid. Afterwards they had transferred them clandestinely to a Khan sister circus far away in the eastern state of Orissa. BBA filed a Habeas Corpus plea on behalf of these missing girls and at the end of July the circus management brought them to Lucknow High Court to be released and repatriated.

Once free, the Roman Circus girls shared accounts of atrocious living and working conditions, daily danger and abuse that were now becoming all too familiar. Worst of all was Khan's violent temper with his slapping girls across the face, dragging them by the hair and throwing them around. They claimed that his violence extended to sexual violence and that he had raped all the girls. One of them, 17-year-old Sita, described how she'd been warned by the other girls that they'd seen Khan eyeing her. One day, just before a show, he grabbed her as she was changing and dragged her to his tent. He met Sita's resistance and screams with a severe beating that left her unconscious. Then he raped her. Such were her visible bruises that she couldn't perform for a few days afterwards.

After gaining her freedom, Gita filed rape charges against Khan but then the case went quiet. There is little justice in India for the female survivors of sex attacks.

In Nepal the media coverage was scathing. A Kathmandu Post journalist who had accompanied the party reported that five of the twelve girls who'd returned to Nepal had not wished to be rescued. He seemed to be prepared to accept that girls' apparent willingness to endure abuse and exploitation in exchange for an income to their families should be respected. In his early written report, ignoring that this was slavery and that the girls had been in the hands of a serial rapist, he questioned if this had been really a *rescue*. He wouldn't have known about Stockholm Syndrome. In due course he realised his mistake and reported appropriately but his early coverage hadn't been helpful.

Overall, I'd been deeply dismayed at the conduct of the raid. Granted, it had been very audacious – it takes a lot of courage to confront armed men even with the support of the authorities. And, in the end, all the girls had been freed. My biggest concern was what I considered to be the excessive media presence that seemed to not only place the journalists at risk but also compromised the control of the rescue. Most of all, I was appalled at a potential rape victim not being given the protection she deserved. With hindsight, I realise now how difficult it can be to rein back the media in Nepal and India. They are much more sensationalist than their western counterparts. Indeed, trying to conceal vulnerable children from the cameras can only prompt the journalists to denigrate the NGO as having something to hide.

Bhuwan and I agreed to differ in our styles and tactics and that our partnership should end amicably. I recognised that BBA had been able to play an absolutely critical role in getting us started but it was time to move on. We'd find another Indian NGO that would allow us to be central players in truly joint operations. Perhaps PNMM might be worth approaching.

Without our support in Nepal BBA couldn't really conduct further rescues of Nepali girls so they seemed to draw a line under the programme. As a final gesture they submitted a Public Interest Litigation (PIL) to the Indian Supreme Court calling for the Court to rule against the use of child labour inside the circuses. PIL's were quite common in those days and viewed by the Court with cynicism; they were perceived as being publicity stunts rather than reflecting genuine concern, but that was as much as they could do.

From e-mail exchanges I sensed Suresh's deepening unease that from here on we would be operating unsupported in India.

Back in the UK I secured the services of Sir Ben Kingsley to make the *BBC Radio Four Charity Appeal* on behalf of our Circus Project. Sir Ben was a perfect choice given his family associations with India and his awesome performance in *Gandhi*. I was honoured to meet him at the BBC studios just before the recording and then watched spellbound as this great actor worked himself into the story as he read through and annotated my script. This told the circus children story against the backdrop of Esther's death and my response to it. As he left the building I was moved when he paused to say:

'As the father of four healthy children it's been my privilege to have helped you in this way.'

The appeal raised £22,000, one of the highest public responses ever to a Radio Four Appeal. But there was a further invaluable spin off as art psychotherapist Caroline Christie heard the broadcast. She responded to the accounts of traumatised children by offering her voluntary services to the charity. Art psychotherapy was rather outside my comfort zone but this was such a timely offer given Shailaja's struggles in managing circus survivors. She had by now received the predicted second influx of disturbed children at the Blue House and was floundering.

Two weeks later the inspirational Caroline went to Nepal and during a two month stay transformed our management of the children. She beavered away showing Shailaja and her care staff how to use techniques involving photography and play. The photography project involved building the girls' confidence and safely exploring their feelings one step at a time through teaching them how to take pictures, choose subjects and then display their images.

The results could be mundane yet very touching. For example, one girl posed by an open fridge. She said that because the fridge was full it made her feel happy and secure. Such an image provided a lead into a relaxed discussion of the food at the circus and other conditions. Caroline encouraged children to build models of their homes using bricks and cardboard which they would use to act out the village family life that had been stolen from them. One girl wrote repeatedly a message to her father 'I am your daughter, I am your daughter.' This was a cry against rejection by her step-mother.

Caroline returned to the UK leaving Shailaja's team members feeling much more confident about their capacities. She had also laid the foundations for our use of art to heal in the ensuing years.

By contrast, Suresh seemed to become increasingly burdened, his smile less ready than before. My concerns were justified when he took me aside one day during my visit that August:

'Philip, I'm sorry but I can't continue in this appointment. It's all too much for me on my own. As you know, I'd hoped to run nothing more than a children's home for you but now we've got all these challenges in India. Now I haven't even got a reliable partner organisation to work with on rescues.'

I felt really sorry for him, realising the courage he'd needed to make this confession. I had to find a way to hold onto this fundamentally good man.

I responded: 'It's me who should apologise for having put you into this situation but please give me a couple of months to see if I can sort something out. This is a great project that is our destiny to do and I know that I can make you proud to be part of it.'

He agreed, but I realised then that Suresh, in spite of his stated resentments about the command of the Brigade of Gurkhas, was actually only really comfortable when acting as someone else's deputy – albeit a very good one. Nevertheless, I could see a solution.

Bev and I had settled very well into a lovely old terraced Edwardian home in Tooting, southwest London, a life of domestic happiness and stability with an excellent circle of friends. Therefore, after dinner one evening I had to take a deep breath:

'How would you feel about going to live in Nepal for a couple of years?'

She put down her knife and fork and stared intently at me, a slight smile on her lips.

'Continue...' she said.

'Well, we're having huge problems over there. Suresh is obviously having a massive crisis of confidence and I think he might resign. And if that happens, the whole operation could well collapse. If I want this circus project to work, I'll have to be there on the ground myself, taking the lead. It'd mean setting up home in Bhairahawa.'

Her reply, given without a moment's hesitation, amazed me.

'We're in this together. Let's do it. And, you know what? I've felt so much recently like we're stagnating here in London and of course I've seen how your mind and your heart have been in Nepal with all these rescues going on. You know I love travelling – the more exotic the better – and I adore those kids in Bhairahawa. It would be exciting to be there with Shailaja. We've got no children, so what's stopping us? It's the opportunity of a lifetime.'

The proposal needed no sweetener, but there was something extra I knew I had to add.

'You know how we've talked about adopting? How would you feel about doing that in Nepal? Gently building a family over there in slow time...?'

She lept from the table and gave me a hug.

'Darling, I'll start packing tomorrow.'

How different this dinner table conversation had been from the one with Esther six years before, when all had been despair and hopelessness. Now Bev and I had everything to look forward to, the world at our feet.

The next morning, I couldn't wait to phone Suresh with the great news that he would be having new neighbours. I told him that I would be able to give him direct support on the ground and that I had pledged to remain in Nepal for at least two years and not to return to the UK until I'd resolved the circus children trafficking issue. This appalling abuse and exploitation of Nepali children had to be stopped and I wanted to be alongside him to play a central role in the fight.

We'd been great friends, family even, and I'd expected him to share my enthusiasm. Instead, there was an ominous and mystifying silence at the other end of the line.

13. No Man's Land

t was the start of our great adventure. Brimming with optimism and excitement, Bev and I moved into our new home on the outskirts of Bhairahawa. We felt hugely blessed to have the opportunity to experience this remote and exotic spot, with great friends living just down the way. And, best of all, we were in the midst of a growing number of ebullient refuge children. We even had the company of a street puppy that we'd adopted on the way through Kathmandu – sadly, there's plenty of them around. We named her Bryher after our favourite island in the Scillies.

I couldn't wait to get to grips with the operational side of the charity's work. Esther's plaque was on the wall, I'd planted a campaign flag and now I would see how far we could go with my loyal friends Suresh and Shailaja. At last I was in the frontline myself. It would be challenging to run the UK side of the charity from afar, but I had very supportive Trustees who would do what they could to back me up. I reckoned we could manage with the role reversal of my visiting UK three or four times per year for meetings and events. So much business could be undertaken by e mail and online fundraising in any case.

Bev and I loved living in the midst of the paddy fields that surrounded the town. From our balcony we could watch an eclectic world pass by – farmers with water buffaloes, oxcarts, children in pristine Western clothes on their way to school, women ambling past in radiant saris. This was a nature lover's paradise with exotic birds and butterflies drifting into the garden.

A birdwatcher's telescope served me well. I could watch the slow, majestic flight of the Sarus Crane as it circled before landing in marshland just a stone's throw away. White-throated kingfishers sat on telegraph wires, plummeting every so often into the ditches beneath. Once I watched an osprey disembowel a rat while perched on top of a lamppost, its red eye prominent against snow white plumage.

Yes, there were some venomous snakes around too, such as cobras and kraits. That meant ensuring that we kept Bryher indoors if there was a snake around, avoiding a fight that she would surely have lost. The other unforgettable element of fauna was the mosquito population that thrived in the swamps. On one occasion I'd asked Suresh why there were bars on the inside of his sitting room door. He replied that he needed them to keep the mosquitoes out. We laughed, but the mosquitos were no joking matter. In this part of the world they carried Malaria, Japanese Encephalitis and Dengue Fever.

In our innocence we didn't realise that our being in Bhairahawa was the last thing that Suresh wanted. Prior to our arrival he'd had four years of a fairly peaceful existence, working from home in his own organisation with no one monitoring him, challenging his decisions or pressing him to meet deadlines. Before the circus work had started there hadn't been much to worry about in his daily life. Thanks to the media publicity I'd generated he was sure of a regular transfer of funds for the running of the children's facilities. He'd the staff he needed for delegation of daily tasks and all he'd have to do to keep me happy was to reply to e-mails and host my quarterly visits.

I can say now, with the benefit of hindsight, that this latter approach is not a valid way to monitor project work in Nepal. Local people excel at laying on a bit of a show for visiting foreigners and at turning on some winning Nepali charm when it's needed. If you really want to know what's going on and gain an understanding of the issues you've got to live there yourself.

Anyway, Suresh must have greatly resented his clear run at things being over. He knew enough of me to realise that he faced the daunting prospect of having a driven person with an eye for detail and strong work ethic living 200 metres along the track from his home. I knew already that he resented authority yet now he had a former British Officer 'telling him what to do' *in his own country*.

This was not at all what I intended to do as this was an equal partnership and it would also have been highly discourteous. Besides, by Nepali law my charity's role was to support projects, not to implement them. Our professional relationship had to be founded on mutual respect rather than diktats. Nevertheless, I was aware of the need for projects to be conducted to the high standard the Trustees would have expected, that we get value for donor money and, most of all, achieve the best care possible for the children. I hoped that I would be able to coax and coach Suresh along towards achieving a rewarding result for everyone, including himself.

Unlike Suresh, Shailaja was overjoyed at our arrival. She could come and sit on our balcony and speak openly, hopeful for change:

'Philip, this centre is being run like a military camp and it's dominated by male attitudes. Just look at Padam and how he controls the children.'

I was already aware of this junior staff member, a former Indian Army Gurkha drill sergeant who'd boxed for his battalion. Padam would parade the children as part of their daily routine. During my visits from the UK I'd found this quite quirky and thought it harmless fun in that it appeared to bring structure to the children's lives and helped keep the refuges neat and tidy. Shailaja saw it differently.

'This is all too strict, man. Children are forbidden to move between refuges, even to see siblings. They long to be free.'

'Don't worry, Shailaja, I'll sort that out very quickly.'

'There's something else, Philip. They don't want to spend money on the children. Suresh's deputy is tight-fisted with money. When Caroline Christie was with me, she had no toys for the therapeutic play activities. We improvised using found materials like old bricks, sticks and corn cobs. I was embarrassed.'

This had seemed quite bizarre to me given the significant funds I had been sending to Nepal.

'Why are they so miserly?' I asked.

'See, in Nepal middle class people object to letting these children who are the lowest of the low having toys and games that they can't afford for their own children. Just go and look in the office. You'll see lots of toys there but they're all kept in a locked cupboard, still wrapped in their original packaging.'

This dog-in-the-manger attitude appalled me. The senior staff didn't seem to comprehend the various ordeals that the beneficiaries might have been through and their need for therapy – and love. Beneficence in Nepal can founder on the rock of deeply ingrained cultural values and prejudices. I resolved that Bhairahawa wouldn't be this way on my watch.

It was lovely to be with the children, these kids for whom the smallest gesture of affection and interest meant so much. Their numbers had been boosted when we closed the night shelter in Butwal. It had been such a success that we realised the educational bar was set too low at non-formal education. The boys had proven themselves interested and capable of attending mainstream school. Dinesh and his friends from the streets added further colour to the mix of refuge children that we had assembled from very different backgrounds. I was interested to see how Kumar Basnet and Bhejendra Pun, the two most recent arrivals from Kathmandu Jail, had gained the respect of all of the children as their surrogate big brothers. They were both great all-rounders with a sporting prowess that matched their early academic achievements and good manners. I was as proud of them as any father could be.

We used to open our home on a Saturday morning to hold three-hour-long art classes for the kids. They'd always turn up early, an excited babble escorted down the lane with Kumar and Bhejendra in the lead. These refuge children were keen to enjoy the atmosphere of a family home for a few hours. We'd have prepared some art activities for them beforehand. Neither Bev nor I are artists but we were very keen amateurs.

Some malevolent person in the area was watching us though for before long a mischievous report appeared in the local press. It stated that the children visited the foreigners' home and afterwards didn't want to talk about what had happened there. On another occasion someone denounced us to the police for proselytising. At that time Nepal was still a Hindu monarchy and anyone guilty of this offence risked prison or deportation. We immediately reported the groundless allegation to the British Embassy and that was the end of the matter. This kind of malice is common in Nepal; frequently sacked former employees can try to get even or it could have been a case of xenophobia. Still, it felt uncomfortable to be in Nepal, helping its children, and to be on the receiving end of such malice.

During the working week Bev interacted with the children on a daily basis, assisting Shailaja and guided by Caroline Christie's many recommendations as well as building on the work of an outstanding visiting volunteer, Marian Bennett. Bev was a hit with the children as it was soon obvious to them that she was showing devotion, dedicated to increasing the fun and learning in their lives. As a steady, regular presence she ran cookery classes, sports days, drama projects and presided over a host of colourful, messy art activities.

The local people, who loved to stare, must have been puzzled at the common sight of this foreigner walking the lanes around the refuge surrounded by laughing kids. The children would look forward to Bev returning from visits to England for more reasons than one. For she brought back wonderful picture story books that couldn't be found in Nepal and set about building a magical library at the refuge.

These children were also very receptive to her story telling. Bev told me how the children had been transfixed by the tale of *Cinderella*, asking her to read it to them again and again. Far from wanting to avoid this traditional tale, it had a resonance for most of those children were themselves unwanted and unloved, had known cruel step-parents and felt the pain of rejection. That had been the central factor in their having been sold. For them Cinderella had been reality with no fairy godmothers to intervene. At least not until now.

It was a challenge for us not to feather-bed children who one day would have to return to the rural poverty whence they came. We had to balance this imperative with the need to create a healing environment at the refuge. Caroline had started this process by creating some personal space by each child's bed. Under her guidance the children drew the outlines of their hands on a piece of paper and then coloured these in as their own statement of identity. They then put their drawings on the ceiling and wall well away from the hands of others. With time and growing self-confidence these were transferred to the walls beside their pillows. In due course they added other drawings and pictures from magazines.

The refuge walls came to exhibit an odd mix of pictures of Bollywood stars, cartoon characters and religious images. Although Shailaja was still a practising Catholic, she went out of her way to ensure that the children followed their religion of choice. So, you could see on the walls Buddhist, Hindu and Christian imagery.

The Christian element was a surprising one in such a predominantly Hindu/Buddhist country. Intriguingly, it was a throwback to the children's time in the circus when they would come under the influence of missionaries who operated in their home districts or, surprisingly, might even get to visit the circuses themselves. The missionaries would encourage them to pray to Jesus for survival and some child performers would even set up little shrines within their accommodation tents. Their subsequent survival would vindicate their faith in Jesus. Besides, it must have been tempting to be seen as a 'sister in Christ' rather than a 'dirty circus girl.'

Bev's rewarding experiences with the children stood in marked contrast with my working environment where daggers had been drawn from the outset. I was shocked and dismayed to fall out with Suresh both personally and professionally. I summoned up all my tact and diplomacy to no avail; he seemed to resent all my suggestions and turned surly. It seemed ridiculous that I should be arguing the case for unwrapping toys to make them available for the children. I was exasperated when he'd make silly and thankless statements such as his view that children should be free to do as they wished rather than being 'organised' through Bev's timetable of activities. Not only did this belittle her major contribution and clear benefits to the children but denied the reality that refuge children left to their own devices would end up watching violent Bollywood movies on TV or wander aimlessly around the refuge building and grounds. His viewpoint ignored the need that traumatised children had for active interventions to help them reclaim their childhoods. Bev felt more than once Suresh's resentment at female staff having for the first time taken such a prominent and successful role in the management and therapeutic advancement of the children. I sensed also a hint of xenophobia coming even from him. He once commented:

'No one can look after Nepali children better than a Nepali mother.'

Some of the children's backgrounds proved this impudent observation to be not necessarily true.

Later that year, an opportunity arose when The Great Western Circus made the mistake of crossing the border into Nepal to pitch its tents at a large regional religious festival. I had a particular interest in this one as it was one of the circuses frequented by trafficker Dani Gurung. Given the historical Nepali antipathy for all things Indian this should have been a soft target for us. However, the operation was complicated in that the Maoists had called a *bandh*[19] which meant that there could be no road travel within the area.

Suresh's field staff took a major risk by posing as national media representatives with signs on their motorbikes. Had they been caught out their bikes would have been destroyed and they'd have been beaten up; the ten-year Maoist conflict was very much at its height. To my frustration, even though I was now living in Nepal, I was still unable to take part as I couldn't pass for a local journalist.

The rescue became complicated when the Chief District Officer delayed intervening after being misinformed by circus supporters that

---

[19] A shutdown as a show of party strength

the rescuers were animal rights activists whose true agenda was to scupper the large-scale animal sacrifice that was a central feature of this festival. He wouldn't do anything to disrupt religious practice. By the time our team got the green light to intervene the circus was already packing up and it had become a race against time. When they finally made it to the circus, they found just four girls inside the compound. The management had been tipped off. Their follow-up search resulted in the team rescuing a further ten girls just as circus staff members were on the point of spiriting them back across the border. These included Sangita.

In an echo of the Kerala rescue, Sangita told us that the circus staff had gained their cooperation by telling the girls that they needed to hide them from 'bad people' who were trying to sell them into prostitution. Later, at the District Administrative Office, four of the fourteen chose to re-join to the circus. The rescuers couldn't prevent their return as the four were all over 18 and were by that stage married into the circus.

The other ten, including Sangita, were more than happy to leave in spite of local politicians and their thugs, termed *goons*[20], trying to persuade and threaten them against it. Seven of the released girls were Nepali nationals, the other three ethnic Nepali from northeast India. Life all at once became a lot better for Sangita as she joined our refuge and started school where soon she was excelling at her studies.

Our field staff went on to instigate Dani Gurung's arrest. He wasn't hard to trace as he was notorious and operating openly within Makwanpur District. Instead, the difficulty lay in getting him charged, given the chronic indifference of rural police officers. A policeman might have little interest in registering a trafficking complaint lodged by a 'dirty' circus girl, especially if friends and family members of the trafficker are bribing or intimidating him. Local politicians can add their voices to the lobbying and angry picketing of police stations. Traffickers affiliate themselves with political parties that then get kickbacks from their sordid earnings and such aggression was the last thing the police needed at a time when the Maoists were targeting police outposts with bomb and bullet. To overcome local police inertia, we would pull in the support of other NGOs and the media or, in extremis, register the cases remotely in Kathmandu.

After getting Gurung charged, the next challenge was to convince a Judge that the circus was indeed a trafficking destination. Nepal isn't a

---

[20] *Goonda* is a Hindi word for 'hired thug'

signatory to the UN definition of trafficking and generally its courts only consider trafficking to involve the sex trade and some slave labour situations. And Gurung's defence would no doubt present the old lie of circus being part of tradition and culture or that it offered an indirect income to impoverished families.

We protected the recently rescued witnesses while they gave their evidence. The stakes were high in this landmark case as Nepali anti-trafficking legislation is very tough. Those charged with trafficking must be remanded in custody and sentences are for up to 20 years without remission. A convicted trafficker also has to compensate his victims.

The Judge accepted the returnees' compelling statements and Gurung received a twenty-year jail term, a sentence that was subsequently upheld after his appeal to the Supreme Court. For me it seemed so appropriate that a legal precedent should be a lasting result in Esther's memory. It would pave the way for the easier conviction of a further 18 male and female traffickers that we identified over the ensuing five years.

In spite of such a success, my daily interaction with Suresh continued to feel like a grind, an unwinnable struggle. I couldn't believe this was the same idealist I'd recruited in Church Crookham and whom I had considered a close friend. It was hard to see a way forward even though I tried so many different approaches to attempt to reignite his passion and open his eyes to new possibilities.

Suresh phoned me early one morning in January 2005. He told me that he had something serious to tell me and asked if I could come to the office. I assumed that a child had run away or suchlike. When I arrived at the office he and his deputy were seated there, looking very sombre.

'Philip, I'm afraid to have to tell you that Kumar Basnet died at 4 a.m. this morning.'

The ground opened beneath me. He continued:

'He became sick yesterday morning and we kept him off school, thinking it was something he'd eaten. Then his temperature soared and we took him to hospital in the afternoon. The doctor admitted him as a case of suspected cerebral malaria. He fell into a coma at midnight and never regained consciousness.'

I was lost for words; there was actually nothing that I could say. Once again, one of the best had been taken from us. I shook Suresh's hand and left the office. As I walked along the path back to the house, an angry red sun was rising, burning off the shroud of mist that envelops the paddy fields in early January. I would have preferred the mist to have stayed a little longer that morning, hiding me from the harsh reality that lay around me, preserving my anonymity for a little longer. Indeed, I wasn't going to change the world. I felt deflated, ineffectual and punch-drunk in the wake of this dreadful news that I'd now have to share with Bev.

In line with Hindu custom, the funeral took place promptly. At eleven that morning we gathered at the cremation site which was in a field by a little riverside. Before me Kumar's body lay on an open pyre. It was wrapped in a white cloth and covered with flowers, but the face that I knew so well was clearly visible. One of the refuge staff, a Brahmin, conducted the ceremony using words that, as at Esther's funeral, I couldn't understand adding to my sense of detachment and impotence. Suresh, acting on behalf of Kumar's father, set the bonfire alight. House mothers wailed in the background. This was neither the natural nor the spiritual order of things. I watched the fruits of my efforts literally going up in smoke to the smell of burning flesh.

It was the 5th January, a day after the fifth anniversary of Esther's death. I felt weary, like packing up and going home.

That afternoon, all the children were called together and seated cross-legged in a circle on the ground at the White House. They had gone to school as usual that morning and were totally unaware that Kumar had died. Suresh delegated to his Deputy the task of breaking the terrible news. As he did so this normally stoical former Gurkha officer broke down. Suresh confided in me afterwards that this had been his reason for dodging making the announcement; he knew he'd have reacted similarly himself. I will never forget the collective cry that went up from the children or the sight of Bhejendra shaking as he wept uncontrollably for the loss of his brother.

After their initial shock and distress, the children responded by setting up a small shrine to Kumar at the White House at which they could leave little messages, memories and marigolds from the refuge garden. A framed picture showed Kumar walking the children down the lane to our house, smiling confidently in the November sunshine just a few weeks before his death. Another of him stewarding the games at a refuge party in our garden. His judo outfit lay to one side.

The following day we held an internal inquiry into the circumstances around his death, consulting in the process with a senior

172

doctor at the local hospital. His conclusion was that all that could reasonably have done had been done and advised us that cerebral malaria can claim a life suddenly. The only way to prevent this from ever happening again would be to treat all standing water within a 200-metre radius of the refuge buildings, this being the flight range of a mosquito. It was an impractical solution to apply to reed-filled swamps that we didn't own. All we could do was to continue with our existing mosquito precautions, accepting that there could be no absolute protection for the children.

It struck me for the first time that perhaps the Terai was the wrong place for our expensively-acquired children's facilities. We should have chosen a malaria-free part of Nepal in the northern hills, perhaps in the tourist hub of Pokhara, or in Kathmandu itself.

Rather than yielding to the urge to go home I decided that, just like after Esther's death, I would meet his head-on and be positive. This death had to galvanise us as a team and if there were childcare and organisational shortcomings, we had to collaborate on addressing them.

The morning after the funeral I walked into Suresh's office and offered him my hand.

'Suresh, we have to draw a line under the acrimony of the previous three months. I'm sorry if I've upset you along the way. Let's be positive at this time and rebuild our relationship. A house divided cannot stand. We must ensure that Kumar's death is not entirely in vain.'

He shook my hand and went beyond that with an embrace. We stood there as two very vulnerable men but were now united in wishing to resurrect something from the ashes.

A couple of days later Shailaja called to see me.

'Philip, I think there's been more to this death than meets the eye. I've found out from talking to the older children at the White House that Kumar had been ill for much longer than you've been led to believe.'

I knew that she was excellent at getting to the bottom of things and in coaxing information out of the children. They trusted her.

'What have they said?' I asked.

'Kumar was ill for several weeks with fevers and night sweats. He didn't want to tell the house mothers.'

'Why ever not?'

'See, the carers are mothers in name only. They don't have deep emotional bonds with the children. For them, they are just doing a job, feeding and clothing the children, sending them to school and so on. I

173

think for these illiterate women, the most they could manage is a one-to-one relationship. Three of them can't cope with 30 children.'

If Shailaja was right, and her insight was always very sound, it appeared that Kumar had been a victim of institutional care as much as of the mosquito. I decided not to raise the matter with Suresh as I sensed that his relationship with Shailaja was already strained and I didn't want to reveal my source. But more importantly, I had only just repaired our friendship and if I had raised this delicate subject that would surely have been terminal. Nevertheless, I was tormented by Kumar's loss, by the realisation of our poor choice of location to site a children's refuge and now also by possible endemic childcare failings.

My sadness, even a sense of guilt, deepened when Kumar's older brother came to visit the refuge a week after the death. He wanted to see where Kumar had slept and meet his friends; they took him to see the shrine. Before he left, he collected together Kumar's scant possessions but made a point of thanking us for looking after his brother, the brother whom we had all failed. It would have been better for Kumar to have stayed in Kathmandu jail. And I felt primarily responsible as, after all, this project had been my brainchild, the mistakes mine.

Professional exchanges improved for a while but underlying tensions remained; fundamentally Suresh still didn't want us in Bhairahawa. At every meeting I continued tiptoeing around a truculent, unappreciative and obstructive Suresh who didn't want things to change. This became very wearing. I suspected worse lay ahead and organisationally we were already in decline.

One evening after dinner I turned to Bev:

'Love, I've had just about enough of professional disharmony and I'm feeling quite demoralised at working with this bloody-minded project partner at the back end of nowhere. Life is just too short for all of this strain. Maybe it's time to break off this flawed relationship and go home.'

This wobble echoed the ones that I'd experienced on the visit with Fionnuala to Kathmandu jail and by Kumar's funeral pyre. Bev responded with a surprising but searching question:

'What would Esther have done in this situation?'

I had no hesitation in answering:

'She'd have stood her ground. She wouldn't have given an inch. In her prime the tougher things became, the more determined she became, the harder she fought.'

For some reason at that moment I remembered again that two-word advice she'd given to a friend who was struggling with an adopted teenage daughter – 'Keep trying.'

'Yes,' Bev said, 'just remember how you told me you wouldn't run from anything after Esther's death. You've been through much worse than this.'

I had thought that by moving to Bhairahawa I would be joining the front line but actually I was fully in No Man's Land as I couldn't count on my allies. Suresh didn't want me there and was making my life as difficult as possible. I resolved there and then that whichever the two of us left the field of battle, it wouldn't be me.

To continue the military metaphor, a few days later a British agricultural consultant called Richard Chambers visited me to discuss ways of generating income for older returnees. A born-again Christian, Richard had spent many years living in Nepal and working within the sector. Beyond discussions around growing mushrooms and farming honey, I told him about the difficulties I was having with Suresh. He said to me:

'Philip, you've made a very public statement of faith, hope and love that's reflected in everything from the international media coverage to that brass wall plaque on the White House with its Gates of Bronze inscription. You've put your head above the parapet and it's inevitable that you're going to get shot at from all sides. This isn't a temporal battlefield. It's a spiritual one. Fight the good fight!'

In practical terms, that would necessitate my splitting from Suresh and it was going to be very difficult for that divorce to be arranged on my terms. Suresh held all the cards. He was on home turf and his independent organisation owned all the refuge buildings rather than The Esther Benjamins Trust. Indeed, his was one of the wealthiest NGOs in Nepal and Suresh could have simply waved goodbye to me and sought another sponsor. I risked losing everything that I had fundraised for – by now seven buildings in Bhairahawa and Hetauda that were probably worth in the region of a quarter of a million pounds.

But the biggest setback wouldn't be a material one; it would be the emotional price I'd pay with the end of my dream, of my response to Esther's death. I wasn't sure how I could cope psychologically with spiritual defeat.

I decided that the only way to break the stand-off was to externalise what had been a harrowing internal conflict. I told Suresh that I was calling his first-ever external evaluation in six years and that

175

this would include an audit of his accounts. I advised him that the person who I nominated for the review was a British man who spoke fluent Nepali after having worked in the sector for the previous 20 years. He knew every trick in the book. This was actually Edward whom I'd consulted in England, who was by nature a very gentle soul, but Suresh didn't know that. This change in approach seemed to unnerve Suresh such that on the eve of the evaluator's visit he handed in his resignation.

This gave me no cause for celebration; far from it. Our friendship had seemed blessed, almost mystical at times, a special relationship that had underpinned those first few years. Besides, I knew that without Suresh's initial contribution we wouldn't have got started. No, I was left feeling very sad. Also, I realised that Suresh's replacement had to be his former Deputy who had kept the purse strings so very tight. He wasn't an obvious choice as Director of a children's NGO but I felt bound to give him a chance. I reasoned that at least the new Director was a physically tougher man than Suresh, a characteristic I needed if the circus rescue programme was to be a success.

This conflict had taken its toll on me and I needed a break. I was feeling isolated professionally and fatigued. I'd said to Bev that although I wasn't that kind of holidaymaker, I could for once see the attraction of an island, a beach and a book.

She suggested that perhaps I should go instead on an art holiday – one of us had to stay in Nepal to support Shailaja and the kids. She thought immediately of a brilliant British mosaic artist called Martin Cheek, who'd taught her on a weekend course long before we met. We checked out Martin's website and were amazed to see he was offering mosaic holidays at Candili, of all places. Bev encouraged me to go for it and, given the connection with Esther, it was ideal to go there without her and enjoy it to the full.

It was only six years since our holiday and the owner, Philip Noel-Baker remembered Esther very well. We laughed as he recalled how she had climbed onto the roof with girl-like enthusiasm to help him get the right angle on a photo of the main house for his publicity material. And how sweet she'd been with his little niece, Maria, skipping around with her, hand-in-hand on their way to a picnic. Overall it felt lovely to revisit the villa with all its happy associations.

Artistically I had great fun experimenting with blending Western and Eastern art. The *Maithili* community of south Nepal/north India paint the walls of their huts with village scenes, wildlife and marriage ceremonies. Inspired by that I translated a wall painting of a bride in all her finery into a mosaic of Venetian glass.

After I returned from Candili a British woman called Caroline Deans came to stay with us in Bhairahawa. Caroline's brother had been an Army dentist with me, and with her profession being pre-school childcare, was keen to find out about our work. One Saturday afternoon the two of us sat down and I told her all about Esther, how I had set up the charity and the way it operated in both UK and Nepal. I shared with her also my experience of coincidences, giving her some examples. In explaining our fundraising support, I mentioned in passing that there was just one church in the UK that supported us regularly, West End Congregational Church in Kirkcaldy, Scotland. She was more amazed than I was to tell me that her uncle had been a former Minister of that church.

Two weeks later, after her return to the UK, Caroline contacted me with news of something that had shocked her even more. She'd been sitting at her work computer looking at the Trust's website with a picture of Esther on the screen. It was the picture I'd taken of her standing in front of a flower bed with a cupid statue at the stately home of Chenies Manor in Buckinghamshire. One of Caroline's colleagues had noticed this as she walked past her desk and paused to tell Caroline that this was her garden; she lived at Chenies Manor. This was once again a coincidence that counted for absolutely nothing beyond confirming for me that something odd *was* going on around me and now Caroline had witnessed this for herself, twice in the space of as many weeks.

Although based in Nepal, I remained Director of the Trust in the UK. One of my main roles was fundraising and I cast that net as widely as possible.

A major fillip came in 2005 when the Master Draper of the Drapers Company of the City of London chose us as his beneficiary charity for that particular year. This essentially boiled down to our being allowed to hold a charity gala dinner in the auspicious setting of Drapers' Hall. The highlight of the evening was an auction with the auctioneer being our guest of honour, the Duke of Westminster, whose daughter Edwina had been one of my first Nepal volunteers. The star prize was a week for two on Sir Richard Branson's private Necker Island, part of the British Virgin Islands. Sir Richard uses the island as his main home but also opens it up to visitors who can purchase a week's holiday for somewhere in the region of £20,000. He donates some of these so-called 'Celebration Weeks' as charity prizes and he did this for us after Edwina had written to him directly.

On the evening bidding was going a little slowly, so in the end the auctioneer bid for the prize himself, a snip at £15,000. Afterwards the lovely Edwina bounced up to Bev and me.

'Guess who's going to Necker Island?' she announced. 'You are.'

The Duke had donated the prize to us as he'd said we'd deserved a break. I'd be getting the beach holiday that I yearned for in the grandest style.

J it Rawat Lama counted out thirty thousand rupees in front of his six year old daughter Nisha and her younger brother Amit. It was the day before they'd leave their tiny home in Humla, Nepal's poorest District that lay in the remote northwest of the country. He was showing them how much he'd collected so that they would understand the huge investment he was making in their future.

Nisha wondered how he had come by so much money, although his recent sale of the family's two goats gave her a clue. But that would only have raised about a third of this sum. She found out much later that her father had put himself in debt with little chance of ever clearing it. For, like most of their community in the village of Srinagar, they were living on the breadline, surviving on barren land that could hardly sustain the goats let alone a family of six that included her mother Shangmo and big brother Karbu.

Their daily struggle had been compounded by the activities of the Maoist fighters who were conscripting young people into their 'People's Liberation Army'. By 2004 their 'People's War' had dragged on for eight years and had taken its toll on their community not only in terms of lives lost but also in breakdown of the local infrastructure. Nisha's school had been closed for the past two years and she'd had to stay at home each day, looking after her baby brother, Basu.

After he'd spread the money out on the table, Jit outlined his plan to Nisha and Amit. This was the placement fee that he'd be paying to a local man called Dal Bahadur Phadera to take the two of them and Basu to Kathmandu and a future. 'DB' would be admitting them to a good children's hostel where they'd have proper food and be able to resume attending school. They'd stay there until they completed their education but DB would ensure that they kept in contact by letters and by telephone calls. They might even get to return home to celebrate the annual Hindu festival of Dashain even though this year they wouldn't be feasting on goat.

Although Nisha didn't like the idea of leaving home, she knew she had to follow her father's wishes and at least this would put an end to her feeling hungry all the time.

DB arrived the next day. Although he was to be their 'uncle' she couldn't help being a little worried. He had been pleasant enough to her and Amit and had dandled Basu, but she sensed that her father was

179

uneasy in his company. It was almost as if he was a little frightened of him.

DB took Jit and his three youngest children to meet the Chief District Officer. He was a very important man who needed to agree that DB could become their guardian so that they could leave the District. The CDO had hesitated over the paperwork as to Nisha's surprise this had identified them as being orphans. Obviously with her father there before him, this couldn't be the case. But DB had been charming and persuasive, while her father had actually become annoyed, telling the CDO that this was the only option he had to give his children a future. Were the authorities about to reopen the school and start a child feeding programme?

The CDO relented and they were off with Uncle DB and an 'auntie' who had joined them. The great adventure started with a trek through the hills on foot followed by a jeep ride down to the major town of Nepalganj. Nisha and Amit had never been in a jeep before but an even greater excitement lay ahead as they boarded the small plane that would take them to Kathmandu.

With all its concrete buildings, vehicles and crowds Kathmandu really was a world apart from Srinagar. After they'd landed DB had taken them to a big building called 'The Shining Stars Children's Home'. It had looked like a palace from the outside but Nisha was shocked by what lay within. The rooms were dark, filthy and crowded with boys. There must have been forty of them and she could see only nine beds. They were all scratching and covered in sores. Worst of all was one boy, Lal, who had a badly scarred face and an eye missing. It looked like he'd been burned but, whatever the cause, he hid his disfigurement under a balaclava. Humla had been bad but this was horror.

The following day Nisha was relieved when DB told her that she and five other girls would be moving on to a better place, a girls' hostel and school that was some distance away. She was upset to be parted from Amit and Basu; she would have cried even more if she'd realised that she'd never see them again.

Her first day of travelling lasted seven hours and took her back to the Nepal plains; she wondered if she was near Nepalganj again. Then she saw the place name, Bhairahawa, where they stopped for the night. The next morning the jeep journey resumed and she nodded off. It must have been an hour later when one of the other girls nudged her awake. Another new form of transport lay ahead; they were about to board a train in a place called Gorakhpur. Nisha's mother tongue was the Humli dialect although she understood a little Nepali. Here they were speaking a different language. When she asked DB uncle what it was he'd said 'Welcome to India'. Nisha knew that her father hadn't agreed to her leaving Nepal but ke garne? She was at the mercy of DB in a foreign land. Also, she understood now why her father had been intimidated by him. DB was quick to slap them for even the smallest offence.

Three days later the train journey ended with their arrival in Coimbatore. It was scorching hot here, a contrast with Humla where the previous week there'd still been snow on the slopes above her village. Nisha could see that the people here were quite dark-skinned and were speaking another language that wasn't Hindi. Life was becoming more foreign by the day.

DB and the auntie took the six of them to the school which she'd expected to be something like Shining Stars. But, no, this was very different and on the face of it looked very pleasant. She had never seen such huge buildings, not even in Kathmandu, dazzling white in the burning sun of Tamil Nadu. There were large letters on the tops of the buildings that she couldn't understand but they must have been the height of a man. She could see lots of pupils, all girls who were dressed in smart white uniforms. They seemed happy enough although she couldn't understand a word they were saying.

Nisha's bewilderment deepened when the school headmistress interviewed them that evening. Through DB she told Nisha that her name was now Rachel and that she had become a Christian. At this school she'd be taught in English and work hard at her studies; she'd learn the Bible. The headmistress pointed to a picture on the wall of the School's Founder and said that Dr Job was now her father. With his bald head and thick glasses, Nisha thought he looked a bit weird.

So began Rachel's eight-year-long stay at The Michael Job Centre. At first, she didn't understand much of what was going on around her but she soon grasped the routine that she just had to blend into. She'd be up at five each morning to join several hundred other girls in a large cold auditorium where they'd sing hymns and recite prayers by heart. That was one way of learning English. After breakfast, classes would run throughout the day, learning about Jesus and his follower Dr Job as they went along.

Now and again, foreign pastors would visit the Centre and she'd be excited until she realised that they'd just come to join the interminable religious ceremonies and take pictures of them. Sometimes it felt like being in a zoo. Of course, Dr Job was a regular visitor too and

181

the girls would have to make a fuss of him. But to Rachel he seemed quite awkward with children and rather distant.

In all her time at the Centre Rachel had no contact with her family and she missed them terribly. Banned from speaking Humli, her sense of separation became even more profound as day by day she lost command of her language too. Although in the company of hundreds of girls, Nisha couldn't have felt more isolated.

14.   Alisha

I watched the girl delicately manoeuvring and gluing the last two pieces of her mosaic into place, spelling out her name, 'Rina'. It was a small but significant step towards retrieving the identity that The Great Indian Circus had stolen from her. What a lovely metaphor this art form had become for reassembling broken lives, while making a tangible statement of recovery and hope for the future. She ran her fingers over her finished handiwork, looked up and smiled. Rina was very proud.

'You won't forget today,' I said to her. 'And every time you feel this mosaic, you'll be touching freedom.'

Martin Cheek's mosaic course at Candili had refreshed and inspired me. After returning to Bhairahawa I thought that I would introduce the little children who attended my Saturday morning art classes to the technique. Granted, I wasn't exactly building on a wealth of experience but they didn't seem to notice that. Initially they would make mosaics out of little coloured paper squares before I progressed them on to using broken bathroom tiles. The kids smashed up these tiles with gusto – a therapy in itself – and surprising patience as they assembled new artworks to site beside their beds.

Encouraged by their enthusiasm and aptitude, I decided to try extending the training to a couple of circus returnees who as teenagers were too old to join school. This had become a huge challenge for me to address as, for example, a 14-year-old girl who had never been to school would not be prepared to sit in classes with five-year-olds and learn the alphabet. For girls such as these I had to find something that would provide an income and mosaic art offered this with the added advantage of some psychological healing.

I set up a small studio at my home and two girls, Rina and Priya, became my first trainees. They weren't exactly dressed for the part as they turned up on their first morning looking quite resplendent in their best saris. However, we gave them plastic aprons and I took them through the basics. Before long they were showing dexterity and attention to detail that rivalled my own as a former dentist.

The concept was a simple one. Through charity correspondence I invited supporters to commission an 'ethical mosaic' for £50 choosing a generic subject such as 'flower', 'bird', 'animal' or 'butterfly'. Then the donor could follow their commission through images that I would e-mail them of work in progress up to the final picture of the girl holding up the finished piece. We'd then site the mosaic at a children's centre such as a school, a disabled day care centre or at our refuge itself. The girl received half the commission as her fee and the remainder served as a donation towards the ongoing child rescue work.

The initiative was so popular that I had to extend the workforce, elevating Rina and Priya to becoming the trainers, giving them a further confidence boost. Volunteer artists came to Nepal to take over from me and inject some genuine artistry into a programme that became a central plank in our management of child trafficking survivors.

The number of circus returnees was building steadily thanks to the efforts of three new Nepali field staff members who were based in Hetauda. We appointed them to fill the vacuum left by the split with BBA. Their remit was simple: Go to India and retrieve girls whose names appear on the Hetauda List. These three were chosen for their toughness and experience, two of them, Bhim and Ganesh, former senior employees within the Indian circuses. The third, Prakash, was a local hard-man. These poachers turned gamekeepers managed to bring back girls in twos and threes, seemingly against the odds. Intrigued, one day I asked Bhim the secret of their success.

'It's through a combination of bravado, bluff, negotiation and persuasion,' he said. 'I've worked in a few circuses in my time – I was a lion tamer – and the owners of the major circuses know and respect me quite well. I think they reckon that if they give me what I am looking for I'll go away; we can stay as friends and their business won't be damaged by a raid.' He motioned towards Prakash. 'Even they are quite scared of him and what he might do if they don't comply. We play the good cop, bad cop game.'

I could see what he meant; there was something of the night about Prakash's demeanour.

In parallel these same staff members were able to track down the traffickers and, using the girls as complainants, have the police pick them up. Sometimes they'd carry out citizens' arrests. Without the circuses necessarily realising it, their performer procurement process was being steadily eroded. However, for this to be successful we needed to win the hearts and minds of local people in communities where NGOs weren't always well received. With a lot of justification Nepali people can accuse NGOs of 'dollar-farming' and 'headline-grabbing', in other words of being self-serving organisations that secure grants for their own staff but in the end do little to benefit needy people. Too often villagers see well-paid researchers coming to their communities to collect data through intrusive questioning. They take up poor people's time to return to their offices and produce reports that get filed away to no one's material benefit apart from their own.

We developed goodwill by directing the finite resources we had towards the neediest families and in the trafficking hotspots. Families appreciated how we provided scholarships, a targeted-scheme that paid for the education of rescued children and their at-risk siblings. At its peak we were keeping around 300 children in school through purchasing their school uniforms and books. We had to be careful of not being seen to in some way 'reward' the families who had sent their children away while ignoring those who hadn't. Therefore, we helped whole communities by building classrooms, provided furnishings and teaching materials.

Alongside that we were providing some good bread and butter social work, practical solutions to address genuine hardship. With Shailaja, I visited the home of Sushma, the young woman who'd suffered the psychiatric episode after her release from the Great Indian Circus. She'd gone on to marry Hari, the lad who'd come back from the same circus and the couple were now living just outside Hetauda, with their baby.

Arriving at the house, I was surprised to find them occupying a fine brick-built house, one of a neat cluster of homes that had been built at the expense of a major international charity. However, as soon as I stepped inside, I was struck by their poverty. There was nothing in the main front room of the house apart from a pile of rags in one corner. Somehow the squalor seemed all the more accentuated by the contrast with the pleasant exterior of the house.

While I paused on the threshold struggling to make sense of the scene, Shailaja had gone on ahead inside. Then she summoned me from the doorway of a bedroom further down the hall. Looking inside, I saw a bed with a blanket covering a strange vertical lump. This was a four-year-old girl, Sanju, who was staying in the house with her father. Hari told us that Sanju's mother had passed away six months previously and since then she had refused to speak or play, running to hide from all visitors.

On this visit I happened to be in the company of Dave, one of my Trustees, and we had a spontaneous discussion as to how to manage this kind of dilemma. Dave had been reading a UNICEF pamphlet and felt well-informed:

'I think the experts would say that the correct thing to do is to support this child within the community and keep her with her father.

The last thing we should be doing is taking her into our refuge. That's institutional care.'

Shailaja was shaking her head even before he'd finished the first sentence.

'I disagree. This is an acutely traumatised child and there's no one in this community who can deal with her issues. She needs to come to us.'

'Couldn't we just take her in for a while then, sort her out and then return her?' Dave suggested.

Shailaja waved her arm around. 'Do you see this girl's father anywhere? He can't be here as he needs to work. And Sushma and Hari can't look after her. They've a child of their own to think about. She needs long term care.'

I added my piece: 'It's quite possible that her father will remarry soon. Then she'll become a stepdaughter and be more vulnerable than ever. She's at huge risk of being trafficked.'

Dave surrendered. A month later I attended a children's show at the refuge and there was Sanju in the front row of a choir, microphone in hand, totally transformed.

It was because of cases like Sanju that our field staff personnel were always welcome in the villages. Indeed, they were the only NGO staff allowed to visit some communities in Maoist-dominated areas; the Maoists shared villagers' cynicism about NGOs, particularly when they were recipients of Western money. Endorsement from the Maoists did not come easily.

He strolled into the bar on our first evening on Necker Island offering an introduction that was quite unnecessary:

'Hi, I'm Richard.'

After exchanging a few pleasantries with each of his guests, Sir Richard Branson excused himself and returned with a chess board tucked under his arm, looking for an opponent. I hadn't played chess in years and even then, I'd been no expert but, emboldened by a gin and tonic, took up his offer. Over the game he asked me about my work but I could see that he was only being polite; his charitable interests lay elsewhere. But at least the chess god was smiling on me. Richard swore at me, twice, first after I took his queen and then at checkmate. We were late in

187

joining the rest of the guests at the dinner table but when we did, he was holding my hand high acknowledging my triumph.

Staying in the luxury of The Great House on Necker was a far cry from the privations of living on the Terai and the work pressures that had so worn me down. It had been a surreal experience to be helicoptered into a little paradise that for a week we would be sharing with only another dozen guests. Some of these were *very* wealthy, others, like us, less so.

I returned to Nepal feeling refreshed and, with renewed clarity of thought, reached the conclusion that it was time for radical change to put our house in order.

First off, I was now convinced that Bhairahawa was the wrong place for the project. Serious misgivings were already there before we had gone to Necker. Shailaja had been sharing with Bev that the kids were missing out on a proper education. In fact, to prove her point she had taken her off early one morning on a surveillance operation. In a classic Shailaja approach, the two of them had crouched behind a wall across the way from the school. They awaited the arrival of our children, who of course looked the part in their pristine school uniforms.

'Now watch,' whispered Shailaja, 'they spend the first part of their day just cleaning around the place and scrubbing out the toilets. See, classes should've started by now.'

Shailaja nudged Bev as the first teacher ambled in an hour late, a newspaper under his arm.

'He's early today,' she said. 'First thing he'll do is go and relieve himself.'

Bev could see that, at least in this regard, the teacher was reliable. Shailaja continued:

'There are three toilets at the school, one for the male teachers, one for the female teachers and one for the 150 children. It's not hard to see where the priorities lie.'

They watched as the other teachers filtered in over the course of the ensuing hour.

'I think they've all turned up this morning but sometimes they don't show at all,' said Shailaja. 'They can be away for months at a time on worthless training courses and there are no replacement teachers.'

Bev returned from her covert investigation that morning shocked by what she had seen and adamant that Shailaja was right. Still, she had to broach the subject delicately.

188

'Philip, I know that you've strong emotional ties to this place, with the brass plaque on the wall of the White House, but we need to move to Kathmandu. These children are being betrayed by their teachers and they're relying on us to do the right thing by them.' She hesitated for a moment as she chose her words. 'You also owe it to Kumar Basnet to ensure that there can be no more tragedies. Let's get the kids out of this unhealthy place. This is our responsibility.'

My second realisation was that we had to downsize and be proactive in reuniting some children with their families. We knew that some parents had been released from prison and, as per the agreement at the time of admission to the refuge, they had committed to take them back. In fact, it was important to return such children as promptly as possible before the released parent seized the opportunity for a fresh start, perhaps finding a new partner who could ultimately become an unwilling step parent. This was a common cultural trend in Nepal. Reunification might require some modest financial support through a transitional period but in many cases the parents weren't so badly off after all.

This need came very much into focus after a released prisoner living in Kathmandu called at the Bhairahawa refuge to collect his two children to join him for the annual Hindu festival of *Dashain*. There was nothing unusual about that apart from the fact that he travelled to and from Bhairahawa by an internal flight, returning his children by the same means at the end of the festival. If he was able to pay for flights then he could afford to have them back permanently. There could be no justification for our continuing to look after his sons at charitable expense when bed spaces could be allocated to more deserving cases, including for circus returnees.

My third conclusion was that we needed a change in leadership in Nepal. Suresh's replacement also lacked the passion that I needed in my project partner if we were to fight the circuses. I had to work with someone who like me was hungry for results. That person was Shailaja who has these qualities but also the vital ones of being genuine and working from the heart. The most painless and politically expedient way to do that was for me to set up a new Kathmandu-based NGO that she could lead and that would focus solely on the circus programme. The Bhairahawa-based original NGO with its flawed leadership would be left to quietly wither on the vine.

The decision taken, we assembled all the 96 children who were in our care into the grounds of the Blue House for one last party.

Beforehand we'd taken advice from Caroline Christie as to the most sensitive way to manage the farewell and the outcome lay before me. Picture albums were piled up on a large table, each one personalised to one of the 32 children who were due to leave us. An album contained pictures of that child with others they'd known at the refuge, an important keepsake of a childhood that we had returned to them. Before distributing these mementoes, I spoke to the group, telling them that they would be forever members of the Esther Benjamins family and that they could count on Shailaja and me if they ever needed us in the future. We wouldn't be hard to find.

The approach worked and everyone was in high spirits, just as at the many other parties we'd enjoyed in Bhairahawa over the years.

Twelve children remained in Bhairahawa as they came from that part of Nepal and for whom we thought there was a good chance of reunification if we could keep them close to their extended families. The remainder piled into two buses for the long drive north.

The kids' excitement wasn't solely to do with enhanced educational and recreational opportunities. One girl told us that she was looking forward to having lighter-coloured skin through leaving the scorching heat of the Terai. Skin colour and status are linked in Nepal and this was how that child felt her prospects could best be advanced. Sadly, she was probably right.

Two days before our fourth wedding anniversary Bev returned to the house one lunchtime, almost breathless with excitement.

'A baby girl has been brought into the children's home down the hill' she said, scarcely daring to believe her own words. 'She's just four weeks old and they say she can be ours. You must come and meet her. She's gorgeous.'

In Nepal nothing is straightforward and for me becoming a father was no exception. In those days foreign adopters had to be married for at least four years before they were eligible to apply yet a single woman could adopt straight away. This was one of those crazy rules that you encounter in Nepal that defy all comprehension. Perhaps with hindsight we should have divorced, allowed Bev to find a child and then re-marry. But we opted for the less drastic option of waiting patiently, counting off the days towards our fourth anniversary on the 7th September 2006.

Meantime Bev had been putting out feelers to children's homes in our part of Kathmandu valley to let them know we were keen to adopt.

I went with her that afternoon to the children's home where I met the owners, Milan and his wife, Abha. In honesty, at that time as far as I was concerned a baby was a baby. But as Abha passed this one into my arms I was immediately smitten. I touched her cheek, she turned her head and, as babies do out of reflex, she began to suckle my finger.

Bev and I looked at one another and we agreed on the spot that we would love to have her. Milan shook our hands in congratulation, Abha hugged us.

'You can come to collect her in two days' time,' said Milan. 'It'll take six to eight months to complete the paperwork with the Ministry but, in the meantime, she can stay with you.'

Bev was thrilled. It was a dream come true to have a little baby to bring up almost from birth but I had a concern.

'What about liability?' I asked. 'What if, heaven forbid, something happens to her while she's in our care unofficially?'

Abha gave one of those little Nepali head wobbles that says nothing and everything at the same time. This was Nepal.

Two days later - and before we got to collect her - Alisha was admitted to the local hospital with suspected meningitis. So, began four weeks of Bev being with her every day in a dirty crowded ward, determined to look after Alisha personally. Nursing care in Nepal can be very sparse and nonchalant; relatives are expected to do their bit in aftercare. During Bev's vigil she was bombarded with unsolicited words of advice from Nepali women who were in the ward. Older Nepali women know better, are quick to proffer opinions and a young foreign mother represented an irresistible target. Still, Bev remained calm and diligent and Alisha pulled through.

Nevertheless, the rollercoaster continued. In March 2007 the Nepali government suspended all intercountry adoption processes. They introduced the moratorium to give themselves time to address alleged malpractice and to introduce a new adoption act. Predictably, after that decision not much happened and the 440 aspiring adopters who were in the system were left in limbo. The impact on us was less than on others from around the world who had taken time out from jobs back home to be with their allocated children in Nepal pending approval; what should have been an acceptable wait of a few weeks turned into months with no prospect of any progress. We were stranded in Nepal as we couldn't leave the country with Alisha even for a holiday and we weren't going anywhere without her.

In the end it took the intercession of the Prime Ministers of Italy, France and Spain to break the impasse. They wrote to the Nepali Prime Minister asking him to intervene on humanitarian grounds and have these 'pipeline cases' approved. All at once the logjam began to clear and on Christmas Day 2007, we found ourselves inside the Ministry building signing our final adoption papers. Now I would have the opportunity of enjoying the unmissable experience of feeling an infant's hand in mine and to be called 'daddy'.

Part 4

Buddha Eyes
Bhaktapur, Nepal

'When you come to a place of darkness, you don't chase out the darkness with a broom. You light a candle.'

- Rabbi Yekusiel Halberstam

15. Changing strategy

Standing by the side of a dusty road in north India one Saturday in January 2007 I sensed the good fortune we'd relied upon for circus rescue had finally run out. The sun was setting and a hostile crowd armed with sticks was eyeing us from across the road. It looked like we were in for a hiding.

Up until then our circus rescue programme had been running well, up to a point. The three-man rescue team had delivered results somewhat against the odds and were meeting the demands of parents in Hetauda. Nevertheless, I was uneasy with that approach. I discussed with Shailaja the circumstances of the unfortunate children and young people whose parents weren't requesting their return. Should they just be condemned to remain in slavery? This was a moot point as we didn't have the funds, infrastructure or experience to deal with mass releases. And we knew that if we brought girls home without parents' support or knowledge we'd be left with the responsibility and additional cost of looking after them. Worse, the families could be knocking on our door demanding compensation for alleged loss of girls' earnings.

I was also very troubled by our inability to take any action against the abusers within the circuses. In fairness, most of the time it was just a relief to see the rescue team return from India safely and to be able to tick off further names from the Hetauda List. Unfortunately, this failure to prosecute meant that serious abuse of rights and of bodies could continue unchallenged. Our impotence became excruciating when I met one nine-year-old girl, Sarita. Bhim had brought her and four teenage girls back from the vicious Moonlight Circus that had been playing in northeast India. Sarita had been recently raped, allegedly by the circus owner, and Shailaja and I had to take her to hospital in Bhairahawa for treatment to serious internal injuries. All we could do at that point was to provide care and protection for the child and that felt pathetic.

Then one morning in late December 2006 Shailaja came to see me. She handed me a picture of emaciated little girls wearing very short skirts and standing inside a dusty, grubby tent.

'We have to act quickly, man,' she said. 'These children are trapped inside the New Raj Kamal Circus which is playing in Uttar Pradesh. Some parents have been down to retrieve them and been turned away with threats. I think they're being sexually abused. This is the worst circus I've ever come across.'

'How big is the circus?' I asked.

'It's small, maybe 20 to 30 girls maximum. But it'll be very difficult. Uttar Pradesh is a lawless State and the owner, Lakhan Chaudhary, is in safe territory. He's a really bad man who will have paid off the police. I believe he's the main rapist.'

I thought for a few moments.

'You know what this means, Shailaja? If there's been sexual abuse going on, we can't just rescue a few girls. We need to bring them all out. And that'll leave us with a large number of returnees as parents won't want them back. But let's do it. We can't afford it but equally we can't afford not to raid these people. I'll find the funds we need somehow, somewhere.'

We agreed to launch the raid early the following month. That would give us two weeks to organise – the minimum time needed to research the families and prepare the accommodation facilities. I also contacted British journalist Tom Bell and his girlfriend (now wife) and film maker, Subi Shrestha, to invite them to document the rescue.

Along with Ganesh and Bhim, Tom and Subi visited the girls' home villages in Makwanpur. Tom interviewed one weepy father who when they met him was already drunk at 11 a.m. Amidst crocodile tears he told Tom how he'd been offered £70 for his daughter – probably an overstatement - and claimed that, as he was sick at the time, he had no option but to agree. Most likely if he'd been paid, he'd have spent the money on alcohol. Clearly his personal interests took precedence over his daughter's and she had been nothing more than a commodity for him. He added that he'd never received the payment and his daughter had languished in the circus for four years.

Following the village visit Tom and Subi went off in advance to see the New Raj Kamal Circus for themselves, which was playing at a place called Hatta, just outside Gorakhpur. Beforehand I'd told them how difficult, if not impossible, it would be to gain access to the circus.

A few days later our team arrived in Gorakhpur. It comprised the three regular rescuers, Ganesh, Bhim and Prakash, two volunteers from PNMM as the Indian link NGO, twelve family members and me. My long wait to take part in a rescue operation was finally over. I caught up with Tom and Subi in their room in central Gorakhpur a few days later to find them indulging in a minor celebration over a half bottle of local whiskey.

197

Tom isn't one who is given to elation but I could tell that they were very pleased with themselves.

'Our visit couldn't have gone any better,' he told me, 'the circus welcomed us with open arms, almost as if they were looking forward to our visit. We were allowed to film the girls in training. They even let Subi set up her tripod so we've got top quality footage.'

'I am sure they were expecting you,' I said. 'They'll have heard all about your making enquiries around Hetauda. And they'll have paid off the police and local authorities. That's why they're so cocky.'

'Ah the police,' he chuckled. 'We even recorded footage of them sitting alongside the circus management. Ganesh challenged them about the sexual abuse that was going on inside the circus and they dismissed that. They told him that was no big deal as sexual abuse goes on all over Nepal also.'

'He's right in that respect,' interjected Subi. 'Most men in Nepal deserve to have their balls cut off.'

Tom laughed again. 'I'd probably better not share a bed with you tonight.'

Next day, we went to the ChildLine India Foundation's Gorakhpur office where we met a young activist called Divya Kanha. He and his Foundation were to play a pivotal role in the operation. From there we went to meet the police chief in Hatta, a gruff lump of a man with heavy stubble.

'Under the Juvenile Justice Act it's your duty to rescue these girls,' Divya Kanha demanded of him. 'It's the Law'.

The cop looked at him with total contempt. 'In this area I am the Law. You mind your tongue.'

Nonetheless he went with us to the circus for what was no doubt a pre-arranged visit. On that first evening the circus freed eight girls after a two-hour stand-off. The circus had already hidden away the youngest girls. Perhaps they hoped that the release of these eight girls, including the daughter of the man Tom had met in Makwanpur, would be enough to fob us off. However, we were determined to stay until all the girls were free.

To my surprise these girls were quick to share stories of their ordeal inside the New Raj Kamal. One girl told Subi how Lakhan Chaudhary had raped her:

'I was new then. I didn't know anything. I was sleeping when he came over. He hit me on the back. It was painful. He hit me again, many times. He said many things. He said that he would kill me. Then he did it.

He said he'd kill me if anyone found out. So I didn't tell any of the girls. I didn't even tell my best friend.' She pointed at the long surgical scar on her forearm. 'I broke my arm when I fell from the trapeze and it didn't set straight. I had to have an operation and the doctor put a bar in to hold the bones together. Chaudhary said he'd take the bar out again if anyone found out about what he'd done to me.'

The next morning, we returned to the police station to trace the fifteen girls who were still unaccounted for. We parked our two vehicles inside the police compound. As discussions were taking place within the station what had seemed initially like a cluster of curious onlookers - commonplace in that part of the world - swelled to become a small crowd. The mood became hostile and hoodlums jostled us. Just then the situation was defused when four more girls were handed over and we withdrew quickly. That was the right decision as we were grossly outnumbered by the circus's goons and unsupported by the police.

Determined to keep up the pressure, we drove straight to the District police headquarters hoping to influence the local police chief's superior. That attempt failed but on the return journey we passed by Hatta police station once again. The lead vehicle with Tom and Subi and some released girls continued on ahead to Gorakhpur while we pulled over at the station to have a look.

From the opposite side of the main road we could see that an open-air meeting was underway inside the compound; it seemed to involve the police, the circus management and their goons, no doubt discussing their next move. The degree of collusion was shocking; we watched circus staff members even using police motorbikes to travel between the station and the nearby circus. The worst we'd had to contend with in the past was police neutrality but this collaboration made for a very precarious situation indeed. In spite of our vulnerability we decided to brass-neck it and go inside the compound anyway. But as we approached the entrance the police guard waved us back.

A few minutes later the crowd emerged from the station and gathered outside the station gates. Many of the goons were carrying lattis. They called over our driver and before we knew it he was being taken off down the road on the back of a motorbike. Our predicament was worsening by the minute. Now there were six of us standing beside a driver-less vehicle that had no keys in the ignition. It was 5 p.m. on a Saturday afternoon and soon it would be nightfall.

We were in trouble.

Immediately Divya Kanha got on his mobile and called ahead to the first vehicle to alert them to the situation. Subi in turn phoned the British Embassy in Delhi:

'A British citizen is in danger of his life outside the police station in Hatta, Uttar Pradesh. We need your help.'

The reply wasn't encouraging:

'Please call back on Monday morning.'

Divya continued phoning everyone he could think of to issue an SOS – please join us with all haste. Fifteen minutes later the terrified driver was returned to us. He was badly shaken and refusing to tell us what his abductors had said to him. We guessed that they'd told him to take us on our way and into an ambush that the goons had prepared further down the road. Our best plan was to stay by the police station which, although far from being a sanctuary, was at least more public than some anonymous bend in the road to Gorakhpur.

Meanwhile, the crowd circled around us and we felt menaced. One goon stood in front of me, tapping his latti on the ground as he looked me up and down. We did our best to appear blithe, chatting and joking with one another although there wasn't much to laugh about. With hindsight I believe it was probably my white face that saved the rescue party as my presence there didn't compute and goons will always hesitate to attack a foreigner. I'm convinced that an all Nepali rescue party in such hostile territory would not have survived.

By six o'clock Divya's desperate calls were bearing fruit. Vehicles began pulling up around us bringing with them a mixed bag of NGO workers - even priests and nuns. NGOs in Nepal can take a lot of justifiable criticism for their complacency and nine-to-five mentality but here was a marvellous testament to the kind of activism that you can find only in the Indian NGO sector. These marvellous people had put themselves in the frontline with us at short notice and on their day off. Before long, our group outnumbered the circus people and the threat dissipated. After some further negotiations at the station our rescuers extracted us, our vehicle in the centre of a convoy with three vehicles in front and four behind.

The Hatta stand-off had become a major incident and ChildLine India Foundation's office in Delhi was applying pressure at the centre. The next day the circus freed eight more girls but to thwart our efforts they returned them directly to Nepal. This left three girls still missing but, in the end, these were accounted for as the circus had sent them to their villages just before our visit, confirming our suspicion that there had been a tip-off. One of these girls was pregnant after being raped by Lakhan Chaudhary. Through spiriting off these three and sending the final eight directly to Nepal the circus was effectively denying us potential witnesses against Chaudhary. By Law the police should have interviewed all the girls at the scene of the crime.

Throughout the whole operation Chaudhary had avoided us, leaving his manager, a guy called Anthony, to act as his spokesperson. My abiding memory of Anthony is of his demonstrating the largesse – and falsehood - of the circus by tossing rupee notes at the girls as they walked away from the police station, free at last.

Tom's report appeared in the Daily Telegraph and Subi's on Al Jazeera television. Beyond that Subi produced a film focussing primarily on Ganesh Shrestha and his rescue activities. In December 2007 I was privileged to be in the audience at the Kathmandu film festival when Subi introduced her film to a full house of seven hundred young Nepalis, most of them male. The first film on the bill had been 'Miss Tibet', a quirky film profiling the candidate for a beauty contest who appeared at times in a swim suit to a predictable audience response. The initial shots from Subi's 'The Circus Shuffle' showed girls in leotards performing inside the circus and attracted similar whoops and whistles. But as the story unfolded and the personal accounts of sexual abuse were related the cinema fell silent. At the end Subi called Ganesh and his two colleagues onto the stage to receive a well-deserved standing ovation and she pointed me out in the audience. This was advocacy at its best from a brilliant young journalist.

Most of the released girls were able to return to their families but we admitted some to our rehabilitation programme. This is where my mosaic activity really came into its own. Seven of the girls joined my studio as a group. This not only offered them the chance of art therapy and an income but prevented them from being rushed into hasty marriages with low calibre husbands. Such arrangements, with the unprocessed psychological trauma, meant the relationships would be doomed to fail. Most of the returnees stayed with the workshop for at least a year and during that time the girls recovered their equilibrium and self-esteem. They'd also earned some decent money and, in a land where money is so important, we found that they married quite well.

When the girls first joined the class, I could see through their body language how I intimidated them. I was a man and maybe they thought I was their new 'Malik'. They would almost cower as I explained the technique, perhaps thinking that I was telling them off. But under the healing power of art the girls relaxed perceptibly. One day a couple of weeks later I entered the studio unobserved since all the girls had their backs to me, busy at work. I heard a sound I will never, ever forget.

They were singing.

Everything I could see in that year confirmed my decision to have Shailaja co-lead the programme. I was in awe of her bravery and tender commitment to the children. Often, she would travel alone into the hills around Hetauda because I couldn't enter Maoist-controlled territory as a foreigner. Yet she did so with determination, returning time and again having scored a further victory. It was really incredible what she could achieve in areas where people were suspicious of strangers and contemptuous of Indians.

One of her most valiant trips had been with Santosh. He was the little boy whose horrific task had been to take girls to be raped in the owner's tent at The Great Indian Circus. He was worried about his little sister, Pramilla, who was still with his unsavoury family and he yearned to join her for the major Hindu festival of Dashain. This falls in September or October and is traditionally a time to be with families when many city dwellers return to their villages. Shailaja had relented to Santosh's repeated requests in spite of his home being in the jungle that lay deep inside Maoist territory. As a white person I could go with Shailaja and Santosh no further than Hetauda; my presence beyond there would only have made her more conspicuous and increased her risk.

We lunched together in Hetauda before her foray into the jungle during which Santosh said something I didn't understand. Then he acted out shooting someone, his hands flicking like recoiling pistols as he made ricochet sounds. I asked Shailaja what he'd said.

'He says that when he grows up, he wants to join the Army so that he can get a gun and kill the uncle who took him to the circus.'

They set off that afternoon, the two of them on Shailaja's motorbike with the boy confident that he could remember the way through the jungle. This should have taken two or three hours but they didn't come back until the next morning. In the meantime, all I could do in that lawless part of the country was wait and worry.

Shailaja reappeared the following day with Santosh and Pramilla.

'That was a journey and a half,' she said. 'As we went deeper into the jungle the track dwindled away to hardly anything. But I had a very good scout.'

Santosh looked up at her and grinned.

'He got off the bike and ran ahead with me following. Eventually we found his home which was really only a shack. Then the Maoists showed up. They were very aggressive. Their leader separated me from Santosh and interrogated me. Then he quizzed Santosh. Our stories must have tallied because they were okay after that.'

'How is Pramilla feeling?' I asked.

'She's really happy, man. See, I couldn't leave her there with that uncle. He'd only have sent her to the circus, or worse.'

The other problem child from the Great Indian Circus had been Ariti. Her restlessness had continued and she had been unable to settle into the comparative comfort of refuge life while being aware of the situation of her siblings. In particular Ariti was preoccupied with the plight of her older sister, Muna, who had taken the wrong decision not to return to Nepal and was still trapped in that circus hell. Moreover, her younger sister, Rita, was in domestic service, another form of slavery in Nepal, and a younger brother, Akash, was living in misery in the village. It would be incorrect to describe him as being at home for he didn't have one.

As the first step in sorting out Ariti's concerns, Shailaja agreed her request to take her back to meet her father and brother in Bara District. When they reached the village, she found that the father was sleeping rough in the grounds of a neighbour's house and his neglected five-year-old son left to wander around the community. When they returned to Kathmandu, they brought Akash with them to join our refuge.

Next, she decided to retrieve Muna by paying a return visit to the Great Indian Circus. We knew that if her father were to go with the rescuers that would offer the best chance of securing her freedom. Sure enough, Muna was convinced by her father's presence at the circus and she returned to Nepal. Once home - and as a grown young woman - she became a solid support to her father, rebuilding the family house with her own hands. Her father stopped drinking, he got his driving licence back and soon afterwards he remarried.

Finally, Shailaja applied some typical cunning and valour in rescuing Rita. She didn't quite know where she was working but had a phone number and was able to speak to the woman of the house. If she'd been upfront about her intentions the woman would have hidden Rita away. In my presence she called her up:

'My name is Pooja Acharya and I have been given your number by my house girl, Ariti. Her younger sister Rita works for you?'

The woman asked what she wanted.

'See, the girl's oldest sister is going to get married tomorrow and it would be nice if they can attend the ceremony together. I could pick up Rita this afternoon and return her to you tomorrow evening. Would that be okay?'

And that was how Shailaja got the address that we visited an hour later, taking Ariti with us. At the woman's house I remained out of sight but I could watch – and hear – the heated exchange that followed.

'It's time for you to release Rita to me permanently,' demanded Shailaja as she held up her NGO ID card. 'You're using child labour and that's illegal. I'll take this girl back to her family.'

'You'd better go away quickly,' replied the woman. 'I'm related to the royal family and I know people who can make your life very difficult.'

Shailaja was unmoved. 'Either hand me over the girl or I'll file a case against you with the police. I know people too.'

The woman acquiesced. Shailaja's brilliant work had brought both Manju and Akash to the refuge. We'd rebuilt a family and Ariti changed overnight.

Rescuing siblings and building bonds between them in the absence of parental relationships became an important element of our work. Another example was the case of an eight-year-old girl called Deepa. A circus trafficker called Kajiman Shrestha had visited Deepa's village in 2002 promising the usual; money, bright lights, stardom and tall buildings south of the border. The eldest of four children and with the family living in penury, Deepa took up Shrestha's enticing offer. A few days later he delivered her to the circus.

Seeing the tents for the first time, she asked Shrestha what they were. He laughed and said that these were the tall buildings he'd told her about. Deepa felt like crying. So began her four years of slavery that ended only when our team had arrived at the circus in 2006. Her rescue had involved one of our staff members physically wrenching her from the grip of the circus owner who'd clung to her waist, not wanting to surrender one of his most talented performers.

The trouble was that Deepa had nothing to return to and joined our refuge by default. For while Deepa had been still with the circus, her father in a drunken rage had beaten up her mother. Soon afterwards she'd died from her injuries. Deepa's younger sister, Manju, had tried to nurse her mother at the end but there was nothing that this child could do to save her. In the weeks after the mother's death the father became involved in sexual liaisons with village women until the Maoist fighters chased him off, telling him that if he returned, they'd kill him. When Shailaja took Deepa to visit her siblings the local Maoist commander asked her if she could take Manju and her two younger brothers back with her to Kathmandu. They had been staying with frail grandparents who couldn't cope.

Confronted with the children's desperate situation, Shailaja could only agree. However, she directed her Hetauda field staff to track down Kajiman Shrestha and bring him to justice. Eventually they found him and carried out a citizens' arrest. Shrestha would spend three years in jail before his case came to trial in February 2009 when the court sentenced him to a further 15 years in prison[21].

Sometimes I'd hear of Shailaja's latest exploit and respond in horror 'She did *what?*' For she is not only courageous but also a maverick. It's only with hindsight that her unorthodox approaches might make sense.

A classic example was how she netted child trafficker, 68-year-old Kirta Tamang. During a visit to Hetauda a local person tipped her off that Tamang had just crossed the border into India with nine children destined for the circus. Two of these were his own grandchildren.

Shailaja didn't bother to alert the police on either side of the border – they're just too slow off the mark and she couldn't risk losing the children beyond retrieval. Instead she summoned a couple of field staff and followed Tamang in hot pursuit. They caught him hiding with the children in bushes by a railway station in Bihar. At this point, rather than calling the Indian police, the team seized Tamang and brought him and the children back to hand him over to the Nepal police. This made sense as there was a much better chance of getting a conviction in Nepal than in India and the sentence for trafficking was more severe. Her tactic worked and Kirta Tamang was convicted of child trafficking and jailed for 15 years.

At the end of 2007 and after having seen Shailaja in action close up for several years, I recommended her for an international humanitarian award. My pen picture ran:

---

[21] Shrestha died in prison in 2014.

'.... She has travelled widely within the trafficking prone areas of Nepal, motivating field staff and interacting with the communities and their children. She is a "people person" and never more comfortable than when operating in this kind of role. Shailaja has shown typical courage, herself going on rescue missions where 'no' is never taken for an answer. She has been directly involved in the counselling of teenage girls who have been intercepted on the trafficking routes and has managed to convince them to give evidence against the traffickers (no small undertaking). As a consequence, agents are now behind bars.

'Shailaja now lives in the midst of 120 children, mainly trafficking victims and their "at-risk" siblings at our refuge in Godavari to the southeast of Kathmandu. It is hard to overstate how fatiguing this must be, day in, day out, with little time taken by Shailaja for holiday. However, she manages with her ready grin. Go to most Kathmandu orphanages and you'll find grim Dickensian facilities. Visit ours and you will see the model of how things should be. I called in there last week, totally unannounced, and found a volleyball competition underway. Shailaja was playing too in the midst of the cheering children, dressed in her Manchester United strip.

'I venture to suggest that you will find within this part of Asia few examples of commitment to social service and child welfare as strong as Shailaja. On the back of her motorbike she has a sticker reading "Catch me if you can". I expect that few ever will.'

She didn't win the award, probably because the kind of people who achieve international adulation are often adept self-publicists and that is something Shailaja certainly is not. Time and again I watched her avoiding speech-making or interviews, often sitting in the back row of any gatherings she attended. But she never took a back seat when it came to confronting traffickers, circus owners and others who were exploiting children.

16. Joe

Friday the 13th June 2008 would be an unlucky day for The Raj Mahal Circus. Our convoy of vehicles carrying around thirty police officers and an equal number of NGO representatives, descended upon it to the clear bewilderment of its solitary guard on the main gate. From the back seat of my jeep Barrister Nandita Rao said:

'Maybe we'll strike lucky and catch one of the circus people beating a performer.'

'Nandita!' I exclaimed.

'Philip, you are not a lawyer.'

This was a return visit to The Raj Mahal. Six months before it had been playing in Chhattisgarh State, central India, and our colleagues at ChildLine India had gone there following reports we'd received of extremes of violence against Nepali girls. As one of the Fateh Khan group of circuses that came as no surprise. On that occasion the ChildLine team had been led by the very capable Kelvin Symon but they'd hit a brick wall. For the circus had argued successfully with the local State Labour Department that restrictions imposed by child labour legislation didn't apply as a circus was a place of entertainment rather than an 'industry'. The authorities freed only six girls and allowed the circus to keep most of its performers, including six minors. The circus even got away with holding onto the released girls' pay on the basis of 'breach of contract'. That meant these trafficked girls had been de facto slaves for six years.

With a strong whiff of corruption in the air, all Kelvin could do was to withdraw and bide his time until the circus moved into the more friendly territory of a different State authority. That opportunity finally arrived in June 2008 when it set up on the cricket ground at Akola, in the State of Maharashtra.

When I joined Kelvin early on the morning of the raid, he was dressed in a track suit and, very appropriately, swiping the air with a cricket bat.

'You've no idea how pleased I am to be here today. Last time I left the Raj Mahal Circus with my tail between my legs, but today I'm going to hit them for a six.'

'How can you be so confident?' I asked.

'We had a great meeting at the District office yesterday and I sense they are very onside. This time we've brought Nandita Rao with us and she explained the situation and the law to them, politely but firmly. They've said that they'll free all the girls if they find that the situation inside the circus is as we describe it.'

'Won't the circus have been tipped off?' I asked.

'Very possibly, but we've been monitoring it since we arrived in Akola, including throughout last night, and no performers have been taken away. I'm sure of that. Today I'll have my revenge, so much the sweeter for being served cold.'

As we climbed out of our jeep at the circus entrance, I could see ChildLine people running to take up positions around the circus to cordon it off. Then, Shailaja and Nandita by my side, we just walked into the circus as if we owned the place. The police fanned out as we entered the ring with the formidable Nandita taking centre stage, an image of dignity and authority in her grey and black sari. Master of the ring, she was in full command of the situation as she literally laid down the law to the circus people and the local authorities.

Listening in to her, I was struck with how far we'd come since the botched Roman Circus rescue of four years before. The operation remained dangerous but we had managed risk properly, including protecting the media representatives who were with us. This time there would be proper legal protocols, no chaos and no running away. We were invincible and on the verge of a major result.

But soon after we arrived the circus owner, Fateh Khan's brother, Siraj, strode into the ring demanding an explanation. He got one, delivered in no uncertain terms by Nandita, as she quoted chapter and verse from the Juvenile Justice Act, bonded labour and minimum wage legislation. He reacted by producing contracts but these were dismissed by Nandita who told him that a law dating back to 1933 made it illegal for parents to write contracts on behalf of their children.

At this point the Head of the local Labour Department who had joined us intervened on behalf of the circus. Counter to our agreed plan to take the performers to a neutral location for interview, as stipulated in Juvenile Justice Act, he proposed that questioning should be done inside the circus. We were suspicious of what might have happened behind the scenes but a quick call by Nandita to his superior was enough to have this sabotage attempt rejected.

The performers were cautious. Women with babies in their arms – former performers – watched in silence. The circus had forced them into marriage after their contracts had ended, binding them to the circus for life. For them we had come too late. The single girls were more outspoken.

'We don't want to leave,' they chorused. 'Why should we trust you? What do you have for us in Nepal that's better than here?'

I could understand their suspicion. We'd heard that circuses had been known to stage mock raids with goons dressed as policemen to identify and beat up anyone who asked to leave. A quick-thinking Shailaja handed the girls her mobile and allowed them to speak with a girl whom we'd freed on the previous raid. That did the trick. Several of the twenty performers were crying as they left the circus but their tears were short-lived. When they arrived at our base, they met girls from that previous rescue whom we'd brought on this trip to provide reassurance. Soon they were laughing, catching up on six months of separation and sharing a proper meal together.

Raids nearly always deliver the unexpected and on this one I was surprised to meet two foreign female performers. One was American the other Italian, working at the Raj Mahal on short contracts. The Italian was a bit crazy and as animated in mannerism as the stereotypical Italian, but I had a level exchange with the American.

'What are you guys up to?' she asked, totally baffled.

'We're freeing these girls from slavery and sexual abuse. Girls have been raped in this circus,' I replied.

Her look of bewilderment transformed into one of shock.

'They've been trafficked from Nepal and we're taking them home. Weren't you aware of the violence?'

'I honestly had no idea. The circus has looked after me quite well and I had my own tent. I was free to come and go as I pleased. The girls seemed happy enough and I assumed that they were being paid. But I guess they couldn't share anything with me because of the language barrier. Why are they recruiting Nepali girls?'

'Because it's a turn-on for men in the audience to see foreign girls in leotards with light skin. An appearance such as yours,' I answered.

She e-mailed me a week later to say that she'd checked out the next day. The Italian woman stayed on.

Throughout the rest of that day Nandita ensured that everything was done by the book and in accordance with Indian law which is crystal clear on the definition and management of child labour and bonded labour. According to the Juvenile Justice Act the girls actually had to leave the circus whatever their stated preferences; bonded labour was by definition illegal and could not be allowed to continue. Even then the official from the Labour Department still continued his subversion, attempting to tone down the girls' statements as they were translated from Nepali to Hindi. All mention of bonded labour was left out of the statements until at Nandita's insistence these were reinstated.

Our team monitored proceedings while working around the clock and going without food. Late that evening it was quite something to witness Nandita grabbing a quick sleep in the hostel courtyard, surrounded by sleeping girls and a swarm of mosquitos.

'Weren't you eaten alive?' I asked her afterwards.

'They wouldn't dare bite me,' she said with a laugh. From what I had seen that day I guessed she was probably right.

'Take a look at this contract,' she said, offering me a document that was, typically, written in English. 'This girl's father sold her when she was eight for 1,800 rupees. And she's been paid nothing further for the past 12 years.'

I made a quick calculation. For her the price of slavery had been a pound a year.

'She didn't see a single rupee of that. She told me that she was only allowed outside once in all that time to visit a temple. The circus made her dress up so that they could take a picture to send back to her father to convince him that she was having a nice time.'

I remembered the similar disturbing photos that I had seen in Hetauda. This was an old trick that had even been used by earlier slave-masters - the Nazis who forced Auschwitz inmates to send reassuring postcards to relatives at home.

Nandita introduced me to one of the girls she'd been interviewing, asking her to hold out her hands. The palms were badly scarred.

'Her trainer cauterised blisters and cuts with molten wax.' She shook her head in disgust. 'The show had to go on at the expense of human suffering.'

I observed to Nandita that one of the girls was particularly solidly built, not at all like a gymnast.

'Was she a weight lifter?' I asked.

Nandita grinned.

'She's a very strong girl. She's the one who used to be placed under the plank for the tractor driving trick.'

That afternoon another of Fateh Khan's brothers arrived on a motor bike outside the hostel where we were interviewing the girls, an implicit threat. Nandita faced him down:

'If you don't leave this moment, I'll report you to the police for attempting to subvert a police investigation.'

He left but we could see him re-joining other circus people who were loitering with intent at the road junction a couple of hundred yards away. I pointed them out to ChildLine staff member, the very plucky Abhishek Pathak, who had been overseeing the surveillance of the circus prior to the raid. He turned to me with an impish smile.

'Shall we take a little stroll?' he asked.

And the two of us walked up the road, passed their menace with deliberate nonchalance and, after a buying a couple of bottles of mineral water at a store, returned past them to re-join our group. We weren't going to show any fear before their intimidation.

As nightfall approached, we relocated to the police station where it would be safer to spend the hours of darkness. At least here the police were on our side. That didn't deter Kahn's brother from returning, boldly entering the station itself. This time Abhishek confronted him. Under the noses of the police he squared up to Kahn, demanding to know if he was trying to threaten him. Kahn had the good sense to apologise, his hands together in supplication, and withdrew.

The collection of evidence continued into the night. At one point I left the building for some fresh air. I crossed the courtyard to stand by the entrance that opened onto the main road. It was 2 a.m., muggy and very quiet. There were very few vehicles around apart from a jeep parked a few metres along the away; I assumed that the driver was one of our NGO colleagues. Shailaja joined me for a chat and the man dropped his head to rest it on the steering wheel.

'I think you'd better come back inside, man,' she said. 'See, that is a circus goon. He's trying to conceal his identity now but I recognise him from the last rescue. He threatened that if I returned to the Raj Mahal, he'd kill me.'

I took her advice.

Behind the scenes the circus management was lobbying local politicians, putting in calls to the police and labour department. In desperation the circus even laid on a lavish dinner for journalists where they alleged that ChildLine had tried to extort the Raj Mahal for money and the raid had only happened because they had refused to pay up. Their efforts were to no avail. Eventually the authorities sent all of the girls home with a police escort to prevent the risk of circus retaliation or abduction.

This had been a textbook rescue that had been dreadful publicity for the circus as the raid had been covered on the front page of the Times of India. This operation marked the beginning of the end of the circus children problem. For later on we found out that a number of things happened after the raid, probably because it had been such a high-profile target and we had wrecked it without any real resistance. First off, the large circuses stopped procuring little children from Nepal. Instead they seemed to seek out more foreign artists to become their new star attraction. In a raid on the Great Prabhath circus in 2010 I even met Kenyan and Russian performers. Secondly, to my surprise, conditions inside the circuses improved. We found out that a group of the major circuses had given their girls the choice of staying under better terms of service or of returning to Nepal. We estimate that the circuses released approximately 350 girls in this way, the same number as we'd eventually free through raids.

The upshot was that over the next two years in raid after raid we'd come to find ever fewer little children and, if there were any, they were Indian nationals rather than Nepali. And we'd meet girls in their late-teens who genuinely wanted to stay on and complete their contracts. They'd told us that if we'd come five years earlier, they'd have left without hesitation but now life wasn't so bad and there was little for them to return to in Nepal.

Of course, the possible continued use of Indian children concerned us but we knew there wasn't much we could do about that as we couldn't assume responsibility for their aftercare since we had no presence in their home areas. Indian-based NGOs could address that and ChildLine was very much on the case. In short, our project seemed to be coming to a natural conclusion. But we still had one old score to settle.

It was well past midnight and there wasn't a star in the sky. By the dancing flashlights we could still see that the small circus pitched in ankle-deep mud in Assam was a dump in a swamp. The young woman we'd come looking had been sleeping in a tent at the rear of the complex. She was confused and disorientated by all the commotion.

'Who are you, what do you want? What's he doing here?'

She'd spotted the brother that she hadn't seen in 14 years. This was no happy reunion.

'We've come to take you home,' Shailaja said.

213

'What, me and my three sons? Are *you* going to feed me?' she asked sarcastically. She knew that there'd be nothing for her at home apart from stigma and a different sort of misery.

Knowing that we had to get her out of there whatever the cost, I took a deep breath.

'Yes, we will; trust us.'

This was the New Diamond Circus, the one formerly known as the Moonlight Circus that we'd managed to rescue Sarita from back in 2004. She was the little girl who'd come to us in Bhairahawa in a terrible state after being allegedly raped by its owner. It was now September 2009 and it had taken us five years to build the capacity to deliver justice at this remote spot. But we were determined to shut this circus down and free all the Nepali performers who were still there.

We'd heard about Saraswati from a former circus employee who'd told us about her plight. A trafficker called Bijay KC had taken her there when she was eight, been forced into marriage with the circus owner at 13 and gone on to bear him three sons. He had died and now her husband's brother, Sarita's alleged rapist Mithun Chaudhari, had taken over the circus and was beating Saraswati.

We acted quickly. After a two-day search Shailaja managed to trace Saraswati's younger brother who agreed to accompany us on the trip. We also took along a journalist, Ujjwala Maharjan, from Nepal's *Republica* broadsheet.

On the way, Shailaja had first called at the Nepal embassy to obtain a letter of support. In spite of a long wait, for reasons best known to the embassy staff, no such letter was forthcoming. She suspected we were being blocked by another major Nepali NGO that had leverage at the embassy and that resented our successful rescues. Sad, but such is the rivalry within the sector. A defiant Shailaja finally stormed into the office and told the obstructive bureaucrat that she would do the rescue with our without embassy support.

After arriving at the Assam state capital of Guwahati we'd touched base with the Deputy Inspector General (DIG) of Police, Munna Gupta. He was an unknown quantity and his attitude would be critical to success or failure. Prospects looked good when, in response to our early morning call, he invited us to visit his flat where he offered us tea and biscuits. He was an urbane, genuine man, very different from the kind of sleazy corrupt cop we'd encountered in the past. After exchanging some small talk, I explained our needs. He listened intently, nodding in agreement. We made no mention of the obstruction at the embassy. Then he said:

'Let's sort these jokers out. I will assign you two plainclothes inspectors for the trip. They'll ensure your security and see to it that you've all the support you need.'

I thanked him profusely and then asked Ujjwala if she would like to ask him any questions before we left.

'So, you're not concerned by the lack of a letter of support from the embassy?' she enquired.

'I beg your pardon?'

I cleared my throat and glared daggers at Ujjwala. Thankfully Munna hadn't quite caught the question, one that could have scuppered the mission.

'Ujjwala wants to know if you need to send a letter of support to the Nepal embassy.' I said.

'That won't be necessary,' he replied.

We embarked on the eight-hour drive to where the circus was based. All along the way the police were great. The District police HQ assigned us an armed escort to the rural police station that was quite near the circus. There the police treated us like VIPs, offering us local delicacies served on banana leaves before taking us on to the circus itself for its midnight shake-up.

Soon after their swoop the police decided to round up everyone and take them to the station. They sat the 15 or so sullen performers in one room while they put Mithun Chaudhari into a back office. Shailaja spotted her long-awaited opportunity. While the police were distracted by interviewing the performers, she slipped unnoticed into Chaudhari's room and pounced like a tiger. She launched a blistering verbal attack on the man who had allegedly raped the little girl that she had tended to back in 2004.

The performers began giving their statements. One boy, clearly with a learning disability, told us how his job at the circus had been to clean up the human excrement in the surroundings of the circus. Defecation al fresco is common in rural India and Nepal. Another lad said that a month before he'd asked Chaudhari for his pay only to be tied to a pole and beaten by three people. Saraswati spoke out:

'That's not true. The circus was just short of funds at that stage. If someone's rude they can expect a beating. That's normal discipline.'

Ujjwala whispered to me that she felt Saraswati should be charged too as she was in cahoots with Chaudhari. I suggested that she

215

wait until Shailaja had had a chance to counsel her before reaching that conclusion. Once again, we were dealing with Stockholm Syndrome. Sure enough, by morning a switch had flicked and Saraswati was telling the truth about her enslavement.

The operation complete, we left Chaudhari in the hands of the police and returned to Nepal with Saraswati and the other Nepali performers. Saraswati was now determined to find justice and bring trafficker Bijay KC to book.

'This man inflicted years of misery on me and ruined my life,' she declared. 'Now it has to be his turn to feel the pain of imprisonment.'

We tracked him down easily as he lived in Makwanpur District. The police arrested him and, based upon Saraswati's unflinching evidence in spite of threats from his family, he was fined 300,000 rupees (£2,000) and given a 20-year prison sentence. In line with Nepali law he also had to compensate Saraswati. The court awarded her the equivalent of £1,500 which is a huge sum in Nepal. Beyond that we kept our promise to provide for Saraswati ourselves, taking her into our own employment as a helper at the Kathmandu refuge where her children were able to join her. The operation could not have been more complete.

In August 2010 two British volunteers, married couple Sandra and Martin, joined us for a filming project. That assignment fell through at the last moment and it was too late to cancel their visit. I had to think of something else for them to do at short notice. As it happened both of them were contemporary circus professionals and Sandra came up with an idea.

'Is there any good reason why we couldn't set up some circus workshops and have some fun?' Sandra suggested.

'I can think of lots of good reasons why not to,' I replied. 'After all that these kids have been through – including rape – it would be obscene for me to even make the suggestion.'

'Of course, it's a totally different circus experience,' she replied. 'I've got some film on my laptop of us in performance. Maybe I could show that to anyone who might be interested and talk them through what's involved.'

'Okay,' I agreed, 'But let me discuss this with Shailaja first.'

Shailaja was more receptive to the proposal than I had expected but had some reservations.

'See, circus is so stigmatised in this society that you'd have to do all of this in secret. I know a gym owner who might be willing to provide training space, but I'd guess he'll be concerned about his image and keeping the gym respectable. You certainly shouldn't involve the media, at least not initially.'

'I think we should try it out and, after all, it will be voluntary,' I said. 'We already know how therapeutic art and the arts can be. I don't know if anyone has used circus skills before for this purpose.'

Sandra returned the next day with the smile of success.

'I'd a chat last evening with a dozen of the kids and told them all about ourselves. They were amazed that anyone should do circus voluntarily and that it can offer a career with a proper salary. You should've seen their faces as they watched my film. They couldn't keep their hands off my laptop. If you agree they're willing to give it a go.'

'Alright,' I said, 'but you won't be teaching "circus"; these are "performing skills" and everything has to be behind closed doors. No members of the public wandering in and out. Nepali people are very curious and they don't understand privacy. We can't allow word to get out. And all the participants should be over 16 so that we can't be accused of exploiting children.'

A week later Shailaja and I slipped into the gym to see what was going on. We watched as the participants literally threw themselves at this opportunity; they were having such fun. Most intriguing was their mix of backgrounds and personal stories. For the students included Aman, who had been one of the first voluntary releases back in 2004, who was somersaulting the length of the gym. Ariti, freed from the Great Indian Circus, was there with her older sister, Muna. Deepa, extracted with some force from her circus in 2006, was wrapped around an aerial hoop. Even Dinesh was climbing a rope with alacrity, one of two former street children who were trying their hand. After my promise to 'feed' her I was delighted to see Saraswati off in the corner spinning hula hoops simultaneously around waist, arms and a leg. All in all, it was a scene of pure magic.

During a training break I asked Sandra if she thought we might be able to develop this into a show.

'We've certainly whetted their appetite,' she replied. 'Having seen their joy, skills and commitment I believe we can, but we'll need a little time and a bit more training expertise. If you are happy for me to do so, I can return to the UK and recruit a few circus professionals to come back with me in a couple of months' time. January is a quiet period for circus shows and I'm sure that I can find people with time on their hands. With three weeks of intense training we can do it if you're sure that you're happy for us to go public.'

I looked to Shailaja for guidance. She shrugged.

'After seeing this, I don't think we should worry so much about going public. They are having a great time,' she said.

'Yes,' I added, 'and we know that most of these children aren't going to make it academically. They've joined school too late. Maybe a show could be a great lead-in to a new form of therapeutic vocational training. Why teach them new skills when they have these ones already?'

And so was born *Circus Kathmandu*. Sandra and Martin returned to Nepal with five colleagues who included a Mexican clown, a costume designer and a gymnast. They worked like Trojans in preparing 'The Devil's Spell' that presented to a full house at the end of January.

This was probably the first time ever that a circus had played in Kathmandu and the British Ambassador was the guest of honour. The highlight of the show involved hoisting a radiant Deepa ten metres to the ceiling dressed as a serpent goddess in a shimmering thirty-foot-long silver dress. As she spun in the air, she was flanked by two other girls who performed mesmerising aerial dance manoeuvres high up, entwined in silk drapes. This show wasn't about tacky, outdated circus tricks; it had assumed the status of art form. At the end of the performance the Ambassador was first on his feet leading a standing ovation.

Knowing everyone's background as I did, this had all been so moving for me to witness. But what I remember most from that evening was the sight of the jubilant performers doing high-fives backstage. This had been a massive step forward as not only had circus entered the public domain in Nepal but also for the first time these young people could be proud to call themselves circus artists. No longer was this activity conducted behind closed doors and there had been an associated blaze of media publicity. We had changed attitudes within society and that is a remarkable achievement anywhere, not least in Nepal.

In spite of the long wait and our trip on the adoption rollercoaster, we wanted to press on with finding a sibling for Alisha. We wanted a boy, which was convenient as by law intercountry adopters were restricted to two children, one of each sex. This rule made no sense either. In the past this policy had led to siblings of the same sex being split up to go to different parents. The problem now was that there was a moratorium on new cases. We had to mark time while the Nepal government got around to signing the Hague Convention on intercountry adoption and for allocations to restart in November 2009. Meantime Bev became a regular visitor to the Ministry, applying charm, pressure and her command of Nepali to ensure we were at the top of the waiting list. She was ready with the mound of essential paperwork we required to satisfy Nepalese bureaucracy.

We were introduced to Joe on paper. The ground rules had changed. The Ministry of Women and Children banned prospective adopters from visiting children's homes to be matched with their babies. Instead the Ministry did the allocations centrally and all we would be allowed to see in advance was a passport size photograph of Joe. To our frustration, this and the associated paperwork arrived at our home in Kathmandu while we were mid-flight returning to the UK for a short visit. We had to endure several more agonising days' wait while a courier brought his papers and photo to us in England. After we finally got to see his serious, dark-eyed little face we agreed without hesitation. However, we had to wait a further four months before we could meet him, all for the want of one last bureaucrat's signature.

When we were finally introduced to Joe this was such a special moment yet also a disturbing experience as his orphanage was noisy and overcrowded. Joe had spent the first sixteen months of his life there. He looked bewildered at the sudden attention he was receiving and we longed to give this little boy all the love and care that he'd been missing. As I sat in the corner of a cramped bedroom that he shared with four other infants, from nowhere he stumbled over to me and kissed me on the cheek. I was smitten.

Under the revised rules Joe's paperwork went through the system fairly quickly and thank goodness we got him just in time. For in May 2010 the British and other governments banned adoptions from Nepal. This decision was largely influenced by objections raised by UNICEF regarding matters such as alleged falsification of documents, weak legal procedures and a lack of transparency on the use of adoption fees; we'd had to pay the Ministry £5,000 per child as a placement fee. Sadly, that suspension remains in place to this day. A lot of children have been condemned to remain in orphanages needlessly while couples around the world yearn to have children and could offer loving homes. I am tormented by the thought of all the Alisha's and Joe's who are out there, trapped in institutional lives, denied a childhood and the chance to realise their true potential. And there's little I can do about it.

In any case I had now also fulfilled the second half of Esther's wish for me – to find another woman *and* to have children. I'd know the joy of carrying my dear son on my shoulders, a brother to Alisha.

April – June 2011.

17.   Shailaja's wager

You might manage to get inside The Great Apollo Circus but you'll never come out alive,' Rahul said to her.

Shailaja was visiting the only Indian circus owner who was running a clean show and who'd become a personal friend.

'Take my good advice and don't go there. The owner of that circus is a really bad guy and a rapist. You'll never be seen again.'

Her visit to Rahul came in May 2011, the month after a landmark ruling by the Indian Supreme Court that outlawed the use of children under the age of 18 as performers. This followed Nandita's submission of an intervention Public Interest Litigation (PIL) on behalf of ChildLine India to back up one that BBA had lodged back in 2004. That one had seemingly been quietly forgotten about. The Court also ordered the Indian government to rescue all the children who were inside circuses and rehabilitate them by June that year.

This appeared to put the seal of sustainability on our work, a programme that had already effectively closed down a child trafficking route with both procurement and demand for Nepali child performers dried up. I saw this lasting result as a permanent memorial to Esther that trumped a plaque on a wall. No longer would the Indian circus cast a long shadow over Nepali children. My stated purpose for being in Nepal accomplished, I advised my Trustees of my wish to return home in July of the following year, my mission accomplished.

Nevertheless, I was keen to see what difference the ruling had made on the ground, if any, and The Great Apollo Circus had been in our sights for a long time. This was the same one that PNMM had raided back in 2003 and the owner had escaped justice at that time. We'd heard that once again there were Nepali girls in his troupe.

'I tell you, there's no way that the circuses can comply with the Court's ruling within that time frame,' Rahul said to Shailaja. 'But they'll get there, maybe within a year or two. The clock is ticking. It is much safer for you to just let this process run its course, including at The Great Apollo. Be sensible.'

Shailaja put down her dal and rice.

'I know that I can make a return journey to that circus and more than that I will bring some children out. Here's the deal. Five thousand rupees says that I can. How about it?'

222

'That's no kind of a bet. Who is going to pay me if you lose? The owner of the Great Apollo?' He snorted. 'Alright then, you mad woman.'

The Great Apollo Circus was operating in Dehradun, an eight-hour drive north of Delhi. We expected danger, also because the owner was a powerful figure who'd be well-protected within that District. To minimise the risk, we decided not to compromise our security by taking family members with us. There was just our four-person team, including Shailaja and my Deputy in Nepal, Bhaskar Karki. However, a duo filming on behalf of Al Jazeera joined us as did an intrepid Hong Kong-based journalist called Ivan Broadhead who was reporting for *Voice of America*.

Beforehand, through internet research I had identified an organisation called Samadhan to act as our host NGO. When it came down to it, there hadn't been much of a choice of NGOs in that particular area. After arriving in Dehradun, I soon realised that Samadhan was little more than a husband and wife team, Renu and Sanjay Singh, supported by a decent American law student intern. What they lacked in numbers they compensated for in hot air.

At our first meeting Renu and Sanjay recounted at length their past exploits in the cause of child rights. Renu talked and talked, stultifying us while the portly Sanjay looked on. Their tales of derring-do included an implausible account of a desert rescue worthy of Beau Geste that they claimed to have conducted in a Gulf State. Obligingly, Ivan kept them talking through a fake interview that they were more than happy to contribute towards, while in a back room Shailaja quizzed the intern who could speak openly when they weren't within earshot.

We went with Renu and Sanjay to meet the District Magistrate (DM) Sachin Kurve, the senior government civil servant within the District. Securing his cooperation would be vital towards achieving a swift and positive outcome.

My first impression of Kurve was not good as I felt his limp handshake. As we were in the company of an international journalist, he made positive statements but over the ensuing days his words were not matched by actions. Although the State police issued a directive to rescue the girls, nothing happened. Kurve stonewalled. At one point he even resorted to hiding in his office while his junior staff told us he'd gone out; by persistence we coaxed a meeting with him fifteen minutes later but we could see that he was just fobbing us off. We realised that this awful man wasn't going to intervene.

The next day a mischievous Ivan went off on his own to confront Kurve. He was wearing a hidden microphone. When he returned to our base an hour later, he was laughing, jubilant at his successful door-stepping of the DM. He played back the terse exchange for us:

'Mr Kurve, why is it that 30 hours since State police issued instructions to free the children at the Apollo Circus at the earliest opportunity they're still stuck inside?' he asked.

'I've passed those instructions on to the competent authorities,' Kurve replied.

'Those instructions were supposed to be acted upon yesterday.'

'They are working upon that.'

'But the Law requires that the children be removed at the earliest possible opportunity.'

'I'm doing that.'

'I saw the District Commissioner of police yesterday and they have been unable to do anything. Why is your office not acting?'

'We're trying. We're taking a legal report.'

'But this has taken two days.'

'Taking the legal report requires so many things to be looked upon.'

'The highest police officer in the State has given the instructions. What's your plan?'

'I will not disclose the plan. We need to conduct the operation in secrecy. The circus operator should not come to know these things.'

'You saw the circus operator yesterday. How can you say he shouldn't know? Why did you meet with him?'

'I have asked the District Labour department to look into the matter.'

'But this is your responsibility.'

'Don't tell me my responsibility!'

'I'm telling you what Indian Law states.'

'I know Indian Law.'

'So, why haven't the children been removed?'

'I'm trying my level best to do that.'

The DM pressed an intercom buzzer. Ivan continued:

'Why have you been speaking to the circus owners and managers? I have that from several sources.'

'I have not.'

Two men strode into the room.

'Take him!' ordered the DM.

'What do you mean, "take him"?' asked Ivan.

'Remove him.'

'One final question – do you think it is satisfactory that these children are still inside the circus after two days?'

The DM began to scream.

'I will not be answering any more questions. Don't argue with me unnecessarily!'

The men bundled Ivan out of the office.

'Is this how India treats foreign visitors?' were Ivan's parting words.

How appropriate that confrontation had been on this occasion compared to my experience of a journalist door-stepping me after Esther's death. This was responsible, investigative journalism at its best.

We spent a further two days in Dehradun going from office to office trying to go over the DM's head but to no avail. We were dealing with a demagogue who didn't appear to be answerable to anyone. This seems to be a throwback to the days of the Raj when the District administrator appointed by the British carried all the authority of the Empire. No one, not even his appointed superiors, could challenge this vestige of Imperial rule.

While all of these shenanigans were going on Renu and Sanjay took increasing distance from us. We gained the distinct impression that they wanted to conduct this rescue entirely by themselves and claim the kudos. Our hunch was that parallel discussions were going on between them and the authorities and a deal was cooking that wasn't altogether kosher.

After four days of zero progress we finally had a breakthrough. One afternoon at around 5 p.m. the intern phoned to tip us off that his bosses were at the circus and that something was about to happen there. We found out later that Renu and Sanjay had gone to the circus with local Child Welfare Committee representatives as a joint inspection team that would reach an arrangement with the circus owner. That was in spite of the fact that under the Indian Juvenile Justice Act the CWC could just walk in and remove any children from the circus without the need for any negotiation or cooperation. But the Chairman of the CWC was the DM himself and he was running to a different agenda.

As soon as we received this message we jumped into our vehicle and rushed to the old military parade ground in the centre of town where the circus had set up shop. Our group consisted of the four of us charity workers, the Al Jazeera duo and Ivan Broadhead. We parked up in a parade ground that was full of people milling around in the late afternoon sunshine in advance of the circus's evening show. The circus was a huge complex comprising an eight-pole tent with an attached fairground that included a Ferris wheel. Like all circuses this complex was encompassed by a high metal fence.

Sitting there, I realised we were lacking the core ingredients for success i.e. the support of the authorities and police complemented by a cooperative host NGO. Worse still, the DM was actively against us. As we sat outside the circus, we hadn't the first idea what was actually going on inside. This scenario made David and Goliath seem like a fair contest; at least David had been armed with a sling. We couldn't enter the circus unsupported and I was at a loss as to how to proceed. I turned to Shailaja who was sitting beside me in the back of the vehicle for inspiration.

'Now what?' I asked.

She responded with her enigmatic half smile. Shailaja seemed to have an instinct for success.

Moments later, something incredible happened. We spotted the back gate of the circus opening and two adults came out with a group of six children. The children were plainly Nepali and still wearing their performance make up. Circus employees were sneaking child performers out of the circus under the stupid noses of the inspection team. Immediately we wheeled our vehicle around to intercept. We four team members surrounded the group in a kind of defensive diamond formation and a heated argument began between Shailaja and the adults. One of them pulled out a scrap of paper with a telephone number to call for assistance but Shailaja snatched it from his hand.

Just then two young policemen happened to drift past on their motor bike and we grabbed them. They provided a vital piece of insurance as a large crowd began to gather around us like curious cattle. While looking inwards towards the group we still had to try and watch our backs. Soon the children began to wail, frightened by all this attention and these strangers. The film crew was having a field day as they recorded a dramatic event that no script could have anticipated.

Ten minutes later Renu emerged from the circus with the CWC representatives in her wake, mobile to her ear.

'We've rescued the children,' she was announcing to someone.

Ivan was having none of that. Incandescent, he thrust a microphone at Renu's face.

'How can you possibly lay claim to having rescued these children? This has been The Esther Benjamins Trust's success.'

226

She ignored him. Against our protests they then tried to brush us aside and take the children back inside the circus to continue the negotiations.

'You can't take them back in there!' I yelled at Sanjay.

'This is an Indian matter and has got nothing to do with you,' he declared. 'We are on official business. Go away now and leave this to us.'

In the nick of time police reinforcements arrived, sirens blaring, and took the released children to the safety of a children's refuge. We followed the group but at the refuge the gates were closed to us. Peering over the gates, we could see that inside Renu and Sanjay were hosting an open-air press conference. We heckled from the outside with shouts of 'Don't believe them!' and 'Liars!' but the reporters were clearly not interested in the truth of our central role in instigating and rescuing these children.

In the knowledge that the children were now safe and realising we could do nothing more as the children were Indian nationals of Nepali origin, we decided it was time to beat a hasty withdrawal from the scene. There was every possibility of circus retaliation and as the outsiders in the equation we were the most likely targets. We were also worried about the DM being part of any backlash and he too was a very dangerous man. We raced back to our accommodation where we downed a very large whiskey in celebration of the children's deliverance before driving through the night to the safety of Delhi.

As we drove off, Shailaja phoned Rahul.

'You owe me some money.'

I had decided that I would be returning to the UK in mid-2012 but even so we once again needed to find a new project area to allow our cross-border rescue work to continue. We had built a network of contacts and an enviable expertise that couldn't be allowed to go to waste.

A possibility arose, once again by serendipity, when in May 2011 our field team stumbled upon a forlorn little Nepali boy who had been held for six months in a Juvenile Correction Centre in Calcutta. He said that he had run away from an abusive stepmother before being caught by the Indian police. Although innocent, he was in free association with dangerous young offenders and his face already bore the scars of his stay. No one at the Centre was doing anything for him, least of all in tracing his family. It fell to us to find his father and secure the boy's release and repatriation to our refuge. He couldn't be returned to his stepmother.

This boy's case prompted us to investigate Juvenile Correction Centres, alternatively called 'children's shelters' or 'observation homes'. It soon became clear that they had become dumping grounds for displaced Nepali children. Or more accurately, for Nepali boys as boys rather than girls tend to run away from home. There were an estimated 600 such centres across India and they housed not just displaced children but also young offenders. The Nepali boys were washed up there like castaways, whereabouts unknown to their families.

They'd be in these places for a variety of reasons. Sometimes a child could simply get lost, separated from parents in a busy street during a family visit to India. More likely the children were runaways (frequently escaping an abusive step parent) or economic migrants who'd gone looking for work that would mean money to them and their families. Some were escapees from religious institutions, including violent Buddhist monasteries. We came across boys inside these facilities who had been working – often happily - in a child labour situation (such as a tea shop) before being 'rescued' by a child rights NGO and taken to a children's home that became their prison. The NGO could then claim the credit for a rescue while the child endured misery. They'd be compelled to stay in the home until the age of 18 at which point the management would discharge them onto the street without prospects and highly vulnerable.

In May we launched a parallel rescue programme in India after Shailaja had found six Nepali children inside a home in Delhi. Beforehand she'd had to trace their families in remote West Nepal. This is no easy task at the best of times given the distances involved and the lack of proper roads, but her pressing field work had to take place during the monsoon season with its associated floods. Bhaskar Karki, my Deputy, had gone off with her on this trip just to gain a feel for what was involved. I'll never forget how he e-mailed me to say

'This woman is mad. She starts at four in the morning and keeps going all day until eleven at night. And she's scared of nobody.'

In the end Shailaja's stamina paid off, finding parents who were astounded to learn that children whom they had assumed to be long dead were alive, if not necessarily all that well.

Soon afterwards Shailaja and the six children's fathers, uncles and brothers set off on a 24-hour bus journey to Delhi to bring their sons home. Their destination, Phulbari Children's Home looked more like a fortress than a childcare centre. The walls were capped with barbed wire while patrolling guards forbad photography even from the outside. The Home's staff refused entry to the party for two hours until our friends at ChildLine India interceded.

Forty-five minutes after finally gaining access the brother of one twelve-year-old boy reappeared distraught. The Phulbari staff had told him that the brother he'd come to find had run away. The home insisted that the boy had somehow 'disappeared' after being taken to hospital for treatment for a minor wound. His brother was doubtful, as there was a medical centre on-site and the details of precisely when the boy had run away were sketchy. His suspicion deepened when the staff refused to show him his brother's file. He had become totally untraceable.

Even with the families' presence, freedom for the other children could only be achieved through a court battle. This risked becoming protracted with the Judge demanding a letter of authority from the Nepal embassy. At this point one father stood firm and said that he wouldn't leave the court that day without his son. Shailaja called in a representative of ChildLine who reminded the Judge of the provisions of the Indian Juvenile Justice Act. Finally, he relented. This operation was a huge result for the children and families concerned but in terms of bangs for bucks it didn't translate well. It had involved (expensive) weeks of research to locate the families and the trip itself had lasted an additional five days. But we had saved five more worlds.

Shailaja revisited Phulbari in June to repatriate a further six boys, five of whom were runaways or juvenile economic migrants. The sixth was a boy who'd travelled with his sister as she was being trafficked through India to the Gulf. After the agent had delivered the sister to a 'recruitment agency' he'd dumped the boy. Just like after circus rescue, the challenges didn't end once the children were back in Nepal. Our imperative was to reunite children with families but for several of the boys this was impossible; they had been runaways from domestic abuse that they didn't wish to revisit. The only option was to join our refuge.

A further objective was to find the trafficker who had taken that boy and his sister to India. He was a man called Narayan Shrestha, a teacher turned trafficker, who lived in Gorkha. This was hatchet country, one of the former heartlands of the Maoist violence. For sure Shrestha would be involved with the party and any attempt to get him directly would be destined to fail or could be life-threatening. Once again, the quick-thinking Shailaja had a trick up her sleeve. Somehow, she'd obtained Shrestha's mobile number and with a wink to me she called him up from inside the police station.

'I am with the Child Welfare Nepal organisation and have a boy with me who has been repatriated from India. His name in Narendra and he's named you as next of kin. Would you mind calling at Lalitpur police station to help us with the handover?'

The next day Shrestha walked into Shailaja's trap. As the police began questioning him about the circumstances of his trip to India and connection with the boy, he turned to Shailaja, the look on his face priceless as reality dawned.

'What's the meaning of this?' he asked.

Shailaja responded with a shrug and a smile. His arrest at the station couldn't have been easier.

18.   Feet of Clay

In early 2011 Shailaja and Bhaskar attended an NGO anti-trafficking networking meeting in Kathmandu. Usually these meetings generate little apart from hot air, but at the end of this meeting a frustrated man stood up. He spoke of the plight of a group of trafficked girls who were stranded at the Michael Job Centre (MJC). Someone called DB Phadera had taken them there eight years previously and since then no one had shown any interest in their situation or in responding to parents' pleas for help.

After the meeting Shailaja and Bhaskar went over to question the man who gave them the basic information I needed to begin my research. This was the first I'd heard of the problem and I was intrigued by the challenge of finding these lost children who'd seemingly been betrayed by everyone - their families, the authorities and NGOs. And of course, by DB Phadera and Dr Job themselves.

My investigation started by reading Dr Job's badly written books including titles such as *Turn your Sorrow* and *Why, God, Why?* that he wrote in the wake of his son Michael's death. I was astounded to learn that Dr Job claimed to have been an understudy for 30 years to someone I'd encountered many years before, Pastor Richard Wurmbrand.

When I was a boy, Wurmbrand had come to speak at my church in Northern Ireland's Bible belt. A Romanian Jew who had converted to Christianity, this intriguing man had a powerful story to tell. For he had spent 14 years in a prison in Communist Romania for his faith, three of these involving solitary confinement in an underground cell. Eventually Norwegian Christians had ransomed him and the regime expelled him from the country to be granted asylum in the USA. From there he continued his work on behalf of the persecuted church, writing 18 books and travelling widely to give talks that raised awareness and funds for his international support organisations. These included the non-profit 'Voice of Martyrs' that continued after his death. His travels included a visit to Washington DC in May 1966 where he gave shocking evidence before the U.S. Senate's Internal Security Subcommittee. In a moment of high drama, he removed his shirt before TV cameras to show scars from the torture he had endured during his confinement.

My response to his moving testimony was to do all that I could as a deeply religious lad; I donated my beloved stamp collection to his then 'Christian Mission to the Communist World'.

Bizarrely, here I was almost 40 years later potentially lining myself up against a protégé of Wurmbrand's. Obviously, the Iron Curtain had long since gone but Dr Job felt he could still implement Wurmbrand's agenda by spreading the Gospel to non-Christian nations where the church was allegedly persecuted. He looked north to find the 'daughters' that God had promised him to replace his only two children, Michael who'd been killed in 1999 and a second son, John, who was killed in a motorbike accident in Dubai in 2007. John had been there operating a small business as his front while clandestinely printing and distributing bibles. Dr Job attributed his death to Moslem extremists but, just as with his Michael's death, that allegation was never proven. These 'daughters' arose from marginalised and impoverished communities in northeast India, Bhutan, Nepal, Tibet and Myanmar. These represent frontline areas for militant Protestant evangelism that tries to upset the applecart of the established religions of Hinduism, Buddhism and Islam.

Dr Job drew upon the services of 'representatives' or 'missionaries' who could procure children from vulnerable families and transfer them over a thousand miles south to the MJC. In the classical trafficking scenario, with children that far away from home and unable to communicate in their own language, he could do what he wanted with them. Or more accurately what he believed God was commanding him to do.

An unpublished UNICEF report from 2005 identified DB Phadera as being the chief villain of the piece in Nepal as he preyed on his home District of Humla. Conditions in the district had reached breaking point in the final three years of the Maoist insurgency, between 2003 and 2006, with schools closed in this remote part of west Nepal. Moreover, their ranks depleted, the Maoists had taken to conscripting a child from each family to join the People's Liberation Army. Playing on parents' fears, DB offered to take children to the safety of Kathmandu valley, promising them a good lifestyle and education. Some of these children were relatives of Phadera's who would possibly be looked after comparatively well in material terms. Others were from terribly poor families like Nisha's who would sell all they owned to meet Phadera's 'placement fee'.

UNICEF's report described how Phadera pressurised the local authorities to obtain false death certificates for their parents. Children could then be declared orphans and Phadera be appointed as their guardian. He admitted the children to his own orphanage in Kathmandu after which, unbeknownst to their families, he'd disperse them to other locations. This represented a gross abuse of his position of trust as 'guardian' for girls who were in the age range of just three to six. If families wished to get in touch with children, they had to pay DB an additional fee for this further service.

Phadera's child victims had three final destinations. Babies would be sent to rogue orphanages that could offer up these fake orphans for international adoption. The Swiss charity Terre des Hommes exposed this very lucrative racket through a film called *Paper Orphans*. He dumped boys in horrible orphanages in Kathmandu, some of which he owned himself, where they became a source of income through begging on the streets. DB's third option was to transfer the girls across the border to the MJC.

Dr Job made Phadera's trafficking very easy. The MJC website described Phadera variously as the Mission's 'Nepal Representative', 'Missionary', 'Good Samaritan' – even on one occasion as 'the Revd Phadera'. Job's staff carried out no background checks for admission of the girls to the MJC, with Phadera's stories taken at face value. Furthermore, the MJC staff didn't consult with the Nepal embassy about the circumstances of these Nepal nationals. This lack of due diligence suited Dr Job in his zeal to recruit future missionaries. DB operated with impunity, covering his tracks very well through forged documentation and with his high-level political connections in Nepal. Moreover, he is a physically dangerous man who threatens anyone who gets in his way with extreme violence.

Whenever Dr Job's staff admitted a girl to MJC they would change her identity. They'd give the child a new Western name (often with a Christian connotation such as 'Martha') and tell her that Dr Job was now her father. Many girls would take his surname as well. The MJC staff also changed all new arrivals' religion to Christianity and added their images and fabricated profiles to the MJC website. In this way they offered all 500 girls to the public for sponsorship in a kind of obscene market place. Disregarding a child's right not only to dignity but also to privacy, the Centre invited website visitors to choose the *'orphan'* they wanted to sponsor. Worse still, the MJC produced toe-curling YouTube films in which the children themselves urged viewers to donate to the Centre.

Needless to say, Dr Job made no effort to reunite children with families or support them within their communities. Why would he do that if these were his missionaries in training? Far from it. Although the Centre's admission procedures were lax, he was rigorous in preventing family contact or reunification. While Phadera was charging families for the privilege of communicating with their children Dr Job was requiring families to make police statements and submit affidavits if they wanted their children back. Had he been genuinely interested in supporting Christian orphans he could easily have provided scholarships for them closer to their homes. No, he had a different agenda. Rather like the circus girls these poor kids had a long, dreary and unrelenting daily routine. From 5 a.m. through to 9 p.m. each day Dr Job would brainwash them with a timetable of lessons interspersed with hymns and prayers. He had created his very own God school at the expense of children's rights and underpinned by criminal activity.

Dr Job's Mission was soliciting huge funding internationally from nine international organisations – in USA, Australia, UK, Germany, Netherlands, Canada, Sweden, Norway, and Switzerland – that allowed him to develop this ghastly monument to child exploitation in Michael's name. The more I read the more I was shocked at the blatant dishonesty of the whole operation, including how the MJC presented these children to the world as the orphaned daughters of Christian 'martyrs'. For sure the Nepal element was neither from Christian families nor orphaned. Their fake profiles carried many similarities, with parents being *'believers'* of varying degree right up to being pastors, who had been murdered by bloodthirsty Maoists for their faith. For example, in his book Turn Your Sorrow Dr Job introduced 'Emily':

'Emily, another of our children at the Michael Job Centre, was brought there in 2002 when she was an eight-year-old. Her parents had been martyred for Christ in Nepal by Maoist extremists because of their Christian work. She was brought to us by our representative from Nepal because none of her relatives agreed to look after her. Like most children who have been through the trauma of losing their parents, she was very distressed. She was a quiet child. After a few months at the Centre, she slowly began to open up. All of us at the Centre praised God for bestowing His grace on her.

'But her trials were not over. When she was 12 years old, she began to complain of headaches. After a thorough check-up, we were shocked at the diagnosis. She had a tumour in her brain. Like any other parent, I was devastated. With great speed we took her to the best

235

hospital and got the best surgeon in Coimbatore to operate on her. Her operation was scheduled for 26 August 2006. I flew from New Delhi to Coimbatore on 25th August to be with her. Many mistook her to be my real daughter. After a complicated surgery lasting seven hours, Emily's doctor told us that the operation was a success. After the operation she recovered fast. She underwent chemotherapy for two years before she was completely cured.

'Her parents honoured God by giving up their lives for His glory. God honoured them through us by giving their daughter life. If Emily had been in Nepal, her tumour would not have been diagnosed. And even if it had been diagnosed, she would not have received the life-saving operation because of financial and medical constraints. Though the journey she went through of being orphaned and of having no relatives to support her was very painful, the bigger picture was beautiful. God had a plan, a plan to save her life and help her to become a "missionary" for Christ. The entire Michael Job family heaved a sigh of relief and thanked God for His mercy. He had saved Emily not once but twice. And we all grew in faith – for we had just witnessed a miracle.'

Dr Job's international supporters adulated him, mesmerised by his falsehood. They yearned to believe that contemporary miracles were taking place before their very eyes in Tamil Nadu. One visitor to the Centre, a Trustee of supporting UK charity 'Love in Action UK', even accorded Emily healing powers. After a visit to the MJC in July 2010 she wrote on her Trust's website:

'The following day, which was the day before I left, I spoke to Emily who had a brain tumour five years ago and became a Christian during that time. She started telling me about all the many answers to prayers she has had. Several women, who had not conceived a child for many years, did so after Emily started praying for them. So many people have been greatly blessed because of her suffering. Indeed, the faith of so many at the Centre is such that even when they pray for miracles to happen, they believe that their prayers will be answered. Spending time with such brothers and sisters in Christ, who put Jesus first in their daily life, enables you to walk much closer with Him too. Our vocabulary has not words to express how good that feels!'

I managed to find out Emily's true background. She was from a Hindu family, a niece of a former MP in the mainstream communist UML party (of which DB is a prominent party member), and Phadera's wife's sister. After her father died from TB and her mother eloped Phadera had taken her south.

236

As I researched the MJC I began to wonder if Dr Job had stepped out of the evangelical mainstream. He affirmed his links with Richard Wurmbrand through his books and organisation's newsletter which was called *Tortured for Christ*, the same title as Wurmbrand's best seller from 1967. Yet I could find no coverage of Dr Job on the main Voice of Martyrs website. Had Dr Job become a renegade? I couldn't imagine that Richard Wurmbrand would have wished to have had any truck with the likes of Revd Phadera or with Dr Job's ruthless child procurement strategy.

It also became clear to me that I had discovered a huge operation that would be difficult and dangerous to break. This had been a challenge that even UNICEF appeared to have backed away from as their report had remained under wraps. Maybe this document had named too many names of people in moderately high places. Moreover, this issue was made doubly sensitive by being entangled with religion and as soon as you go there you risk upsetting religious supporters and faith-based organisations which are part of the development sector network. UNICEF's apparent inaction had condemned these girls to remaining in Dr Job's warped regime for at least six years.

It has to be said that there is an argument that at least the girls were being fed and educated which is more than they would have received in Humla. Maybe the deceit, brainwashing and indoctrination represented a small price to pay in return with the end justifying the means. I couldn't subscribe to that viewpoint and I knew that Esther would have condemned this. For sure she wouldn't have looked away. I decided once again to act in the spirit of Esther Benjamins.

During our rescue planning phase, a spy came to our office. He was Netra Bhandari, parent of one of the lost girls. Unbeknownst to us until much later, Bhandari was also brother-in-law to DB Phadera.

Very discreetly - and without networking with other Nepali organisations to maintain secrecy – we'd invited Nisha's mother Shangmo, her brother Karbu and Bhandari to a meeting. They confirmed statements they'd made to the Humla District Child Welfare Board saying that they had not given permission for their daughters to be transferred to Tamil Nadu, to have their names changed to Western ones or for a change of religion. We offered to assist them with retrieving their daughters but there was a catch. Our support was conditional upon their being willing to give evidence against Phadera after the rescue. This had been our approach with the circuses; using the survivors to bring the traffickers to justice. They agreed to cooperate but, to our surprise, the following day Bhandari sent a message that he would go to Coimbatore independently. So already the word was out even before we'd left Nepal and Phadera knew our full agenda; we were after him.

Next, I had to notify the Trustees of the forthcoming rescue and set a budget for the operation. I pointed out that although we would be going with two family members to retrieve just four identifiable girl relations there was every possibility that we could end up with a mass release. This was based on previous experience where all the girls within a circus would seize the chance of freedom and ask to leave. Should this situation arise we would need to provide for the released girls' needs for quite some time post-rescue as part of our duty of care. The Trustees agreed that this could be funded from available rescue funds.

Finally, we obtained a letter of support for the operation from the Nepal Foreign Ministry. We'd also tried Nepal's Central Child Welfare Board but it refused to endorse the trip. Its then Director told us not to waste our time and to allow Maiti Nepal to deal with a problem of this scale. We ignored that guidance as enough time had been lost and we knew that Maiti Nepal didn't enter India to conduct rescues. However, we did decide to take a journalist with us who could witness the rescue and possibly provide some leverage with the Nepal embassy in Delhi and with the Indian authorities. She was Rubeena Mahato who wrote for the Nepali Times.

In spite of Rubeena's presence, our visit to the Nepal embassy was profoundly disappointing. Unbelievably they refused to give us an audience, eventually only issuing a one paragraph letter of support after we'd waited for two hours. We went from there to meet with our friends at ChildLine India and the formidable Nandita Rao. We were delighted when Nandita agreed to down tools and join us on the next day's flight south to Tamil Nadu, via Mumbai.

The mission didn't get off to the best of starts. The two family members who accompanied us were Shangmo and Karbu, Nisha's mother and older brother. Shangmo only spoke the Humli dialect but we managed as Karbu could act as an interpreter since he spoke both Humli and Nepali. It was hard work encouraging Shangmo along as before this operation she had never travelled in a car before let alone in a plane. But on the flight south Karbu developed severe abdominal pains and Bhaskar and I had to break the journey to admit him to hospital in Mumbai. The remainder of the party continued with Shangmo thereafter totally unable to communicate with them. Bhaskar and I resumed the journey the next day leaving the unfortunate Karbu in hospital with a case of suspected gallstones. We caught up with the rest of the team just after they had entered the MJC.

Arriving at the Centre I was struck by the enormity of the campus with its unappealing white blockhouses carrying the names in massive lettering of Richard Wurmbrand's late wife Sabina and Dr Job's two ill-fated sons. There was a school going from kindergarten up to grade 12, a 'college' offering 23 disciplines and a teacher training college. The MJC also boasted an auditorium and extensive sports facilities. On the face of it this was a far cry from what had been on offer back in Humla, but the fraud and perverse religious agenda were rotten. And the facilities aside, the quality of the educational output had to be called into question as not everyone is academically capable of completing grade 12, let alone obtaining degrees.

Attendance at the Centre by this stage had reached a staggering 1,041 with 541 'orphans' studying alongside 500 girls from local, well-off, Hindu families. These latter were paying monthly fees for education, food and accommodation, an income that subsidised the care and education of the 'orphans' on top of the sponsorship income. No doubt this extension of service to the local non-Christian community also offered some measure of protection. Therefore, through fundraising from child sponsorship and from international donors, Dr Job must have been reaping a rich harvest of money.

Unlike with the circus rescues, there was no need for police back up. Although the Centre would later lie that we had stormed in and seized the girls, the exchange was quite gentlemanly, at least initially. The local Child Welfare Committee was as supportive and discerning as we'd hoped they'd be. Because of the tip-off Dr Job must have known that we were on our way yet he'd chosen to stay at home in Delhi. A coward lurked behind all his posturing and rhetoric.

The MJC's Principal met us in Job's absence. In spite of being ostensibly a staunch Christian, she started off our exchange with a massive lie. Just like Raza Khan at the Roman Circus, she denied that there were any Nepali girls at the Centre. We showed her the children's pictures and profiles that we'd downloaded from their website and she then admitted the truth. Over the ensuing three hours of investigation our patience wore thin. It became patently obvious that there had been no proper child admission documentation.

239

At school lunchtime I found it so strange to meet trafficking victims who were dressed in pristine white school uniforms and speaking excellent English. This was a far cry from the dingy circuses. Once more, just like that first visit to Kathmandu Central Jail, I felt a strong sense of the surreal. But that link to Wurmbrand left me in no doubt that again I was standing in precisely the right spot.

While I reflected on this déjà vu, Rubeena Mahato was interviewing some of the girls who were excited at their possible return to Nepal. They sang the National Anthem for her and for us rescuers. They'd memorised the words from the mobile ring tone of a Nepali who had visited the Centre. One girl said to her:

'I want to go home. I wouldn't mind walking all the way to Nepal.'

Rubeena also witnessed Shangmo being reunited with her daughter, not that Nisha recognised her. She's been so young when Phadera had taken her away. Unfortunately, they couldn't communicate as Nisha no longer spoke Humli. Here was very obvious damage that PP Job had inflicted upon this family In Christ's name.

'I want to speak to Dr Job now,' I insisted just after lunch.

'You can't do that,' replied the Principal. 'Dr Job sleeps in the afternoon until 4 p.m. in the interests of his health. He has high blood pressure. I'm sorry, he cannot be disturbed.'

'Madam,' I answered, 'I don't think you have grasped the gravity of the situation. Can I remind you that the Disciples woke up Jesus when there was a storm on Galilee? Why's this guy so important?'

Nandita's patience snapped. 'If you don't wake him up now, he'll find himself waking up in prison. Now do it.'

The Principal relented and Nandita, Shailaja and I got to speak to the great man on the phone. His reaction to Shailaja was more reminiscent of Pontius Pilate rather than of Jesus.

'My work is complete. As far as I'm concerned, you can take all the children that are staying there.'

So much for his devotion to Emily. I asked Shailaja to pass me the phone:

'Dr Job, we've found a real mess here and it's one of your making. Your organisation will need to fund the return of these children to their families and their aftercare.'

I found it hard to believe just how meek he was in reply. All he could say was 'Yes, yes, yes.' This was far from being the firebrand preacher I had expected. He must have been a total walkover for someone like Phadera.

By this stage the local Child Welfare Committee had concluded that this whole business stank to high heaven, so to speak. The Committee members took the decision, as the local authority, to remove all the Nepali children from the Centre and to hand them over to us for repatriation. The CWC gave the Centre 15 days to provide them with their child admission documentation.

Shailaja and the girls set off on a week-long train journey across India that paused again in Gorakhpur where Nisha had last been seven years before. Here the children became the responsibility of the local CWC, one of whom had strong personal connections with Maiti Nepal. Predictably, he attempted to hand the children over to Maiti Nepal but we knew this was not in the girls' best interests. They had now built a relationship with us as their rescuers and this should be the foundation of their rehabilitation and reintegration. The attempt failed and Gorakhpur District Magistrate directed that the party should be repatriated without further delay.

At this point, Bhaskar and I who had returned to Nepal separately drove nine hours through the night from Kathmandu to meet the group and help prevent any further glitches or attempts at hijack. We'd invested so much time and money in this operation and in gaining the girls' confidence that we wanted to see this through to completion ourselves.

As we approached Bhairahawa in our jeep Bhaskar took a call on his mobile. It was Shailaja:

'DB Phadera is waiting here for you.'

A very excited group of girls greeted our arrival in Bhairahawa. They had clearly bonded well with Shailaja during the journey north. However, in their midst was the menacing, swaggering presence of DB, determined to spoil the party. Snake-eyed, he was watching our every move, assessing the threat to his operation. Netra Bhandari was by his side. So was another of his goons called Jagat Dhami, a lean-faced black belt third Dan in karate. DB was intent upon reclaiming the girls and to a certain extent that was his right. For within the 23 girls he and his henchmen had some relatives, including 'Emily' and DB's own seven-year-old daughter, now called 'Hosanna'. DB rebuked her for having returned to Nepal although she'd had no choice in the matter.

Jagat Dhami must have been disappointed that there was to be no physical confrontation in Bhairahawa that day. Once again, my white face (rather than my brawn) had provided some protection. We settled for eyeing one another and just like outside the New Raj Kamal Circus, our giving the appearance of not being rattled. Still, the threat was very palpable as DB took pictures of us. In response I photographed him. Eventually the District authorities passed the buck by ruling that the police should take all the girls to Kathmandu where the formal handover could take place.

Once back in Kathmandu the 23 girls became divided into two groups. The larger of the groups was under the control of DB either through these girls being related or by his influence over their parents who were from higher caste families. The smaller group, that included Nisha, was mainly drawn from poorer Sherpa caste families who weren't to be intimidated by this thug. These children's parents either reclaimed them or agreed that they should come under our care and protection.

DB didn't waste time in launching his backlash. He took 'his' group of girls from office to office claiming that the girls' education had been disrupted by a bunch of ill-advised adventurers who were headline-grabbing and dollar-farming. He accused us of doing nothing to help the girls post-rescue. Of course, as I mentioned earlier, we had budgeted for providing for all the girls in advance of a possible mass rescue.

The main reason we weren't helping DB's group of girls was that they were in his hands while he used them as a tool against us. The second reason was that the fine folks at the MJC had taken a dog-in-the-manger approach, refusing to issue educational transfer certificates. Without these documents we couldn't admit the girls to a new school in Nepal. Such was their interest in the girls' welfare. MJC continued to lie by alleging that we'd repatriated the girls based upon a false pretext i.e. they believed they were going back to Nepal merely for a holiday. In fact it was the Coimbatore Child Welfare Committee, as the investigating authority, which had sent them home for good, not us.

The Nepal media got onto the story, of course, and for the most part accepted DB's stance. The papers pilloried us for our rash actions. I suppose our being naïve, meddling foreigners is an easy stereotype to sell to journalists in a land where xenophobia is never far beneath the surface. The normally insightful Republica newspaper printed a front-page report damning us for what we had done. Their journalist accused us of having conducted a fake rescue and alleged that we had failed to take proper responsibility for the consequences of our action. He described the operation as having been an 'apparently impulsive act' when it had been nothing of the sort. The report quoted the local police chief, Deputy Superintendent of Police (DSP) Puja Singh, describing this as 'a hasty act' even though this had been nothing of the sort. The girls' release had followed considered examination of Michael Job Centre records (or lack of them) by the local Child Welfare Committee. But according to this narrative, we were cowboys while DB was the true philanthropist. Or Good Samaritan, depending upon your viewpoint.

The most vicious media attack came from a Nepali television channel called Avenues TV that produced a venomous 20-minute report on national TV. They followed that with their camera crew trying to force entry to our children's refuge before being turned away. In a subsequent broadcast they interviewed Phadera and filmed him issuing death threats against us. He announced:

'The concerned Ministry should take us seriously and if they don't for us the final option is to set the organisation on fire. They won't expect to die. We will create agitation...we know what to do....where to find those people and we know how to give "treatment"....and we really will.'

The alarming thing was that the Revd Phadera was making these statements from within the Social Welfare Council offices – a government building. He was rampant. It felt to me like we were very much out of our depth, caught up in a riptide that could take us right out of Nepal. No one dared to speak out to defend us.

Perhaps, as with the deportations of the Jews in the 1940s and with Hans, the onlookers justified their inaction by using the same old cop-out of our having brought this situation upon ourselves. Most pathetic of all were the fellow NGOs who preferred to stay out of trouble.

One NGO even seemed to toss us an anchor rather than a lifeline. DB's agitating group's itinerary in Kathmandu had included the office of Maiti Nepal. DB didn't go in person as he'd have been known very well there, so the front man for this visit, and at subsequent press conferences, was his brother in law, the spy Netra Bhandari.

After their meeting with Maiti's Founder, Anuradha Koirala, she phoned me up to hear what this was all about. I gave her the background, advised her of Netra's infamous relative and suggested that he was manipulating her organisation. After quite a pleasant chat she urged me to help the girls - which we had been trying to do - and we agreed to speak again one week later. To my horror, that very afternoon, and in response to the Avenues TV coverage, Anuradha called up the Nepali Prime Minister. During a live televised radio phone-in, she told him that an 'organisation' had been acting inappropriately. I have no idea why Anuradha took this needless action, but it was very unhelpful and served only to strengthen a trafficker's case against us.

The only voice that spoke out on our behalf was journalist Rubeena Mahato. Indignant, she wrote a follow up article in the Nepali Times in which she stated, based upon what she had witnessed at the rescue, that we should be 'commended rather than condemned'. But we were in the firing line. To paraphrase the eighteenth-century Irish statesman Edmund Burke, evil was triumphing while good men did nothing. The papers besmirched the name Esther Benjamins and for the first time Nepalis were sending us hate mail.

We stayed calm and I decided to temporarily close our office building so that it couldn't become the focus for street protest or physical attack. Instead we set up a virtual office in the lounge of the nearby Summit Hotel and in that respect, business continued as usual. I also had to take personal security measures, siting an armed guard on my home. We recruited a tough former Gurkha who would shadow Bev, Alisha and Joe on their daily walk to and from school. In previous rescues I'd felt fairly safe after returning from the circuses but now the threat was now literally very close to home.

The response from the authorities was mixed but largely negative. We registered a written complaint with the police regarding Phadera's trafficking. The police wouldn't accept this as a so-called 'First Information Report (FIR)', as its investigation would have made it mandatory by law for Phadera to have been taken into custody. Again, police officer Puja Singh blocked us. She admired Phadera as being a local hero for saving these children from a life of penury in Humla. So what if there had been some fraudulent activity or dodgy religious intentions? The material end justified the means. Also, Puja had every reason to tread warily. If she hadn't taken this line there'd have been every possibility that through Phadera's political clout she'd find herself posted out of cushy Kathmandu to some far-flung part of Nepal – like Humla. Exchanges at her police station became heated with Phadera coaxing his large group of family members to harangue our small team.

Bhaskar Karki told me to stay away that day as he felt the presence of a white face could be counterproductive. With typical courage Bhaskar and Shailaja stood their ground before their accusers. This gave Puja the opportunity to show her power by locking up Shailaja, Bhaskar and Phadera for 24 hours, ostensibly to calm the situation. At their release she reminded them that she had the authority to detain them for much longer. You don't want to mess with the Nepal police where physical violence against detainees is endemic.

As his next move the devious Phadera encouraged seventeen parents from the larger group into registering a formal complaint against us with the Ministry of Women, Children and Social Welfare. The Minister in turn ordered the NGO governing body, the Social Welfare Council, to investigate our actions. This was a one-sided inquiry from the outset. Although DB's own NGO was also registered with SWC no questions were asked of its role in the illegal transfer of children across the border to India even though we showed a letter naming them as the involved party. The Ministry instructed SWC to take 'strict action' against our team even *before* the inquiry had been conducted. We were called to the SWC to give an account of ourselves. This presented no problem as all our paperwork was in order and we had worked in conjunction with both the Indian and Nepali authorities all the way. When I asked the SWC inquiry team if they would be interviewing Phadera one of its members told me with a wry smile that they'd already done so and found him a 'very aggressive man'.

The SWC inquiry ended up finding in our favour subject to our providing for all the girls. We assured them that this had always been our intention. By contrast we received short shrift at a follow-up meeting at the Ministry where Puja Singh and representatives of the Ministry and the Central Child Welfare Board ganged up on us. The CCWB challenged us to state on whose authority we had conducted the rescue. Of course, this hadn't included CCWB as they'd declined to write a letter of support (for whatever reason). We responded that we felt we'd had enough official sanction to proceed given our prior written agreements with the SWC, the Foreign Ministry and (eventually) the Nepal Embassy. The Director of CCWB asked silly mischievous questions like what we had been doing with the girls during the long journey back from MJC. He knew fine well the distances involved and the struggles required to overcome Indian bureaucracy at Child Welfare Committee level.

Eventually the meeting broke up with our being left in no doubt about the fragility of our position. It was obvious we weren't going to have any success with prosecuting Phadera; we'd been lucky not to have been thrown out of Nepal.

Back in India in the immediate aftermath of the rescue Hindu activists had demonstrated outside the MJC, correctly accusing the Centre of proselytising. The local Child Welfare Committee's continued investigation found more non-Nepali children not to be orphans and they sent 46 girls to Assam and Bihar in northeast India. In October the Child Welfare Committee withdrew MJC's registration under the Juvenile Justice Act. Later we were encouraged to learn that the authorities had instructed for the total closure of the MJC with the directive that all children were to be returned in batches to their parent countries under the supervision of the Child Welfare Committee. In contrast with the resistance in Nepal everything seemed to be going our way in Tamil Nadu.

Then history repeated itself with everything falling quiet in India after a rescue. Little further information emerged with the Indian authorities being tight-lipped about the investigation. Meanwhile Dr Job used his local political connections to ensure the Centre's survival. Increasingly it looked like the Child Welfare Committee was going to lose this battle. On his website Dr Job acknowledged the support of Tamil Nadu Chief Minister Dr Jayaram Jayalalithaa in protecting his Centre. He described former actress Dr Jayalalithaa as being 'very religious' and instrumental in the repeal of anti-forcible conversion legislation in 2005.

In spite of her Christian ideals Jayalalithaa had a reputation for extravagance. She holds two Guinness Records for the wedding with the most guests and the largest banquet/reception from the marriage of her foster son in 1995. Forty corruption cases had been filed against her and in the past, she had even served a short prison sentence for bribery. In common with Dr Job she held the belief that she could do as she wished with Divine sanction. Dr Job was confident enough of the support of this political heavyweight to decline the invitation to attend the Coimbatore Child Welfare Committee's inquiry. In another show of cowardice, he sent a deputy in his place while he embarked on another of his foreign tours where he could bad-mouth us to naive supporters.

Meanwhile, I had set my sights on Dr Job's international support. My first target was his supporting UK charity Love in Action. I had written to the charity after the rescue to share the UNICEF report and our findings, politely inviting them to help us sort out the mess. There was no reply. I wrote once more, explaining that there was now significant UK media interest in the case and suggesting that it might be in their charity's best interests to respond and to be seen to be cooperating. Once again, they gave no reply. Probably they thought I was bluffing but a few days later our work received half a page of coverage in the Daily Telegraph, the UK's largest broadsheet. Journalist Dean Nelson's article with its unmissable headline 'The Indian Preacher and the Fake Orphan Scandal' laid it all out, naming and shaming Love in Action. Dean gave examples of the fake orphans whom he'd spoken with and reported how Love in Action had provided Dr Job with £18,000 in funding between 2007 and 2010. The charity had declined to comment to him too. The article sparked an e-mail from a Christian minister in the south of England. He congratulated me on the exposé as his church had once hosted a visit by Dr Job and they'd hadn't liked the cut of his jib at all.

My third letter to Love in Action having met with no reply, I then wrote to the UK charity regulatory body, The Charity Commission, inviting them to investigate Love in Action for involvement in child trafficking. The charity shut down in December 2011.

My background reading revealed that the MJC's main international support aside from Love in Action came from the USA and Holland. At first it seemed like I'd had a good meeting of minds with the prime mover in the USA, a Maryland-based Vietnam veteran, Tom Cropper, who doubled up as a Director of the MJC. He replied at once to my initial approach pledging his support in the interests of the girls. Again, I showed him all my evidence but before long he was writing complete nonsense in his blog:

'Three months ago, the government of Nepal changed. It is now controlled by the Communist Party. Christian persecution is increasing dramatically now in that country. Today, the government of India, based upon the demands of this new communist government came for 40 of our girls (of Nepali descent) at the Michael Job Centre for Orphan Girls and took them away.'

Nepal was certainly *not* under Communist control and nor was Christian persecution on the rise; the country had in fact become very liberal in respect of religion. By mid-November he wrote to me that he felt what we had done had been a mistake and that we were now on opposite sides. Soon afterwards, in January 2012, he visited Kathmandu to follow up on the girls' welfare. Sporting a Stetson, my staff spotted him rubbing shoulders with DB even though I'd told him all about his sordid background.

The Dutch sullied themselves too. In January 2012 I learned that representatives of 'Hulp Vervolgde Christenen' (HVC – 'Help Persecuted Christians') were in town. A very excited Katharina Tomoff and Micha Luedecke, my friends from our German supporting charity, Hatemalo, came to my office one afternoon. That morning as they'd been having coffee in their hotel, they'd been astounded to overhear my name being mentioned at an adjacent table. Kathmandu is indeed a small place. They had tuned in as best they could to what was a meeting between a group of Nepalis and two foreigners, taking surreptitious photographs as they did so. Unfortunately, they could only catch snatches of the conversation, but based upon my prior research I could identify one of the foreigners as being Jan Bor, the Director of HVC. I worked out that one of the Nepalis was DB's brother-in-law, the spy Netra Bhandari.

That evening, with a certain sense of mischief, I wrote to Bor for the first time, letting him know that I knew he was in town. I suggested that if he was on a fact-finding visit then perhaps the most appropriate thing to do was to meet with me and I could tell him everything he needed to know. Bor didn't reply but his companion, HVC Board member Abwin Luteijn, agreed to meet at a local hotel to see my research material. His conclusion was that Phadera was 'probably' a bad man but he still found our action inappropriate. After an hour or so I realised the meeting was pointless and left. In the eyes of these people I was the devil incarnate for having disrupted the Lord's work.

A line was drawn under this particular episode in 2011 when our Trust picked up the tab for the cost of the returnees' continued care and education in Nepal. This had always been the charity's intention from day one. Although many of the girls and their families continued to criticise us, I can only hope that one day all of these girls who were exploited for financial and 'spiritual' gain will understand and appreciate what we did for them. Most likely they won't, but personally I have no regrets and with hindsight wouldn't have done anything differently.

As for Nisha, she was one of six girls who joined the excellent Ama Ghar children's home run by the lovely, genuine, American woman, Bonnie Ellison. Some months later, a relative called to collect Nisha as the family wanted to see off her younger brother at the airport. He was on his way to join a Buddhist monastery in south India. Because of China's now defunct one-child policy Tibetan monasteries in India were struggling to find Tibetan children to train as monks. In desperation, they began sourcing Nepali children from Humla and other mountain regions who have a similar appearance. It seems that religious trafficking and associated deception isn't just a 'Christian' phenomenon. On this occasion different religions were splitting up the same family.

S he was tired of being hungry all of the time.

That had been her school friend Ganga's reason for getting married. As Radhika Yadav walked home from the ceremony that afternoon she wondered if Ganga's yearning to have a full stomach would become reality. Most likely not, since she hadn't married well, her father unable to afford the dowry that would have bought her a better husband. In Sarlahi District, southeast Nepal poverty embraced poverty, poverty to deepen. And it would be propagated to another generation with the inevitable pregnancy that would follow within a month or two. That was the Nepali way. Ganga had now become her husband's property and his family would expect her to contribute towards its overall good by producing a son. The sooner, the better.

A pair of orange butterflies arose in a vertical dance above the rubbish that lay in the ditch by the track. She stopped to watch them weave their meandering path skywards and then they were gone. Maybe she too could rise above destitution and make something of her life.

Unusually for a girl of 15 from her village, Radhika was still attending school. Ganga had been the last of her former classmates to get married. Some had married when they were 12 or 13, pressurised by parents who knew that the younger the girl, the lower the dowry. A first period and the girl would be gone, parents ensuring that she remained untarnished by an illicit relationship that would set village tongues wagging.

A girl had no choice about who to marry; that was a parental decision that could have been taken place behind the scenes several years before. The only alternative was to elope as Ashmita had done. She'd crossed into India with a boy from the village a year ago for a love marriage. She hadn't been seen since. Perhaps she was doing alright now. Would she be any worse off than her sister Savita who'd had two children by the time she was 14? One of her babies had died. The doctor had said that she'd married too young to be a mother.

She picked some flowers from the wayside bushes as she strolled along, assembling a posy of reds and yellows.

A doctor, yes, Radhika would love to be a doctor and help her community. She could wear a white coat and wrap a stethoscope casually around her neck. Her father, Rajkumar, had been very good about keeping her at school, saying that he wanted her to achieve her potential even if, like all daughters, she would ultimately be lost to

250

another family. Often in Nepali families the parents send their sons to private schools and daughters to government schools as sons are worth investing in. But Rajkumar had made no difference between her and her 11-year-old brother Rajan. Radhika loved him for that. It cost money to keep her at school although it was supposed to be free; her father had still had to pay for her books, stationery and uniform and of course sacrifice what she could have earned by dropping out early. He didn't mind as he said that she was clever and worth it. Radhika hoped that she wouldn't let him down with her class 10 results. He'd already said that she could do 'Plus Two'[22]if she did well and after that she might qualify for a scholarship to medical school. She'd heard of a few of these being available to poor families.

Radhika enjoyed marriage ceremonies even if they were so often framed with sadness and false hopes. These and religious festivals were of course social occasions when for some time you could dress up, dance, chat and pause reality for a while. But that day she'd had to excuse herself from the festivities a little early as Rajan was on his own at home. Her mother had gone in for an operation and she and her father would be away for a few days. As she arrived at her hut everything was unusually quiet for a Saturday afternoon – most people were still at the ceremony. There was no sign of Rajan. He was probably still playing in the jungle. She'd seen him go off that morning with his homemade wheel on the end of a stick, trundling it proudly down the track.

As she entered the hut she was grabbed from behind.

Radhika thrashed and fought as best she could but he was too strong for her. She cried out but there was no one to hear her – the man pulled off her shawl and stuffed it into her mouth. He raped her. Radhika fainted from the pain.

She was aroused by Rajan's scream. He'd found her sprawled on the floor, half naked, her pretty clothes covered in blood, flowers scattered on the floor. The man had fled. Radhika asked Rajan to run and fetch auntie who was still at the ceremony but not to speak with anyone else. As soon as they were back auntie called their father but he was a few hours away and, as it was now late evening, unable to return until the following day.

Meantime neighbours had gone to find the attacker – Radhika knew him. He could expect a severe beating. Auntie took Radhika to the health post as she was still bleeding. After that she stayed the night with

---

[22] Grades 11 and 12 – Higher Secondary education

her, helping her to wash but keeping her clothes as evidence for the police.

But when Rajkumar returned he wanted the rapist to get more than a beating. He approached the Chairman of the *panchayat*, the village assembly, to seek justice for his daughter. The assembly of village elders, all men, met three days later. Rajkumar was shocked and horrified at their decision. They ruled that, as no man would now want to marry a rape victim, Radhika and her assailant should become husband and wife. They were both single so there could be no obstacle to the arrangement. Rajkumar would have to pay the rapist a dowry of 500,000 rupees (£3,300) to seal the deal. He protested that his daughter's life had been ruined and that this was also unaffordable for him. The panchayat knew that he eked a living from selling cosmetics in a wayside stall. The only concession they would make was to reduce the dowry to 300,000 rupees. Rajkumar felt that he had to accept the ruling as refusal could have led to the panchayat expelling him and his family from the village.

He tried to borrow the money from friends and neighbours but they were poor too. Time was against him as Radhika was to be married in one week's time so he had to sell the little bit of land he owned at the back of his house to raise the dowry. Next, he had to steel himself and deliver the money to the rapist's family four days before the wedding. But when Rajkumar arrived at the house he found that the boy and his father had both absconded.

Enough was enough. Rajkumar decided to take Radhika to the police in Birgunj, a two-hour bus ride away. He took Radhika's blood-soaked clothes with him in a plastic bag. At the station they were shown into the bare back room that the police used for interviews. Two male policemen sat behind a desk, one of them lounging with his arm over the backrest as if awaiting some entertainment. His knee was jiggling in lewd anticipation. Radhika was given a seat before them, Rajkumar had to remain standing. They weren't offered tea.

'How many times were you raped?' began the first policeman.

'I don't remember,' murmured Radhika.

'Did it happen on the floor or on the bed?' asked the second.

'The floor.'

'Was this your first time? A pretty girl like you must have had a boyfriend or two. Look up and tell me the truth, child.'

Radhika's eyes met his, but her tongue refused to move.

The intrusive questioning was interrupted when the door opened and an inspector of police strode in, vainglorious in his crisp blue uniform and peaked cap. The reclining policeman jumped up and offered him Radhika's seat. Rajkumar could see that he was a Brahmin from the hills so he couldn't expect much off him. Or at least not without a bribe.

'Why have you waited so long to come here?' he demanded from Rajkumar. 'This is very suspicious. How do I know you aren't lying?'

'I hoped this could be settled in the village,' he replied. Then he opened the bag and the inspector peered inside, his aquiline nose wrinkling.

'If you'd come to me first, I could have got you a better deal. The boy would have had to pay you,' the inspector said. He smirked. 'And we deliver quality beatings. We have a female constable who is a real professional. She never leaves any bruises.'

The inspector instructed the constable to file the complaint, but Rajkumar was unconvinced. He knew that often the police would record cases in a fake register, tricking the complainant. To get into the real register and ensure the case progressed he'd have to pay for it.

As a last resort Rajkumar went from there to the office of the local paper.

'I've made a mistake and been belittled by everyone because I am poor,' he declared to the journalist. 'Our panchayat didn't allow me to make decisions and I had to agree to what they said. But now I will not tolerate this and I will fight for my daughter's rights. I need everyone's help in this.'

The truth was that there wasn't a great deal that Rajkumar would be able to do. The local media outcry would soon blow over and the police would be half-hearted about finding the rapist. Radhika's physical injuries would heal but the mental scars would burn long and deep. She had become a social outcast in the village and could plan on neither a marriage nor a career. Her childhood, her life, her dreams had come to an end.

19.   Journey's End

In January 2012 I took what must have seemed to friends, family and charity supporters as being the most bewildering, even callous, of decisions. I notified my Trustees that after 13 years in the driving seat I would be moving on following my return from Nepal. To leave the charity that I had founded and that bore Esther's name was not a decision that I took lightly. Of course not. But I knew it was the right one for a number of reasons.

The first – and simplest – of these is that my personal vision had changed from what it had been in 1999. In my ignorance, I'd founded the charity to set up a children's home in Esther's memory. That wasn't much of a vision but, as I have explained, it was all that I could conceive of at that time given my limited insight. It was only after I began working in Nepal that I became drawn into the challenge of fighting child trafficking which, as it transpired, was a more appropriate activity to undertake in Esther's name.

This shift in vision had been controversial from the start. I've described how back in 2003 the Board of Trustees was divided on whether or not we should take on the circus traffickers. Thankfully history has proven that the Board took the right decision at that time even though, granted, we were fortunate that no one was killed in the ensuing confrontations. In spite of getting Board agreement, reservations lingered about adopting such an aggressive stance and were propagated down through the years. The Trustees worried like hell about the circus rescue operations and they were right to be concerned given what we were up against. And I couldn't fault them their worries as it's part of a Trustee's remit to consider and mitigate risks.

Board concerns reached a peak during the Dr Job affair. That operation proved to be very costly not just in financial terms but also in negative media coverage in Nepal, some of which I suspected at least one or two Trustees came to believe themselves. Such is the power of the trafficker. This, together with the heightened danger that accompanied the rescue in the form of Phadera's threats, gave the Board the collective jitters. A couple of Trustees argued that this was a time to consolidate, protect our funds and ensure a secure future for the children already at the refuge. This viewpoint reflected a reversion to our original vision and I can't criticise them for remaining true to that. It was me who had changed, or, more accurately, evolved.

I contended that we shouldn't allow the refuge to become an end in itself and we had to continue the audacious rescue work alongside Shailaja. If we did so I believed the funds would look after themselves. But I lost that argument and I found myself being reined back. The charity seemed to have lost its fighting edge – an aspect that was so quintessential to Esther's spirit and values - and there was nothing I could do to address that from within.

After a great deal of thought - and many sleepless nights - I concluded that staying on in any capacity and risking a conflict would be unseemly and terminal to the Trust. I gave the Trustees a generous six months' notice of my intention to leave and to allow them time to reorganise and define their future, more limited, goals without my influence. That was the responsible and mature thing to do. I felt that I had achieved something really appropriate and substantial in Esther's name – the closure of not one but two child trafficking routes – and I could certainly settle for that.

By any standards mine had been a remarkable journey in terms of practical achievements. My charity had raised millions of pounds and made a lasting difference to the lives of so many children in Nepal. I estimated that we had freed 700 children from the circuses alone, half of these from our rescue operations and the other half released voluntarily by the circuses to avoid our unwelcome attentions. A further 150 children could be added to that whom we'd brought out of prisons, off the streets, out of Indian 'children's shelters' and from the Michael Job Centre. And critically we'd put 19 traffickers into prison with legal rulings in both Nepal and India that ensured a sustainable result.

The immediate knock-on effect of my departure was that Shailaja and Bhaskar left too, unenthusiastic about working with anyone else. If truth be told, I think all of us needed a break after the intensity of the previous eight years that had been so draining physically and emotionally.

For my part I had things to attend to in our personal lives back in the UK. We had to find a new home (our London home had burned down in 2011) and Alisha and Joe had reached an age where we wanted to get them settled into school. Moreover, we had to cater for the needs of my increasingly frail in-laws who were now both well into their eighties (since deceased). The family – including our two Nepali dogs – relocated to live in Devon, southwest England. But I also needed the time and space to reflect upon what had also been a very spiritual journey. It had been a true leap of faith for me given my lack of charitable and personal credentials back in 1999. It would be easy to point to my success as being the reward of keeping that faith through all the vicissitudes of living and working in Nepal. That is certainly a valid conclusion, but I returned to the UK with some profound unanswered concerns that I needed space to ponder.

For one thing I had to reflect upon the old conundrum of human suffering in the presence of, we are told, a loving, benevolent and omnipotent God. Why did Esther – like so many other good and genuine people – have to suffer and perish while the wicked people I encountered seem to be such inveterate survivors who go on to die in their beds? Why did those Nepalese children that I helped have to endure such an unspeakable start in life, robbed of their childhood and innocence? The conventional Christian religion that I was brought up in certainly didn't give me the right answers. In fact, all it seemed to offer was patently wrong ones.

For example, in the month after my return from Nepal I took a short holiday in Brittany. Curiosity drew me into the American cemetery at St James, the scene of fierce battles and the bloody sacrifice that followed the D Day landings. The immaculate ranks of 4,410 headstones echoed the soldiers' discipline while the lawns were as close-cropped as a GI's crew-cut. In the midst of such numbers I could still see the human factor; 83 headstones bore the Star of David, Jews who'd stood a fighting chance against Hitler, and this fallen legion included 21 sets of brothers. But I was struck also by a wall tablet inside the memorial chapel that carried the lofty words of a prayer that surely can't be right in the midst of such carnage:

'O God
Who art the Author of peace
And Lover of concord
Defend us
Thy humble servants
In all assaults of our enemies
That we
Surely trusting in thy defense
May not fear the power
Of any adversaries.'

Self-evidently, the occupants of this cemetery hadn't been defended and a dreadful burden of sorrow had been visited upon their loved ones. I don't believe this reference to an 'Author of peace' is altogether a biblical concept either. On the contrary. For just a few lines after the Gates of Bronze reference in Isaiah it reads:

'I am the Lord, there is no other;
I make the light, I create darkness,
Author alike of prosperity and trouble.
I, the Lord, do all these things.'

An 'Author of Trouble' rather than of peace seems to rest better with my experience and for that matter with the Hindu deity of Shiva, the 'destroyer'. As I understand the Hindu faith, destruction goes hand in hand with creation or re-creation. Without the destruction a better set of circumstances can't arise. So did the 'Author of Trouble' visit Himself upon Esther and me? If so, I could only infer that this cruel visitation was necessary in the interests of the greater good. Perhaps both of us had to go through this hell for me to rebound with the determination I'd need to take on the circuses and Phadera. If I am right, this is an excruciating conclusion and the inference of such a ruthless God is chilling.

The second question which I had to struggle with is why the Divine silence? Or, in my case, why only the enigmatic, almost teasing, winks and whispers of coincidence? After what I have experienced I haven't the slightest shred of a doubt that God exists, a viewpoint that Jung had reached by the end of his life. In a television interview from that time he described this as being for him not a case of 'belief' but of 'knowledge'. Also like me, his was a mysterious God who is inadequately defined by religions. More than that, he wrote that 'One of the main functions of organised religion is to protect people against a direct experience of God'. But I still can't understand the coyness.

The only half satisfactory answer I can find to the dilemma is that without this silence there would be no call to have a faith, the faith that when mobilised has the power to move mountains.

There was a third and most difficult question that I had to contemplate; had Esther's death been 'worth it'? Ultimately only she can be the judge of that in terms of what has been achieved in her name but I can guess what she would say. From a personal perspective I have to try and balance her loss against a reality that makes for an uncomfortable admission: After her death I went on to live life to the full and in a more rewarding way than I could ever have imagined. I chose the freedom she'd have wanted for me and the fruits of that were not to be missed. I have been privileged to work with real heroes and never felt more alive than during my time in Nepal. The buzz of entering a circus, resolute yet without the slightest idea of what was going to happen next, has been unforgettable. How can I compare the exhilaration of rescuing hundreds of children from these circumstances with what would have been the professional alternative of restoring teeth? Moreover, beyond these temporal experiences I have tuned into an all-important spiritual dimension that would otherwise have gone unnoticed. If only there could have been some other way of accessing it.

Notwithstanding all the positives - personal, professional and spiritual - there can be no entirely happy ending to the story. That's due to the scale of the tragedy that propelled me onto this path in the first place combined with a refractory sense of loss. But paradoxically these two leave me permanently restless and have become empowering factors.

Finally, Carl Jung wrote, 'As far as we can discern, the sole purpose of human existence is to kindle a light in the darkness of mere being.' I managed to relight Esther's candle, find purpose, and through my future work in Nepal that candle can burn brighter still.

Let's see what happens next.

F ather Barnabas chose to start his day early; by 5 a.m. he was sitting at his little desk, ready to start his daily devotions. This usually gave him a clear hour before the first of the day's phone calls could intrude. Nepalis liked to call at first light, apparently indifferent to the privacy and possible sleep requirements of a 65-year-old priest. That way, at least, the caller could be sure to speak with the intended target whatever the consequences.

Nevertheless, he had been pleased to arise early that morning as the 11th June 2018 was a minor highlight in Father Barnabas's spiritual calendar. It was the Feast Day of his namesake, Saint Barnabas. He'd chosen the name for himself when he entered the Jesuit order forty years before. For he admired Saint Paul's travelling companion, he who had left his homeland and creature comforts to spread the Gospel far afield, perhaps in a more low-key way than the rather bombastic Paul. Just as he had swapped the canals and beaches of Kerala for the mountains of Nepal to be a witness for Christ, aspiring that his deeds should speak louder than words could ever do.

According to his Roman calendar, the Feast Day lessons to reflect upon were from Acts 11 and 13, Psalm 98 and Matthew 5, the Sermon on the Mount. In the first of these he read how Barnabas had left Jerusalem to visit the early church in Antioch:

'When he arrived and saw the grace of God,
he rejoiced and encouraged them all
to remain faithful to the Lord in firmness of heart,
for he was a good man, filled with the Holy Spirit and faith.'

He paused to gaze out of his window. Torrential early monsoon rains smothered the dreary landscape in sodden embrace. Yet the dawn was now beginning to claim ascendancy over the night, heralding another day's toil for the women in the tea estates that were becoming defiantly visible in the near distance. The lone trees that were scattered through the plantations and that provided shade by day stood inimical in the half-light, rising like skeletal fingers from the poisoned earth. The insecticides and herbicides used in tea cultivation made for few bugs, butterflies or birds, beyond the undiscerning mynah birds that scavenged everywhere. In this dismal place Father Barnabas found little call for rejoicing and, rather than being filled with faith, he had come to know only personal doubts and frustration in the twilight years of his ministry.

Soon it would be the third anniversary of his transfer from picturesque Tipling, a mountain community in the west of Nepal, which enjoyed Mount Ganesh as a majestic backdrop. He had exchanged what could at least superficially have been seen as a rural idyll for this dull and downtrodden society on the eastern Terai. In Tipling there had been a certain sense of dignity and pride even in the midst of the poverty but in Jhapa the people had long since lost their self-respect and spirit. Most of them were at best in Limbo since reconfigurations of the border that had happened generations before had left ethnic Indians living within Nepal. Life had continued much as before but these people were effectively stateless, lacking the citizenship that gave them any rights in either country.

Rather than being a witness for Christ, Father Barnabas had become witness to servitude and docility. In this dreadful place a person slaved away in the tea plantations picking 26kg of tea in exchange for a couple of dollars a day. The poverty was compounded by endemic alcohol abuse and depression was widespread. The social impact was devastating with child marriages, high infant mortality, sexual abuse and the highest girl suicide rate of any District in Nepal. This was a far cry from Kerala which enjoyed the best literacy and life expectancy of any State in India.

His frustration stemmed primarily from an inability to speak out against the wrongs of local society. Unlike in Tipling where he'd had a voice, this was a tight knit community that was wary of outsiders. As a foreigner and a Christian within a Hindu heartland, his position was particularly precarious. If he attempted to rock the boat, he'd be the one who'd end up falling out or, more accurately, thrown out. Rather than being in a position to condemn, the best he felt he could do was to show compassion and console. He'd do his rounds of the mud hut homes, offering words of comfort, especially trying to inspire the young ones in the midst of their misery.

This included encouraging attendance at the school that his Order had set up back in 1999 to provide free education for the children of the workers. Exam results were, at best, average as there was no scope for home study in such pitiful domestic circumstances. Also, the curriculum went no further than the tenth grade and the only real option for most of the girls was to marry and follow their mothers into the tea plantations. Wherever he looked, he saw only hopelessness and despair. Being passive didn't come readily to him; he was falling short of his calling and Jhapa felt more like Hell than Limbo.

It was 5 a.m. and Josephina had been up for an hour. Although just 16, she was already two years married and, as was the custom, living at her husband's parental home. She hadn't wanted to drop out of school but it was her father's wish that condemned her to a kind of domestic slavery at the whim of her mother-in-law. Cinderella-like, her day's chores began at 4.15 with cleaning the house, preparing food, tending to the chickens, anything really. Her one-year-old daughter, Rabina, was of course quite a handful while all this was going on.

By 6.30 she would be in the tea plantation to drop Rabina off at the childcare facility. This consisted of nothing more than a large tarpaulin supported by four corner posts and one in the middle, the infants under the supervision of a very old woman who was too unfit to pick tea leaves. Her task was made easier by the children being tied to the posts to stop them wandering off in search of their mothers. Every two hours or so the mothers would be allowed to return to the rudimentary shelter to breast-feed their children and settle them down. Aside from these breaks Josephina worked solidly through the day until 5 p.m. when she wound her way home in time to cook for her in-laws. Every day was the same apart from Saturday when the slavery was entirely confined to keeping her mother-in-law appeased.

Josephina saw nothing of her husband during the days and very little of him in the evenings either. Most of the time she had no idea where he was or the nature of his nocturnal activities but when he finally did return home he'd invariably have been drinking. Then the drama would begin as he asserted himself as the man of the house, his father a semi-invalid. Her husband gave her no support with bringing up Rabina but he did often talk about his wish for a son. The realisation of his dream would make Josephina's nightmare complete.

In the midst of her monotonous isolation, her stagnation, Josephina did look forward to Father Barnabas calling by. He'd drop in ever so casually to say hello on Saturday afternoons after morning Mass. Josephina felt like she had been one of his favourite pupils when he taught her English at the Catholic school. He'd discouraged her from dropping out but this hadn't been her choice. As an adolescent girl she was expected to be meek before the adults in her life; she had no voice. Now he urged her to try and look on the bright side of life and think of her lovely daughter but thoughts of Rabina and a future possible son only deepened her anguish. She had an all-consuming sense of desolation and couldn't see a future for any of them, born or unborn. Over the previous month she'd feigned illness when Father Barnabas called as she lacked the energy to see him or anyone else and fake happiness. She left that bluff to her mother-in-law. Josephina sensed that there was only one escape, she had hidden the rope and this grey morning would be her last. She knew which plantation tree she'd use.

Father Barnabas had just completed reading the second lesson, Psalm 98, when the phone rang. It was ten to six. As he took the call he winced. He contemplated absently the picture on the wall of a white-faced Christ with his sacred heart exposed, a pierced hand pointing to this symbol of his divine love for humanity. He replaced the receiver, put his weary forehead to the desk and prayed for the repose of Josephina's soul. There was no hurry to respond to this early morning call. Josephina was gone and he could call at the home later in the morning to console once again. He who had been powerless to intervene in any meaningful way and prevent another Jhapa girl from hanging herself.

Feeling suddenly very old and careworn, he returned to reading the Feast Day's third lesson, the Beatitudes from the Sermon on the Mount in Matthew 5:

'Blessed are the poor in spirit, for theirs is the Kingdom of heaven. Blessed are they who mourn, for they will be comforted. Blessed are the meek, for they will inherit the land.'

He closed his bible and murmured to himself, 'No Lord, not in Jhapa, not in Jhapa.'

The cockerel crowed in the garden outside.

Epilogue

"Three Ways"

One Sunday afternoon in August 2012 Dr Job suffered a massive heart attack while taking rest after lunch (as was his wont) and died soon afterwards. We are told that that morning he had delivered a particularly inspiring sermon to a church group in Hungary. He told his listeners that Christians should not be mere preachers of the Gospel, but demonstrators of it. His demonstrable legacy, the Michael Job Centre, continued thanks to the personal support of Jayalalithaa, although she in turn suffered a fatal cardiac arrest in December 2016.

The MJC does seem to have rebranded though, presenting itself these days as a benign centre for 'empowering the girl child through education'. Its evangelising agenda is now downplayed, however on websites such as that of their Swiss funder, EKU Foundation, can be found the myth perpetuated that the MJC exists for orphan girls. Wondrous signs continue unabated with the same site telling of a coconut tree that is bearing fruit after just two years. An agricultural engineer is quoted as saying, 'This is a miracle, which can only be explained by the fact that this plant has been nourished by the tears of the orphans.'

Dr Job's evangelising agenda has survived, mediated primarily by his Dutch co-workers. HVC evangelists are spending an increasing amount of time in Nepal itself as they use former MJC girls for outreach in their home District of Humla. In the HVC 2014 film *Gevonden Dochters* ('Found Daughters') girls are shown heading back to their villages for long-overdue reunions, incongruously overdressed in designer trekking gear. I wonder how the locals perceive this given that the girls can no longer communicate with them in their native dialect. A 'Pastor Philip' is leading this groundbreaking first missionary expedition but the film reveals that there is an additional presence who is spoiling the party – none other than Phadera's henchman, the black belt, third Dan, Jagat Dhami seen joining the girls on their outbound flight from Kathmandu. This bizarre situation is explained in a series of articles from 2013 in the Dutch religious paper *Reformatorisch Dagblad* which covered this church-planting project. The first deeply misleading report opens by saying that HVC has longstanding contacts in Humla through the Michael Job Centre. It was there that the Foundation came into contact with 17 christian girls aged 14 to 18 years old who wanted to return to Humla to bring the Gospel to their relatives. These girls were amongst hundreds who were procured by human traffickers (at least here there is an admission of trafficking). It continues by saying that the girls were sent home in 2011 at the insistence of the government, but happily they managed to stay in touch with HVC Chairman, Jan Bor aka 'Uncle Jan'. Happily, he has been able to facilitate the trip. There is no mention of HVC's involvement with the original trafficker. A subsequent article stated that the bodyguard of the human trafficker (i.e. Phadera) was on the flight because his boss was unhappy with the visit. He had tipped off the police and District authorities but Pastor Philip had been able to negotiate that the trip should continue on the strength of its associated humanitarian purpose.

That purpose was the apparent long overdue reunification of a father with his two daughters, 'Anja' and 'Miriam'. Abwin Luteijn described witnessing the moment everyone had been looking forward to:

'This happened in a very Nepalese way; I had to push the girls towards him. It became a clumsy welcome. Starting with a *Namaste* (good day) as if strangers, then a sort of handshake and half hug. And of course it made sense, as they hadn't seen each other for ten years and didn't recognise one another. Later that day they talked a lot. At the end of the day I asked the girls if they were now familiar with their father. They answered in the negative but were very happy to be with him and back in Humla with their relatives.'

There is another explanation for the awkward welcome. Shailaja recognised the father in the accompanying picture. He had come to Kathmandu in 2011 to collect his daughters after their first return from the Michael Job Centre. This wonderful reunification that the article likened to the story of The Prodigal Son was 'fake news'.

The HVC outlook on Phadera clearly became muddled. In an interview for the Dutch broadsheet *Trouw* in 2013 Jan Bor made an apparently amoral admission: 'I know that he [Phadera] is known as smuggler but he has very good connections at Government level. According to the girls, he is good for them. I allow him his value.'

In Gevonden Dochters Luteijn presents a different story. Profiling 'Anja' the film states: 'Phadera is one of the most notorious human traffickers in Nepal. During the Maoist war more than 1,300 children disappeared through him. The civil war brought him wealth. Phadera lives in the most inhospitable part of Nepal, the Humla region. In the village where Phadera lives he is well-regarded. There they do not know about him trafficking children as slaves or prostitutes. And, in order not to arouse suspicion, he even helped children from his village escape during the Maoist war. He also helped Anja, who lived near to him. Phadera took her, together with 21 others, to MJC in India.'

Notwithstanding their Damascene revelation, I remain denounced in the film. We are to believe that I became involved in a situation I didn't understand and harmed girls who had been Phadera's unsuspecting victims, forcibly repatriating them to Nepal.

As for DB, he's still a free man and his political connections will ensure that he remains that way. He may even be going places. In May 2016 the Nepal government nominated him to be one of the Members of the Karnali Development Commission. Karnali, which is in the Far West of Nepal, attracts huge amounts of foreign money ostensibly to be invested in infrastructure development. This is alarming. Perhaps there are bigger fish to fry these days than through the comparatively modest proceeds of child trafficking.

Of all the circus owners that we had to contend with, to the best of my knowledge only Lakhan Chaudhary received a custodial sentence, and even then, only a modest one considering the scale of his crimes. However, Haji Alim, former politician, child rapist and one of the two brothers who owned the Great Apollo Circus met with a worse fate. One morning In October 2018 he was found shot dead in his bedroom, a pistol and empty cartridges by his side. It is unclear if this was a case of suicide or murder. Violent death runs in the family. Back in 2013, following a family dispute over property, his third wife was stabbed to death by Haji Alim's son from his first marriage; he is currently in jail.

After I left Nepal Bhaskar became a stockbroker while Shailaja went to work for another NGO. By mid-2014 she was becoming restless. Her new employer appeared to be not quite sure how to use her. The solution was to try to accommodate this square peg of a dynamic woman into the round hole of a desk job. All Shailaja wanted to was to be out in the field, rescuing children. In late 2014 she resigned to set up her own NGO which, at my suggestion, she called *ChoraChori*. This is the Nepali word for 'children'. Without too much difficulty she managed to coax Bhaskar out of his retirement to become ChoraChori's Chairman.

As Shailaja was registering ChoraChori, I cautioned her that in all likelihood I would be unable to support her financially as, unlike in 1999, I had no pot of cash to draw upon that could launch a new charity. Nevertheless, the old rescue team had re-formed and I was invigorated by that. I registered ChoraChori with the UK's Charity Commission in January 2015. In spite of my expressed reservations to Shailaja, the UK charity got off to a positive start with, once again, just the right people coming along at the right time to lend their support.

Operationally, we decided to carry on where we left off with our previous Esther Benjamins Trust work in rescuing displaced children from Indian children's shelters. Since late 2015 Shailaja has rescued 147 of these kids at the time of writing, mainly boys, most of whom she has managed to reunite with their families. The few who can't go back to families, for whatever reason, are staying at the former Esther Benjamins Trust children's refuge that was closed down soon after I left Nepal; we have reinstated it, bigger and better than before. We've even built a brand-new child trauma management centre on the same site. We saw this as being essential given the incidence of mental health problems in returnees due to the abuse they had experienced in India; some boys were diagnosed as being suicidal, an issue close to my heart. The trauma management centre has been designed with lots of light and space so that we can continue to make therapeutic use of the arts, the approach that was so powerful in the past.

In my final years in Nepal I had become increasingly aware of the horror of child rape that seemed to be rife in rural areas and especially on the Terai. In press reports I would read of little girls who would be attacked, often by relatives, sometimes by powerful higher caste men who, like the circus traffickers before them, could operate with impunity. My heart would break not only at the horror of it all but also at what lay ahead for them. They could expect inconsiderate, inappropriate and aggressive police interviews, with the girls so young that they might lack the vocabulary to describe what had happened to them even if they were in a fit state to do so. The police would be much more likely to broker financial deals rather than to investigate properly (there is no use made of DNA evidence in Nepal) and enforce the law. If the case got as far as a court a rapist could pay for a full legal team to counter the government-appointed prosecution lawyer who might have little interest in the case anyway with death threats discouraging him and the witnesses. Under these circumstances the assailants would get away with their crimes. And after all that there'd be no proper trauma management and victims would be for ever stigmatised in their villages, if they were even allowed to remain at home.

No NGO would want to become involved in such a distasteful and dangerous situation but in May 2018 ChoraChori stepped into the breach. We are supporting families emotionally and practically as they pursue justice, making use of ChoraChori's own lawyers. Shailaja has been as active and determined as ever in the community, visiting victims and their families; the former has included one eight-month-old baby.

She has been tracking down rapists and bringing them to book. She enticed one absconding rapist back from India after tricking him into believing he would be attending a meeting that would lead to a financial settlement. Plainclothes policemen were awaiting him and he was arrested.

Our trauma management centre has been of central (and unique) benefit admitting girls like Radhika who will benefit from the therapeutic art approach that we have used in the past alongside a new central technique called Theraplay that visiting British volunteer psychotherapist Debbie Mintz introduced. Just as Esther did 35 years ago with Holocaust survivors, we will work hard to restore self-confidence and belief in humanity in our beneficiaries. Also, we have begun income generation training to girls from Jhapa District, the District that is a hotspot for sexual abuse and that has the highest girl suicide rate in Nepal. We will introduce hope where there is currently despair, giving girls a way out of the de facto slavery of the tea plantations.

With hindsight, I can see how a window of opportunity opened between 2004 and 2012. The right combination of people came together and we had just enough resources to allow us to take on the circuses. We proved that child trafficking can be defeated with courage and especially if good people get behind us instead of looking away in a wish to stay out of trouble. Also, if I have learned anything from my time in Nepal it's to refuse to be overwhelmed by the scale of an undertaking. Have faith, make a start, the unexpected will happen and efforts can be amplified.

The other experience I have had in Nepal has been setback after setback. You build up and then have to rebuild after it gets knocked down. It's important to be stoical and not disheartened by such occurrences. Twenty years down the line I'm still here, still fighting and as defiant as ever. If we can find the substantial funds we need – much more than before as we aim ever higher - that window of opportunity can open once again and the best may be yet to come.

I am donating 10% of the sale price of Gates of Bronze to ChoraChori. But I really need your financial support now for the massive struggle that lies ahead as Bev, Shailaja, Bhaskar and I strive to bring child rapists to justice in Nepal while helping the victims. The management of survivors is going to be so much more challenging than with the circus returnees – and very expensive. If you are able to help us with a donation then please visit the ChoraChori website. Alternatively, you can send us a cheque to the charity address: *Three Ways, Ledstone, Kingsbridge, Devon, TQ7 2HQ, UK.*

Also, if you are writing or re-writing your Will in the coming time please do consider making a small gift towards giving traumatised and vulnerable Nepalese children a chance through our rehabilitation, education and training programme.

For further information about ChoraChori and its work, or to join our small group of dedicated supporters, feel free to e-mail me on Philip@gatesofbronze.com

Thank you so much.

Philip Holmes